JIM BROWN LAYS IT ON THE LINE IN HIS HARD-HITTING AUTOBIOGRAPHY, *OUT OF BOUNDS!*

On *TV AND THE NFL:*
"It started looking like the Ziegfeld Follies out there. One team scores, ten guys party for the camera. Big 300-pounders shaking their ass. What the hell does that have to do with football?"

On *RUNNING:*
"Sundays were mine. I thought, one break, maybe two, I'd run wild. By the time I walked on the field I thought I was God. Don't kid yourself: Walter Payton, Gale Sayers, O.J. Simpson—all top runners have felt the same way."

On *COPS:*
"In the eyes of the police I'm more than just famous. I'm big, black and arrogant. There are cops in Los Angeles who would love to be the guy who sent me to San Quentin for 49,000 years."

On *COCAINE:*
"I hear people say athletes should stop using drugs because they're role models. These people are naive about drugs. A guy strung out on cocaine cares about setting an example for kids? He cares about stuffing his nose with cocaine. Period."

On *THE MEDIA:*
"If you're famous, the American media will exploit you. The media is also America's safeguard. A lot of them are bastards, but I'd rather have those bastards than no media at all."

"ONE HELLUVA GREAT SPORTS READ."
—LARRY KING

THE PEOPLE BEHIND THE HEADLINES
FROM ZEBRA BOOKS!

PAT NIXON: THE UNTOLD STORY   (2300, $4.50)
by Julie Nixon Eisenhower
The phenomenal *New York Times* bestseller about the very private woman who was thrust into the international limelight during the most turbulent era in modern American history. A fascinating and touching portrait of a very special First Lady.

STOCKMAN: THE MAN, THE MYTH,
THE FUTURE   (2005, $4.50)
by Owen Ullmann
Brilliant, outspoken, and ambitious, former Management and Budget Director David Stockman was the youngest man to sit at the Cabinet in more than 160 years, becoming the best known member of the Reagan Administration next to the President himself. Here is the first complete, full-scale, no-holds-barred story of Ronald Reagan's most colorful and controversial advisor.

IACOCCA   (3018, $4.50)
by David Abodaher
He took a dying Chrysler Corporation and turned it around through sheer will power and determination, becoming a modern-day folk hero in the process. The remarkable and inspiring true story of a legend in his own time: Lee Iacocca.

STRANGER IN TWO WORLDS   (2112, $4.50)
by Jean Harris
For the first time, the woman convicted in the shooting death of Scarsdale Diet doctor Herman Tarnower tells her own story. Here is the powerful and compelling *New York Times* bestseller that tells the whole truth about the tragic love affair and its shocking aftermath.

Available wherever paperbacks are sold, or order direct from the Publisher. Send cover price plus 50¢ per copy for mailing and handling to Zebra Books, Dept. 3114, 475 Park Avenue South, New York, N.Y. 10016. Residents of New York, New Jersey and Pennsylvania must include sales tax. DO NOT SEND CASH.

JIM BROWN

OUT OF BOUNDS

ZEBRA BOOKS
KENSINGTON PUBLISHING CORP.

ZEBRA BOOKS

are published by

Kensington Publishing Corp.
475 Park Avenue South
New York, NY 10016

First Zebra Books paperback edition: September, 1990

Printed in the United States of America

To Kenny, Ed, Maggie,
the Wallace family,
and Big George.
Thank you so much.

J.B.

To Mary Kay,
for her optimism,
grace, and love.

S.D.

OUT OF
BOUNDS

ACKNOWLEDGMENTS

Special thanks to Basil Kane, Wallace Exman, and Walter Zacharius, who had the imagination to see it, the resolve to get it done.

The Authors

1

PSYCHOLOGICAL

THE BRONX, NEW YORK. Yankee Stadium. October, 1963. Winter is moving in. So are the New York Giants. And they're attacking my eyes.

I wasn't happy, wasn't quite surprised. Though you'll always find scared individuals, the prevalent nature of the professional football player is that of a soldier of fortune. He's trained and willing to bust people up.

The Giants were sophisticated assassins. Maybe it was living in New York: guys like Frank Gifford, Jim Katcavage, Andy Robustelli, seemed hipper, classier, than the average guy in the NFL. I had big respect for the Giants. They were football intellectuals, the smartest team in the league. Also the most calculating. Other teams would have one or two thugs who'd randomly jump you, hit you in

11

the head. New York did *nothing* helter-skelter. The Giants would determine, as a unit, who they were going to get, then go out and get him. I used to envision them in their dressing room: "Look, today we're gonna fuck up Jim Brown's eyes. And here's how we're going to do it."

Loose rules. Hard men. Not a lot of cash. It made the old NFL a primitive place. I accepted the standard rough stuff, knew it was part of my sport. Still, the first time I carried the ball against the Giants, I knew something was *up*. We used to wear those two-bar masks; the bottom of the nose to just above the eyebrow was exposed. As I was going down my first carry, a guy stuck his hand inside my helmet, scraped my eyes. Next carry, my eye got hit by a forearm. As the first half went on, I guess the Giants got pretty blatant. Rosey Grier, their huge defensive end, started screaming at his own teammates: "WHAT THE HELL ARE YOU DOING THAT FOR?"

Me and Rosey were real friends, the Giants knew it. I don't believe they sent him that morning's memo.

Rosey even confronted the officials, told them his teammates were after my eyes. The officials didn't call anything. I'm not singing the blues: in our era, that was not unusual either. The game was not remotely as commercial, refs weren't out there to protect careers. Guys got away with serious mayhem.

For me that particular day, that presented a problem. In boxing, guy hits you in the groin, ref is dreaming about his chick, it's simple: you crack the *other* guy in the groin. To keep it semi-clean in

12

football you need the official, especially if you're a guy on offense, particularly a runner. A runner can't really retaliate, all he can do is go nuts, start a fight. Then his ass is ejected, the defense is grinning.

I came in at halftime against the Giants, sat by myself. It was a strange, memorable moment. Time diffuses memory, and people today think I was all power, speed, and instincts. I did have those talents, but a major part of my edge was psychological. Normally, I was the one who messed with people's minds. Now the Giants had penetrated mine.

Sitting alone, I was thinking, *Damn. Do these guys have me? Do I complain? Do I start a fistfight? Have they broken my will?*

I was scared. Not physically. You can't play in the NFL, not for long, if you're frightened of taking punishment. No way you can play running back.

What scared me was the Giants' tactics. Specifically, I was afraid that those tactics would stop me from performing. In my entire life, fear of not performing is the greatest fear I have ever felt.

I wasn't alone. Bill Quinlan, a defensive end, was one of the roughest, toughest guys on the Cleveland Browns. He would throw up violently before every single game. Quinlan's boogieman was inside his stomach, tearing away.

Being the star of my team, perhaps the most scrutinized man in the league, my boogieman was twenty feet tall. The pressure on any big star is somehow unique. You're in the dressing room before the game, younger guys are glancing at you, veterans depending on you, 60,000 people want to

13

be entertained—brother, you *can't* have an ordinary game.

That shit would scare me to death. I'd be trying so hard to concentrate, start thinking, Wow! I think I would rather not be here.

At first when I had those thoughts I was miserable. I felt so damn guilty. Then I talked to other people, not my teammates or opponents, but men I respected in other professions, and learned that fear is perfectly natural. It's essential—if men didn't blink when you threw something at their eyes, if they had no fear, they wouldn't survive. I learned that fear is a gift from God.

I was set free! Once I admitted I had fear, I used that sucker. Made it my ally. *Okay, I have a contest this afternoon, and I am Fucked Up. By gametime, can I take this totally messed up feeling, pull my stuff together? Can I come face to face with the Devil—and still perform?* When I discovered I could, it was a hell of a piece of knowledge. By kickoff, I could grip my fear, transform it into power.

Unfortunately, during halftime against the Giants, I forgot all that. I didn't have a fucking clue. Not only had they rattled my mind, the Giants had messed up my eyes. I felt like I was looking through a thick curtain. Then halftime ended. End of soul search. I thought, *Man, I got a game here. They go for my eyes again, I'll deal with it then.*

I never discovered what I would have done. First time I got the ball, I broke a long one—touchdown. Next time we got the ball, I scored another strong TD. That was that: the Giants stopped going for my eyes. I think I know why. I've always felt that competition, stripped to its essence, is a battle

14

of will. Skills, conditions, even luck may vary. Only one thing is constant: break an opponent's will, you'll beat him every time. Control a man's mind, his body will follow.

The Giants probably didn't know it, but on that day, they came close to breaking *me*. When I wouldn't succumb, I think they lost *their* will. And we beat them, 35-24.

There was still the matter of my eyes. Two days later they were still blood-red and blurry. I pulled aside one of our coaches just before practice.

I said, "Coach, my eyes haven't cleared up. Maybe I should go see the doctor."

He said, "Yeah . . . can you go after practice? I don't want the other guys to think you're hurt. It would screw them up."

So I practiced, then I snuck to the doctor that night.

Looking back it seems a bit crazy—no one's eyes are tough. Yet I understood the coach's point of view. I was the star of my team. I had to play Superman for the inspiration of my teammates. Taking that position is an awesome responsibility, and you have to be a certain type of animal to even want it. I loved it. Loved setting a standard of durability for my teammates. Loved knowing the other team spent a large chunk of its week discussing me, how they might stop me, and if they did manage to stop me, they would then tell tales about that. I was the fastest gun in the West.

Of course there are no Supermen. And I was no myth. I was just a man.

I say that now, but no matter how obvious, I

would never make that statement when I was still in the NFL. If certain guys wanted to think I was otherworldly, I'd be the last man on earth to dissuade them. Mystique is a powerful force.

That's not to say I was acting out there. The NFL isn't like making movies. When a pissed off Ray Nitschke is trying to hurt you, it's about as honest as it gets. That time I practiced despite my bad eyes? In part, yes, it was for my teammates. It was also for me. To never miss a game in my career, to practice for nine years in Cleveland's wind and cold, to deal with guys like Night Train Lane and Jim Hill, who would try and take your head off, it required a certain mental position. Mine was simple: I didn't want to be hanging out in the training room, screwing around with doctors. I didn't want to be weak. I wanted to be a bad motherfucker.

To maintain that state of mind, I had to develop a process. During games, for instance, I almost never drank water. Part of it was simply old-school thinking: I believed water, even a little, might physically slow me down. But the jugular issue was my mood—maintaining it. You drink water, you feel good. You feel satisfied. Just like you do after having sex. Very few men, after sex, want to get up and run wind sprints.

When I was on a football field, the last emotion I wanted was satisfaction. I'd look at water, not drinking it, as a test. Three hours of football. I will not deviate. I will not acquiesce. I am a warrior.

Before the games I'd sit alone. The Cleveland Browns were never a rah-rah team—that wasn't Paul Brown's style, nor was it our players'—so I didn't have to deal with a bunch of speeches. I'd sit on a bench, enter what approached a trance. And I would hate it when some old pro would come into the dressing room; I'd have to leave my trance so we could talk. Even if I loved the guy, it was not my time to sing and dance.

Once the hitting began, every time I was tackled, I'd get up slowly, deliberately. Like most things I did as an athlete, this was calculated. I knew the Browns wouldn't grade me on how I looked *between* plays. I also discovered quickly, there were times I had no choice, had to get up slowly. Maybe my head was still ringing from a blow or I was seeing black, or I couldn't breathe from a shot to the kidneys or my arm was bent as God had not intended or the nail on my big toe had been bloodied and knocked right off. It's not like guys were out there and nothing hurt. Shit, almost everything hurt. Throwing a forearm against a man's helmet—it will hurt. Sometimes what hurt the most was the ground. When the field was frozen, you banged it with a frozen elbow, it would hurt right to your teeth.

Whenever I would hurt, I'd never let the defense know. If I was still fucked up by the time I got back to the huddle, I'd hide behind those big offensive linemen so the defense couldn't see me suffer. The key in the NFL is to hit a man so hard, so often, he doesn't want to play anymore. You let the defense know you're hurt, next play they'll be twice as motivated to finish the job. By getting up with leisure every play, every game, every season, they never knew if I was hurt or if I wasn't. I was screwing with their heads, trying to save my own.

Some defensive players did a lot of talking.

You'd be climbing off the dirt, they'd stand right over you, all defiant, like your mother-in-law on Dexedrine.

"Gonna chop you up today."

"Come on back, Big Jim. I got some more for you."

"You ain't gonna get no fucking yards on me."

Even for a pro, my focus was abnormally sharp: when guys would talk trash, I damn near didn't hear them. I was out there to produce, not chitchat. Even when guys would get through, hit a nerve, I never responded. I gave them the Joe Louis stoneface. I would stand still, emotionless, not say a word. It was partly my nature: I don't do a lot of woofing. When I get angry I tend to get very quiet, go inside. It was also by design. I knew it's the quiet guys who are scary. You never know what's going on in their head.

Guys would try and bait me, distract me from the task, but I was committed to restraint. I also believed in playing the game as a gentleman. I didn't dislike the thugs in the league, actually felt we needed more on the Browns, but it was not my style. I only broke my own code, got wild, on two occasions.

The first was against the Giants. After that game in which they'd gone for my eyes, I made a vow to myself: anyone ever hits me again in my eyes, fuck being a gentleman. I'll repay them with a forearm. I never used a fist when I wanted to punish someone on a football field. I considered my forearm the more dangerous weapon.

Sure enough, the very next time we played New York, it was late in the game, they were blowing us out, when Tom Scott, one of their linebackers, tried to get his arm inside my helmet, club me in the face. I put the forearm on his cheekbone, this time the vision of the refs was perfect. They tossed me out of the game.

I was ejected one other time in my career. We were in St. Louis. It was our regular season finale, we'd already clinched the conference title. Gale Sayers was a rookie, he and I were neck and neck for the NFL lead in TDs, and my linemen wanted me to score a few, take the title. Third quarter, near the end of a play, my back was turned when a guy named Joe Robb smashed me in the back of my helmet. I was outraged. We were going to the NFL championship, the Cardinals were going home, this guy was clearly trying to injure me.

I decided to put something on him.

The next time we called a pass play, I pulled aside our tackle.

"Do me a favor," I said. "Let this guy come through kind of easy."

Our tackle let Robb come through. I crouched, knees bent, almost to the ground, bolted up, struck him in the head with a forearm. For good measure, karate kicked him in the stomach. The ref was right there, I was gone, Gale won the race for TDs. I didn't care. At least I put two on that sucker's ass.

Those responses were entirely uncharacteristic. I usually took my "revenge" another way: in the other team's film room. I knew if I ran over a man on Sunday, or misused him on a fake, made him look feeble, his coach would run that play more than once. The players would go Woo! They'd laugh and give that guy grief. I liked knowing that. Even though the game was over, my presence was still being felt.

Even when the real season ended, the game within the game never stopped. At the Pro Bowl, I'd play with guys who were normally opponents. They would saunter over in the locker room.

Guy would say, "Hey Jim, remember I hit you in the head with that forearm? Hurt, didn't it?"

"Forearm? What forearm? Didn't we kick your ass that day?"

He'd walk away grumbling. Then he'd start drilling my teammates. "What's he like? Doesn't he ever get hurt? Who is this guy?"

Except for a few close partners, my teammates didn't know either. I didn't reveal much of myself. I knew guys went home for the summer, or to the Pro Bowl, talked to players from other teams. If they talked about me, I wanted them saying I was this strange, aloof, mysterious type of cat.

I didn't want to be understood.

I didn't make as many friendships as some guys, but the ones I made had depth. And I wasn't there to be a good old boy. If you're a public relations person, you try and be the best public relations person in the world. The Cleveland Browns didn't pay me to do public relations. They didn't pay me to be mediocre, or even good. They paid me to perform at a mental and physical level that was awesome.

So I tried to block out all the peripherals. In the case of awards and trophies, that was easy for me: I didn't give a damn about either. When I did win plaques, I gave them away. In part, it was the racial climate of the times, and my social consciousness: if they wouldn't give me respect as a human being, then I wouldn't accept their accolades for being a Football Star. I knew if you didn't have both, you hadn't won anything.

Just on a sports level, I felt the trophy system was bogus. My most brilliant year in the NFL, when I deserved the MVP, I didn't win. The season they gave it to me, it could have gone elsewhere. What's the significance to that? And what should I have done with my MVP trophy? Put it on my mantel, brag to chicks, when I knew I probably didn't merit it? I gave my MVP to a buddy. He was delighted, put it on his restaurant wall.

One year I won the MVP in the Pro Bowl. They chose the winner in the fourth quarter, announced that I was it. I proceeded to fumble, lose that fumble, and the other team won the game. I felt ridiculous.

Trophies are given by man, and I didn't need any man to justify what I did. You know, I gained a lot of yards in my nine years, and most of them I don't remember. That's not humility. It's arrogance. I set my standards so high, no one could be harsher on me than I was. If there's one thing I hated, it was making stupid errors. When we won the NFL title, our defense was courageous and nasty, shut out Johnny Unitas and the Baltimore Colts. Winning the NFL title was the tangible peak of my career, one of my loveliest memories. I played pretty well, made my contribution. You know what single play sticks out in my mind? I could have scored a TD, but I grabbed the goalpost with my hand, instead of touching it with the ball.

The ball was ruled dead at the one. DUMB! And I'll see it in my head forever.

Sundays were mine. I didn't need any fan or writer or awards person to collaborate with me. I didn't need pacification. I knew when I performed, knew when I didn't. Even if I rationalized my ass off about other matters, I was brutally honest about my performance. That's why I would generally avoid reading the sports sections when I was playing. I knew they'd put thoughts in my mind that shouldn't be there. Knew as a star, they'd give me too much credit or not enough. And they'd base it on some false criteria that had nothing to do with the true value of the performance.

"Jim Brown gained 101 yards. He had a great game."

I might have played lousy that day. For instance, once I went over 100 yards against Pittsburgh. My linemen were opening clean, relatively massive holes. I was in the secondary all day. But I kept veering, instead of cutting. I should have had 220 yards that day. But since I got my "100 yards," people said I played great.

"Jim Brown got seventy-two yards today. He had an off game."

Man, I did wonderful things in those seventy-two yards. Our quarterback was out, the defense was stacked against me. Our play calling was predictable. I had to spin and buck and churn, fight off Bob Lilly and Herb Adderley and Lee Roy Jordan, just to get two yards. A less determined runner might have lost five.

Mark Twain wrote it: "Do you want the statistics or the facts?" I was looking for facts, at least as

I saw them. It was inevitable that the general public, the collective press, would have different standards than mine. And to play in the manner I demanded of myself, I needed to forget about stats and cosmetics, attempt to free my mind of clutter. Then I could bring order to Sunday's chaos.

2

WARRIORS

I First Ran Into Sam Huff in college. I was at Syracuse, Sam played for West Virginia. Senior year, we beat them down there. Early third quarter I took a handoff, the hole opened wide, there was Sam. I broke his nose, busted his teeth, knocked him cold. Hi, Sam.

When Sam arrived in the NFL, he didn't bring a lot of pure skill. Yet Sam was a unique individual —he was so addicted to detail, every time he walked on the field he had an edge. Sam knew every item about every man out there, including first names of the damn officials, and what kind of game they were likely to call. That much dedication requires extraordinary will. Sam's will and his brain made him one of the most effective middle linebackers in NFL history.

Sam was no chump off the field. When he got to the Giants he saw that I was getting a forest of press. He realized if he linked his name with mine, he could also get the serious ink. That's exactly what happened. When people talked about Brown, they often talked about Huff. When CBS awarded Sam with a prime time special, words by Walter Cronkite, Sam became the NFL's first defensive superstar.

Sam must have really appreciated my help: he'd follow me all over the field. Led by Tom Landry, the Giants' defensive staff eventually devised a scheme in which their linemen would shield our blockers from Sam, freeing him to move in, try and bash me. Actually I think Sam talked them into it; when they had some success, they were smart enough to adopt it. The Giants had always keyed their defense to shutting me down. This was the first time they took a man, Sam, and let him mirror my every step. It was effective. Along with Detroit, no one played me tougher than the Giants.

Sam often made the tackle, or at least slowed me down until his buddies arrived, so Sam got most of the credit. He also knew precisely how to work the press. In the week before our games, Sam would herd some reporters, stress the importance of our Personal Rivalry. Sam would tell the writers, "Man, if I can get through and bust Jim a couple of times, we can win this thing. If I can stop Jim, it'll be a hell of a day. Because he's the greatest in the game." That was the set-up. If Sam played well on Sunday the headlines would deliver the punch line: Huff stops Brown! Giants Win!

Jimmy Taylor said Sam was a dirty player. A

lot of people did, but not me. Even when Sam's teammate, Rosey Grier, told me Sam was out to get me, I thought Rosey was exaggerating. I always thought Sam was trying to win, never believed his goal was to hurt me. Sure, I saw Sam jump late on some piles. Big deal. It was part of the game then. No one played for big money—even allowing for inflation, what the owners gave us was *not* big money. What drove us was pride. I don't know if the old game was better or worse. I know it was nastier.

It had to be, the rules encouraged rough play. When a back circled around the end, go for a little pass over the middle, defensive guys could stick out their forearm, catch you in the neck. That could knock you out, but it was legal. So was hitting a guy in the back of his knees when he wasn't look-ing, another sweetheart move that could end a ca-reer. The headslap couldn't maim you, only knock your brain out of your ear. Now outlawed, all that used to be legal and standard, and you have to look at Sam Huff in the context of his era. And I don't think Sam was dirty.

Only once in my career did I get angry at Sam. At the bottom of a pileup he started twisting my head. I just grabbed his wrist. I have strong hands. I squeezed, wouldn't let go. I waited until everyone else had climbed off the pile, still wouldn't let Sam get up.

I said, "Sam, that's not like you. That's not your style."

He said, "You're right, Jim. Sorry man."

I let go. Though we played the Giants twice a year, Sam and I had no more problems. In fact,

Sam would hype the hell out of me. He knew if he was out there telling these wonderful stories about me, I'd have to tell wonderful stories about him. Sam would hit the banquet circuit, dive right into his rap about me. He loved to tell about the time he stopped me a couple of consecutive plays, then stood over me gloating: "Look at you, Brown. You stink." Later, with the Browns needing a touchdown deep into the game, Sam said I broke one for fifty yards. And I called to him from the end zone, "Hey, Sam, how do I smell from here?"

On the circuit, that was Sam's heavy artillery. When I was on the cover of *Time,* Sam even told it to them. And he made it up! He was lying his ass off! And I did the same damn thing. I'd get on the circuit, make shit up! *Yeah, Sam Huff is an animal. Tried to rip my damn ear off!* We all did it. When you're on the circuit, if you don't make stuff up, people go to sleep. They *want* you to blow some smoke up their butts.

Sam did promote himself, but that was no reason for people to turn on him the way they did. People started saying that Sam hogged headlines, was more adept at PR than MLB. I hated that. More than any defense I ever played against, New York played team defense. They were football's version of the Celtics—each guy's responsibility was related to the next guy's. Sam was an integral part of that unit, and the Giants had one of the stingiest defenses in football. To deny him his due is ridiculous. Sam's where he belongs, in the Hall of Fame.

When people started dogging Sam, you started hearing more and more about Joe Schmidt. Schmidt played middle linebacker for the Lions,

28

never got much press, was highly respected within NFL dressing rooms. We didn't play the Lions very often, when we did I understood why other guys talked up Joe. When Schmidt latched on to you, that was the end of the play. I was very big on giving guys the forearm, sliding off. I couldn't pull that with Joe.

Ray Nitschke hit anything mobile. Ray was surrounded by talent, but he was the soul of the Green Bay defense, and Lombardi knew it. I never thought Ray got enough credit for his versatility. Everyone knew he murdered the run, but Ray was also a former fullback, had good football speed, was pretty nifty against the pass. There are certain plays that still haunt me, Ray made one of them. My final season we went to Green Bay to play the Packers in the NFL championship. The field was ice, our running game was largely negated. Blanton Collier put in a pass play for me. A bomb. I loved bombs. I snuck out of the backfield, got behind them all. Two yards from the end zone I saw the ball was coming short. No one was around, it didn't matter. My hands were open, waiting . . . Nitschke got back. He leaped, knocked the damn ball down. Ray stole seven points, we lost by ten. I still have dreams of Ray Nitschke, depriving me of what was mine.

Today I'll see Ray at an occasional golf tournament. He does the same thing every time. First he engulfs my hand in his own—Ray's got these big, gnarly hands—and he'll squeeze it. Then he'll look me in the eye and say, "Jim, come on back in. Work with these corporations, you can make some great money. We love you, they're gonna love you. Don't stand outside all the time."

I know what he means. Ray knows he's on the inside of society, while I'm kinda out here on the fringe. He's letting me know if I ever want in, he can make room for me. When he says, "We love you, they'll love you," Ray means he'll *make* them love me. I never take Ray up on it, but I love him for asking.

Maybe I'm just biased—to me a linebacker is the ultimate football player. And Chuck Bednarik may just be the prototype. They used to call him "Concrete Charley." He played both ways, of course, and he was leathery and fierce and borderline dirty. I was watching him once on TV, one of those nostalgia shows about the old NFL, and he admitted that one time he kicked me. I didn't recall it, but there was Bednarik on the film, running into the pile, giving me a little kick in the ass. When they cut back to Chuck he was laughing.

Chuck hit me as hard as I've ever been hit in my life. On a straight dive up the middle, both of us propelled by running starts, Chuck lowered his head, I dropped mine, BAM, we both stumbled backward like we'd been Mike Tysoned. I briefly saw darkness, don't know what the hell happened to Bednarik. After I regained the light, I refused to look at him, didn't want Concrete Charley to know he'd almost put me under.

I can't talk about middle linebackers without getting to Dick Butkus—he might track me down, try and take my head off. I played against Dick one time. I didn't have to play another. I had eyes, I could see him. Physical animal. Played every down in a frenzy. Dominator in the middle, at a time when every team needed one. Butkus wasn't content to tackle. He'd try and rip out hair, put a helmet through a chest. Butkus was unequivocally out of control. The ideal linebacker.

The one time we met on the field, Dick was playing for the college all-stars, nothing memorable occurred. After I retired I'd check him out on the tube. He'd intercept a pass, instead of running for the goal line, he'd cross to the flanker or runner, shake the ball in their face. They'd freeze, in fear and awe. *Do I try and tackle this dude? If I do, will I regret it in a large way?* Butkus played in the 1960s and early 1970s, the era of the great middle linebackers—Nitschke, Bednarik, Schmidt, Mike Curtis, Huff, Lee Roy Jordan, Willie Lanier, Tommy Nobis—but I think no man ever did it better than Butkus. I don't think anyone today comes close. When football players sit around, discuss guys they admire, they talk about Butkus. Football is hitting. Butkus is the ultimate hitter.

For different reasons, I also had huge respect for Roger Brown and Alex Karras. Since they played for Detroit I didn't face them much, which was okay: Alex and Roger both played tackle, we liked to run up the middle, they didn't let us run up the middle. Alex had those twinkle toes, which initially surprised me for a man his size. Then I looked closer, realized Alex wasn't all that big. For a tackle he was actually light, cat-quick, and guys had trouble blocking him squarely. Alex was also a master at the karate chop to the helmet, and a very determined sort who genuinely despised being outplayed. Next to Alex was Roger Brown. The guy weighed 300 pounds, and he'd be out there scratching you. So you're not only getting hit, you're getting scratched while you're getting hit. Football players *hate* to be scratched. That's girl's stuff.

In tandem, Roger and Alex scared the hell out of our line. Offensive linemen are a singular breed to begin with. Linebackers are killers and thugs and some defensive backs are little killers and thugs. Defensive linemen get to be mean and creative, so offensive linemen must be cool and precise. They're large men, but they have to constantly adjust to the charge of the man across, always staying conscious of their footwork, so their game is essentially mental. If they get psyched out, as a runner you have a deep problem. So you have to keep them encouraged, praise them and pet them, let them know you understand what goes on down in the Pit.

I was always much tighter with my offensive linemen than our guys on defense. I didn't know much about the guys on defense. I had to run through those guys every day at practice, and they'd be talking their own talk. My linemen were my lifeblood.

It used to get funny: you could tell by watching our linemen who we were playing that Sunday. Their demeanor told the entire storyline. If we had a game against a team with no defensive line, guys like John Wooten and Gene Hickerson were all laid back, having their fun. Talking big: *I'm gonna kick this guy's ass! Gonna beat him up! Run over me! I'll open the holes!*

Next week we'd have Detroit—Roger and Alex

—my boys would be humble! "Damn, I'm gonna need some help. I can't exactly handle this guy straight-on. I think a double team is called for." They'd arrive at practice early, watch film that night until their eyes ached, as serious as accountants. What made it comical was that there wasn't any lying or bullshit about it. Forget the games that athletes and reporters play on each other: when football players get together, discuss what they can and cannot do, they're straight out. Offensive linemen may be the most honest beasts in the jungle. Wooten would watch Roger on film, his eyes would open wide. He'd always say, "Damn, I gotta play against this *big* bitch."

Against a team noted for its pass rush, they'd practically pay the coaches to start our first series with north to south running plays: they wanted to charge straight out and deliver some punishment before we started passing. They knew what defensive linemen would do on pass protection: bash a neck with a fist; probe a groin with a knee; step on a leg, keep running. At the prospect of knocking the living crap out of a quarterback, defensive cats turn evil.

As I recall, our linemen didn't woof much the week of a game with the Rams. The Fearsome Foursome was wicked. Deacon Jones. Secretary of the Defense. Flamboyant. Crazy. Ridiculously quick for a man his size. The guy who made them coin the word Sack. Rosey Grier. Immense. Impossible to defeat with brute force. Sweet and gentle out of shoulder pads. Loved to sing, pick a guitar. Lovely human being. Lamar Lundy. Defined the term Unsung. Steadfast. A mass of muscle. Would have starred on any other team. Merlin Olson. Loved the old-fashioned, man-to-man battles in the Pit. With both hands at once, he would hit guys across the earholes in their helmet for stereo ringing. Put him in the lineup for ten years, worry about something else.

With a line that formidable, the Rams didn't need any assistance from the NFL. They got it anyway, at least I thought so. After Rosey suffered a serious injury, I picked up the paper one morning, read that Detroit had traded Roger Brown to the Rams. I said, Wait. What the hell is that? They still got the Deac and Merlin and Lundy, Rosey gets hurt, boom, they get Roger Brown?

I was sure that trade was bogus. And it wasn't until that trade that I started thinking: yes, pro football is a business. I used to think it was a sport, but it has to be a business. Because no owner, not one, should want Roger Brown, a star, a *300-pound* star, to move to the Rams. With Roger, the Rams are as good as they are with Rosey, perhaps better. And Detroit and Los Angeles are both in the same conference! The league must want the team in Los Angeles to remain strong. A thriving team in a critical market is good for the networks, what's good for the networks is good for the league. Man, these owners are doing some *business.*

As Cleveland Browns, we did a little business of our own: one time we put a bounty on the head of John Henry Johnson. John Henry played fullback for the Pittsburgh Steelers. I considered Detroit, Philadelphia, and Pittsburgh the three dirtiest teams in football—John Henry was Pittsburgh's principal thug. He was a street-brawling SOB who used to drink shots with Bobby Layne. On kickoffs, John Henry had this quaint habit: he'd sneak up on people, break their jaws with his forearm.

One kickoff, John Henry shattered the jaw of our backup fullback, Ed Modzelewski. John Henry broke two different bones, Ed was all fucked up. After the game, our team passed around a hat. Each man stuck $20 in the hat: whoever messed up John Henry would get the pot. Man, they never touched him. He'd dance and move and taunt. If John Henry somehow got cornered, he'd slug it out, or bite people. Though we never stopped trying, we never got John Henry. The ante kept growing.

So did Big Daddy Lipscomb; depending on the time of year, Big Daddy went anywhere from 280 to 320. Amazingly, he was also fast enough to run down halfbacks from behind. Daddy's strength was unrivaled. With most tacklers, even if they had a firm grip on me, I could lean forward, push off the earth with my legs, fall ahead for a few extra yards. Not with Daddy. He would grab me with each of his hands, where my shoulders meet my arms, jerk me up out of my lean, slam me to the ground. Goddamn!

I first opposed Big Daddy in 1959, my third year in the NFL. It was the first time the Cleveland Browns, with me on their side, would play the Baltimore Colts. They had splendid Lenny Moore to run the football, but they also had Johnny Unitas and Raymond Berry, lived mostly by the pass. We were a ground team, everyone billed it as a classic matchup. The fans were excited, the press was excited, we were excited. Then I wasn't so excited:

Daddy decided he would kick my young ass. He announced to the press that he would personally "Get that Cleveland cat."

Other guys had said they would Get Me, but their names weren't Big Daddy. Properly motivated, Daddy could disrupt an entire offense. Watching film didn't cheer me—Wooten kept complaining that he had to face another Big Bitch. I wasn't exactly scared, wasn't exactly stupid. I gave Big Daddy, Sunday's encounter, considerable thought, came up with a plan.

I knew not to make Daddy angry, knew I couldn't whip him physically. I decided to con him. I knew a little bit about Daddy. Though his body was oversized, inside he was a little boy, who hated to be scolded. When he was, he would pout and refuse to perform, and that's why his career was uneven. If you gave Big Daddy praise, he was a pussycat. If you gave him enough praise, maybe he wouldn't break you up.

Sunday in Baltimore. Noon. Despite our friendship, I knew Big Daddy had been working up a hate for me. During pregame warmups, I marched right through several Colts, up to Big Daddy.

I said, "Hey, Big Daddy, how you doing? How's your family? You're looking good, man."

Big Daddy was suspicious. I kept on talking and smiling, Mr. Chummy. Finally . . . Daddy smiled. He said it was damn good to see me, too. I told him to have a super game, got the hell out of there. The other Colts were glaring at me.

Well, I had an excellent day. My offensive linemen and I, without the knowledge of the coaches, devised a new blocking scheme: whatever direction their defensive men wanted to go, they would encourage them, push them that way; I would survey the situation, have the option to choose my hole. I'll talk more about this later, because I wish we would have done it my entire career. On that day against the Colts, I wound up scoring five TDs, including a long one for seventy yards. Everyone on the offense was feeling fantastic. Except for poor Bobby Mitchell.

With me out of the picture, hate-wise, Daddy decided to tear up Bobby. Daddy was visibly angry, wanted to hurt Bobby, put him out of the game. Bobby knew it. After Daddy flung him down the first few times, Bobby started scooting out of bounds to avoid him. Daddy only got hotter. On one of Bobby's sweeps, Daddy chased him across the sideline, over the bench, damn near into the stands.

Meanwhile, I did something I never did: kept talking the entire game. "Big Daddy, you're kicking ass. How's that pretty girlfriend? Daddy, we *got* to get together later."

I lugged the ball thirty-two times that day, but Unitas, carving us up, nearly beat us. We held on, 38-31. Poor Daddy never even knew I fooled him.

After the 1963 season, Daddy died. The stories out of Baltimore attributed it to drugs; I believe the papers said he overdosed on heroin. None of the players who knew Daddy believed it. We'd spent time with him—there wasn't one of us who believed he was on drugs. The reports of his death were so mysterious, we suspected wrongdoing. Some guys checked around, they could never prove anything.

A few months before he died, I got to play with Big Daddy. By then he was a Pittsburgh Steeler, we were teammates on the East in the 1962 Pro Bowl. That regular season I had broken my wrist: it was the first time in my career I didn't lead the league in rushing—Jimmy Taylor won it that year. Though I played all year, my wrist didn't begin to heal until the last few weeks of the season. Since my numbers were way down, certain people were suggesting my career was washed up. They happened to be saying the same thing about Daddy.

During Pro Bowl warmups, Allie Sherman, the Giants' head coach, now in charge of the East, walked up to me.

He said, "Jim, I'm gonna use you a lot. I know what people are saying and I know you hurt your wrist. But you're the best runner in the league. Get ready."

I loved Allie for that. I had always liked him, considered him a friend though he was the opposition. His faith in me now, when I was getting dogged, pumped me up. Excited, I went to find Daddy.

I said, "Look, Allie is in my corner. He wants me to have the ball and my wrist is feeling good. I'm gonna win this MVP."

"Jim," Daddy said, "if you got the MVP, I guess I'll go for Lineman of the Game. Shit, I'm still the Daddy."

Once the game began, every time I came to the sidelines I'd give Daddy a pat on the butt. I'd say, "Daddy, you're doing great, man. You're shining. Keep hustling, brother." Then Daddy would come off and ask me, "Jim, how am I doing?" And I'd tell him he was kicking ass. This time it was no con. Daddy was fantastic, going sideline to sideline to drag people down. One time he saved a touchdown, caught Dick Bass from behind.

After the game we both got our trophies. Usually trophies never moved me, this time it did. Back in the locker room I looked at Daddy. He was holding his award to his chest, as a child cradles a puppy. When I think of Daddy, I like to remember that.

One of the charms of the NFL, for me, was that tough guys came in all sizes. Larry Wilson and Pat Fischer were big as peanuts, but they rattled your senses.

I'll never forget Larry Wilson. Number 8. They said he was 5'10", 170, but I think that was generous. I always prided myself on recognizing talent at an early stage, and I designated Larry for stardom the first game we played. Larry didn't give me much choice.

We're playing the Cardinals. I turn the right corner, cut back hard against the pursuit, now I'm flying, this forty-yard TD will feel very nice— CRACK—I'm hit in the ankles, wrapped up, I go down, straight down. I've been running full speed, and this is a solo tackle. On the ground I'm thinking, What is going on here? I look up, see this little No. 8. Funny-looking guy.

A series later, I come around the end again. About to shift up, about to break it. Whack. Same tackle, at the ankles. I look up, number goddamn 8 again. That's *two* TDs this little sucker has ripped me off.

Back on the bench, I sit with my offensive linemen. I say, "Man, that number eight is a motherfucker! You guys watch him. He's gonna be a helluva player."

They think I'm crazy. They never heard of him either.

After that game, Larry Wilson would become one of my all-time personal favorites. Larry used every ounce of what he had. That's the finest compliment I can pay him.

Pat Fischer, who played for the Redskins, reminded me of Larry. His sideburns were bigger than he was, but Pat was one of those guys you never wanted to turn your head on. One of the funniest moments I had in football involved Pat. I was getting ready to sweep, the Redskins called a blitz, Pat came in just as I got the football. Pat picked me up on his shoulder. When you're off the ground you have no leverage, so no power, and Pat carried me back for five or six yards, dumped me on my butt. The image was so comical, Pat was 170, I was 230—the entire stadium, and we were in Cleveland!—broke out laughing.

People are surprised when I say this, but little guys often gave me the largest problems. With their hits, they were *accurate.* Agile and low to the ground, they'd zero in on my ankles. Sometimes they'd flip me straight in the air, I'd crash on my shoulders or my neck at peculiar angles. At first, the little guys puzzled the hell of me. They were always sticking their bodies into bigger bodies, yet they'd walk away, unhurt. At 230, even I felt those shots. No meat on their bones, why didn't they?

I saw the truth when I played with Fischer in the Pro Bowl. After practice I was slow in getting showered, the guys had all left by the time I was dressed. I saw Pat sneaking into the whirlpool. He was suffering, hobbling, grimacing. I thought, Okay. Now I understand. These guys just hide their shit!

Something else about old guys from the NFL: their current civility can fool you. You know Irv Cross, the commentator on CBS? Upbeat, preternaturally pleasant Irv? Watch him on Sunday mornings, you'd trust him with your newborn. On Sundays past, Irv Cross was a menace. Irv Cross is one of the biggest hitters in NFL history.

Jim Hill was another guy who would try and rearrange your spinal cord. Jimmy played cornerback for the Cardinals, I played against him when I was a rookie. First time I ran to Jimmy's side, he rushed up, I figured he'd try to tackle me. He tried to murder me. Smashed me flush on my chin with a vicious forearm. While I was lying on the field, Jimmy stood over me talking: "Yeah, I got you now. You better *not* get up." I stood up, wobbled to the huddle.

I got the ball two plays later, Jimmy ran up from his corner. I can still see it perfectly: Jimmy closed his fist. He tensed his arm. I knocked the daylights out of him with *my* forearm! Caught *him* on the chin. Jimmy got up pissed, and that was the beginning. For the rest of my career we ran at each other with forearms cocked. The only question was who could unload quicker.

Jimmy was a cornerback—he had to be cocky. If a corner gets burned, it's six points. If he doesn't bounce back immediately, they'll toast him again. So you don't want some cat who's into introspection. You want a guy who's arrogant, even overbearing—you want Lester Hayes. Or those two little guys at Cleveland, Minnifield and Dixon. They're tiny but they think they're giants, so that's how they play.

One of the toughest, finest, most supremely confident corners of all time was Night Train Lane. He was big for a corner, 215, super-fast, and would stick you and maul you. The guy was so incredibly good I hope you got to see him play. The Train might get beat deep twice in an entire season. Might.

The optimum moment I ever had against the Train came in a Pro Bowl. I broke one around the side and it was just me and Train. He hit me square, but I dropped a shoulder, knocked him down, and scored a long touchdown. My pride was flowing: very few men on this earth have ever knocked the Train down one-on-one.

He and I are close friends, a few months after the game we were playing some golf. I was teasing him about my TD. The Train let me finish getting off.

Then he said, "Jim, there's something I better tell you, brother. The only reason you were able to knock me down was because I had appendicitis. Right after the game they had to put me in the hospital. If my appendix wasn't messed up, you never would have knocked me down."

Damn.

There were certain quarterbacks who used to torment me. I'm talking about late in the game, a tight game, when I was on the sideline watching them drive their offense, knowing it was out of my hands now, all I could do was *sit* there, helpless. For me, those final minutes were mental murder. And the deadliest guy in the league was Johnny Unitas.

No matter how many times they drew his blood, I swear Unitas was impossible to intimidate. Some guys thought he held the ball a split second longer than he needed to, to symbolically spit in the eye of the defense. As a passer Johnny had no limitations, could throw it long or underneath, could float it or sting your hands. One of the highlights of my career was playing for a team that twice beat a club that had Johnny Unitas. For me, Johnny's the consummate NFL quarterback—my favorite of all time.

Another guy I admired was Y.A. Tittle. If you're a statistics man, you'll never even glance at Tittle. He reminded me of an old truck, didn't sound good, didn't look good, kept on crossing that desert while all those pretty new cars were stuck on the side overheated. Tittle would bang up a knee or a shoulder, stay in the game, then throw the crucial pass at the critical time and he'd beat you. When he was with the Giants, in my opinion, Tittle *was* the offense. They didn't have Gifford or Alex Webster yet, and they used the same three plays over and over: Long pass, dive up the middle, the famous Y.A. Tittle screen. Somehow, Tittle won anyway. I'll never forget that famous photograph of Tittle on his knees in the end zone bleeding from his bald head. By then his career was over, but the man was still a champion.

Bobby Layne was a cowboy. Loved booze, dingy bars, women who had a pulse. So tough it was funny: right until he retired in 1962, years after the league had made them mandatory, Bobby refused to wear a face mask. Safety? To Bobby it wasn't right. Bobby defied every rule—didn't throw a tight pass, couldn't run, drank too much to have a hard body—but he had no choke in him, and that's the man who's feared the most at the climax of a competition. In those last two minutes give me Bobby Layne.

At QB, another guy I favored was Joe Namath. NFL-wise, Joe was revolutionary. With the women and the Fu and the minks and the white spikes—the Namath Attitude—he taught some coaches and execs, confirmed what sports fans knew all the time, that it's the players who make the game.

And yet I never thought of him as Broadway Joe, not in our personal relationship. One on one, Joe was in total contrast to his image. He was one of the shyest, humblest, most caring guys I knew, and Joe did wonderful things for black guys on the Jets. He tried to land them commercials, supported them during their contract negotiations. Johnny Sample, the Jets' outspoken cornerback, said Joe, without being asked, generally did everything he could for the brothers on the Jets.

One time Joe was in Hollywood, wanted to check out the Candy Store, a famed private club on Rodeo Drive. Joe said, "Jim, can you get me in there?" I told Joe I'd meet him there later that evening; in the meantime I said to just head over, tell them who he was, they'd let him right in.

I said, "Hell, you're Joe Namath. You don't have to tell them, they'll know."

When I arrived at the Candy Store Joe was still standing outside, waiting for me, so he could enter as my guest. He didn't *want* to do the "Hey, I'm Joe Namath" thing. I thought that said a lot about Joe and the way that he viewed himself.

Though as a person Joe was much more substantial than his image suggested, as a quarterback I thought he was *over*rated. With New York as his stage and all that charm, especially after he guaranteed and made good on the Super Bowl win over the Colts, Joe was God. I think Joe was a courageous quarterback, a genuine leader with a rapid-fire release. I do not think his performance matched his legend. Held back by those terrible knees, I don't think Joe had enough big years to stand him with the top quarterbacks ever. I never put him in a league with Unitas, or even Dan Marino.

What separated Joe was dash. He had it in spades and for that Americans loved him. For his charisma, even more for his class, Joe's got my affection, too.

3

PEOPLE
AND ROOTS

As a young boy I didn't know my father, had to
settle for the legend.

The legend was plentiful. My father's name
was Swinton Brown, everyone called him Sweet
Sue. They said he'd played some amateur football,
been fast enough with his fists to earn cash in the
ring. They said he could dance or gamble into the
morning. Mostly, they said Sweet Sue was a lover.
Perhaps he once loved my mother, but I don't really know. I was born James Nathaniel Brown on
February 17, 1936. Sweet Sue left a couple weeks
later.

He moved north, later found another wife,
had a whole bunch of babies. I wasn't mad when I

learned that; I actually felt good for him, that he had his own family. But I never loved my father. I didn't even know him. Only saw him three or four times in my life.

The first few times I was glad to see him, and curious as hell. I'd heard so much colorful talk, I wanted to check out the flesh and blood. His visits were pleasant but brief, I couldn't learn much about him. As I got older and he stayed away, my curiosity faded. What remained was a cool recognition that this man was not a part of my life. The rare times we did meet, we made a pact, unspoken, but very real: when I was a little boy, he had done nothing for me, so when I got older, I would do nothing for him.

I was in my forties when my father died. His wife knew my mother, she didn't even call her. Instead she called the police, asked them to contact me. I was at my home with Big George Hughley, my best friend, when the police called me and gave me her number. First I phoned my mother, then my father's wife. She wanted me to come to New York where they'd been living, basically to caretake my father's other family, beginning with the funeral. She spoke to me as if we'd known each other for years. It did not feel sincere, and what I dislike most of all are things that aren't real. They confuse me. When something is real, even if it's bad, I feel safer.

After Big George left, I sat down by myself at the little table off my kitchen where we sometimes play chess until six in the morning. I knew if I went East and played the role they desired, it would be hugely symbolic. For me, that's all it would be. I didn't even know these people. Sweet Sue was dead, yes, but it didn't bring me any remorse, not really. We never talked, never saw each other all those years. He was a stranger, and it felt like a stranger had died. He was blood, but I look at blood the way I do my friends. If blood loves you and treats you right, then blood has meaning. But I've also seen blood kill blood.

I called back my father's wife. Gently, I told her that I wouldn't be present at the funeral. I've never felt bad about it.

And I've never really missed having a father. There was no man in my childhood house, but there was plenty of love. Until I was seven I was raised by my great-grandmother. She was very old, my life was beginning, but we were family, for true, and she was the most important person in my life. Her name was Nora Petersen. To me she was Mama.

My natural mother, Theresa Brown, left our home when I was two years old. She was young when she had me, Sweet Sue had cut out, decent jobs were scarce. Like many Southern blacks, my mother migrated to the North, where she had a steady job lined up, as a maid on Long Island. With Mama, I remained where I was born, on St. Simons Island, a quiet, dreamy islet just off the southern coast of Georgia.

I got old-time religion in a hurry. On Sundays I was a churchgoing fool: Mama would send me up to seven times a day! Most of the people in our church were Baptists, and accordingly emotional. They'd faint and scream and cry and fan those fans. I'd grin when no one was looking.

Going to church wasn't a prerogative—Mama made it the law. For such a wispy woman, she could kick some ass. When I'd stay out too late, try and sneak back in, she'd be waiting with that damn switch of birch, whale on my behind. I never ever got mad at her, because I knew she loved me. Mama loved my mother, too. When I'd wonder aloud about her, Mama'd explain that my mother was almost a child herself when she had me, didn't have the know-how with children that she, Mama, did. "Someday," she'd say, "your mother is going to send for you."

I don't know how it got started, but people seem to think I grew up dirt poor in a cabin. Neither is true. Mama worked as a domestic, so did my aunt, and my uncle Bubba, who owned a taxi in New York, would sometimes come down and bring us money. I never paid much attention to how, but I knew we were getting by. We had food and clean clothes, and our one-story house was big if a little old.

We shared the house with my grandmother, Myrtle Johnson. Myrtle was an alcoholic, not a very private one. A frozen memory of childhood: Myrtle, in the backwoods, or on the main road, falling down drunk. She was a total wreck. I'd see her, my stomach would get strange with embarrassment. I'd look at the damn bottles, think, *Not me. Nothing will ever run my life.*

Then she just stopped, or at least it seemed that way. After twenty-five years, Myrtle quit booze. To me it was unreal and glorious. From the day she went sober, my grandmother was one of the most beautiful, loving human beings I have ever known, and she became the rock that held my family together.

When I was playing pro football, Myrtle contracted cancer. She didn't want anyone to know, didn't even want to stay in the hospital. All she wanted was a new bathroom for our old white house. Man, that's all she wanted. I had that new bathroom put right in, she was so excited, and proud. Right before that I had finally convinced my mother, who'd been content living in Cleveland, to move back to the island and take care of her mother. I don't think I ever loved my mother as much as the day she returned to St. Simons Island. I came back to visit, went in Myrtle's new bathroom, ran the water loud, cried like a baby. I knew Myrtle would die happy.

While she was dying, I spent a lot of time back on the island. Myrtle would tell me things I'd done when I was a little boy, things I remembered, but never dreamed that she would, due to the booze. She was hurting, she knew she was dying, she never once cried the blues. My entire life that's inspired me.

Myrtle died while I was back in Cleveland. The morning of the funeral I flew to Jacksonville, Florida, about eighty miles from St. Simons Island, and I made the drive in a rented car, beneath the pine trees and the filtered sunlight, and it was lovely. I don't know if I've ever felt so serene. Myrtle had beaten the bottle, she'd spent her last days with her daughter, and she had been ready to leave. The funeral wasn't sad at all. It was beautiful.

Myrtle's love for me had been fierce and unconditional. So had Mama's. To me, black people in the South seem to love stronger. I've never felt more love than I did as a child on St. Simons Island. The black folks on the island would watch out for their neighbors, share food. Someone would roast a bunch of oysters on a piece of tin roof, then pass the word to invite people by. If it was oysters or some shrimp, people would always save me some, even if I was out playing. Everyone knew I was soft for it.

I was a rambunctious, tough, pretty happy little kid. I thought about the fact that my parents weren't around, but I didn't sulk. My family was Mama and Myrtle and the community, and my childhood memories, except for my brushes with racism, are mostly sweet. Organized sports hadn't yet hit the island, so we were natural little men: we carved slingshots, made boats out of boxes, sailed them in the pond where folks said there used to be alligators. We'd roll tires, hitting them with sticks while running at full speed. We played our own brand of stickball with a bat made of wooden board. We even figured out ways to play during storms. Mama's house sat about three-quarters of a mile from the beach and the more volatile tropical storms would whip the ocean right up to our door. We would snatch our mama's wash basins, float around in the flood water. What's more fun than that?

Maybe it was the island's grandeur that made us feel so good. We had rapturous sunsets, skywritten swirls of royal and baby blue, all pinked-up by the vanishing sun. The magnificent moonlight would wash over our roads, illuminate the darkness. The island soil was so rich you could just about live off it. There were trees everywhere, with scuppernong grapes and oranges and pecans and figs and bananas and every type of melon. Men could go fishing or shrimping in the morning, eat that night like kings. The island's lump crabmeat is the most succulent I've ever tasted, better than any restaurant in San Francisco.

There's a whole string of islands that stretch along Georgia's coastline, and their history is comparably fertile. On nearby St. Helena Island, the first school for blacks, Penn School, was established in 1961, and the first black teacher, Charlotte Forten, taught there. Martin Luther King formulated plans on St. Helena for his historic march on Washington. On my island, there are forts from battles in the Civil War, and burial grounds full of Indians. On St. Simons, still, there are some Gitchi people, a mix of French and black, who sound Jamaican. People think Georgia is Atlanta. If they went to the islands, they'd witness another world.

Sadly, a lot of the history and culture is getting bulldozed, literally. White developers and land prospectors now outnumber black natives. Many of the blacks are selling their land to the whites. My mom still lives on St. Simons and we're holding onto our land. I'm afraid we're in the minority.

The time I spent on St. Simons, the heritage I was passed down, will always inform who I am. Historians say the men and women who were born on the islets off Georgia and South Carolina are descended from West African tribesmen, who were captured then abducted to the islands as slaves.

One of those tribes, the Ibo warriors, were kidnapped to St. Simons Island. Rather than live out their lives as slaves, the Ibo marched into the ocean to their deaths.

4

CHANGE

When I Was Eight years old, Mama put me on a train with a big box lunch. As Mama had assured me, my mother was calling for me.

When I arrived in the North, my mother was working in Great Neck, New York, as a domestic. Her employers were the Brockmans, a witty, easygoing Jewish couple who made me feel welcome. As part of my mother's arrangement, the Brockmans provided her with an apartment over their garage. Though I missed the island, loved Mama deeply, the reunion with my mother was nice. I hadn't seen her since I was two.

That train ride brought me to a strange new world. A white world. On the island, white folks lived near the beaches, black folks lived in the middle, and except for a pair of little white boys I befriended, my world was essentially black. Great Neck was a suburb on Long Island, virtually all white, decidedly affluent. I would have liked to have had the time to breathe deeply, make sure I was still residing on the same planet. Right away I had to start school.

I went to school in nearby Manhasset, where I got the one surprise I hadn't expected: Manhasset Valley grade school was predominantly black, although the suburb of Manhasset was mostly white. My first day, first *recess*, I got in a fight. My mother, excited about my arrival, had dressed me in new clothes, sent me to school in a taxi. That morning when they gave us recess, a black boy made a wisecrack, said I looked "pretty," then he shoved me. I reacted on the spot, Georgia-style: I tackled him, pinned his shoulders with my knees, hit him with a schoolboy right only his mother couldn't love. The closed circle of kids started chanting, "Dirty fighter, dirty fighter." I stopped fighting, climbed off the boy who'd pushed me. I was mystified; how did these boys fight up here? Back home no one called it dirty fighting. On the island I'd been known as a fighter. No one could call me a bully, but if another boy messed with *me*, I was a buzzsaw. I didn't care if a boy was bigger or older, I'd fight anyone who started with me first. That was unusual, and the other kids, even Mama, thought I was crazy. Once a big boy jumped me in the woods, scared me, hurt me, so I bit him. He was shocked and frightened, turned and ran home, where I heard he got a whipping from his mama for letting a little boy whip his butt.

I had one of those nothing-goes-right days the

summer before I was due to start high school. The Brockmans said they were moving to Los Angeles! My mother had to find a new job, and she and I had to move. That hurt, because I really liked the Brockmans. They bought me my first basketball, put up a hoop for me in the yard. I still owe my nice little jumper to the Brockmans.

We moved right where Great Neck met Manhasset, and I later enrolled at Manhasset High. In retrospect, this was one of the key events of my life. Supported by local money and high ideals, Manhasset High was one of the country's finest public schools. Both the educators and the coaches treated the students with respect. I was one of the school's few blacks, and I was voted Chief Justice of the Supreme Court. I felt loved at Manhasset, on and off the playing field.

I was also spending time on the street being a wise guy. With several other athletes I created a gang, the Gaylords, and I was voted President. Our gang was not too dangerous: mostly we cruised from town to town looking for chicks, preferably from rival schools, and when that led us into trouble we'd fight with our fists. At times we carried switchblades, but we never chose to pull them in a fight, and none of us did any jail time. Later, after I quit the Gaylords and went to college, some of the fellas who stayed in Manhasset turned into pretty strong gangsters.

The people at my high school and sports kept me from falling in too deeply with the Gaylords. I won thirteen letters playing football, basketball, baseball, lacrosse, and running track in three years of varsity competition. By my senior year I was all-state in football, basketball and track. I averaged 14.9 yards per carry as a halfback, also played linebacker. We had our first unbeaten season in twenty-nine years. In basketball I averaged 38 points a game as a physical forward who could shoot. I also played some baseball, pitcher and first baseman, threw a pair of no-hitters, got a bunch of press, though I wasn't that good. Casey Stengel was managing the New York Yankees, he offered me a minor league contract. I declined. I knew I didn't have the skills to make it to the majors. And I preferred the physicality and excitement of football.

To come play football, Ohio State offered me a four-year athletic scholarship. About forty other colleges were in the running. To help me decide, I leaned heavily on Ed Walsh, my high school football coach. I played for Ed thirty-five years ago. I still benefit to this day.

In a suit Ed looked small. In his coach's shorts and T-shirt, you could see he was all bone and muscle. Ed wore glasses, rarely raised his voice, radiated great inner strength. His message was clear and consistent: a man without principles could never be great. And the color of a person's skin meant nothing to Ed. Bigotry was beneath him.

One Easter my mother and I were battling. She was young, pretty, and this dude started hanging out at our house. I was even younger, pigheaded, didn't want no dude messing around with my mother. My rap about my mom was, Don't be saying shit about my mother, and don't even *think* about messing with her. That's my *mother*.

Everyone needs a lover, but I was too territorial to even consider that. One night my mom was putting on a new dress, I knew the cat was on his way over. I had muscles by then, big enough to fight him, and if I saw his face again in our apartment, I told my mother I would kick his sorry ass.

"Well," my mother said, "you could leave."

That was the law to me. She tells me to leave, I'm gone. I went right to Ed, told him I was leaving home. He didn't tell me I was a bum, or Gee, Jim, can you come back later? Ed invited me to stay at his home. He said to pack some stuff, bring it over, stay with him and his wife while I decided if I was doing the right thing. I told him No, thank you, but never forgot the moment. Ed was a white man, who invited a black kid to live at his home in the 1950s. And meant it.

I stayed instead with my first real Main Girlfriend, Henrietta Creech, and her wonderful family. She was the head majorette at a rival school. I took her to my high school dance, wooed her on the floor to some blues by B.B. King. I fell for her hard, and when I was in college, I came home and got Henrietta pregnant. She gave birth to Karen, my first daughter.

I'm not a man prone to regret, but I should have married Henrietta. After she had Karen, I knew she wanted to marry me, but she was so strong, she never harped on it. Henrietta just started raising Karen by herself, with the help of her parents. I've felt guilty about that all my life. I made a choice—if I was going to finish college, have an athletic career, I felt I could not take on a wife and child. I'm not sure what I would do if I could go back, I might make the same choice. And yet, I've always felt what I did to Henrietta was terrible. If people are going to crucify me, crucify me for that.

Today Henrietta lives in New York where she produces commercials. To this day she never got married. She's been in my corner since high school, emotionally, and when I've needed her, financially. I still look at Henrietta, wonder why I could never be that good a person.

Eastertime, junior year. I was still living with the Creech family, still angry at my mother. I wanted to go to church for Easter, felt insecure because I didn't own a suit. As usual, Ed Walsh was Mr. Clutch. He drove me up to Harlem, to 125th Street, where white men don't normally tread. Ed took some money out of his own pocket, bought me a suit.

Ed was the best football coach I ever had, in every way, including major college ball and the NFL. He cared about his players as people, we could always talk freely to him. That's very important to me in a coach. If something's wrong, let's find out what it is. Should I be doing something differently? Tell me exactly what you want, I can do it. Just don't get mysterious on me. If I don't know what's happening, I can't perform.

When I screwed up in class, Ed never wrote me off as a punk. I recall the first time he told me I had a chance to play professional football. He said, "But you have to go to college first, and you won't go to college unless you start trying harder at your classes." Ed was right; I'd been fucking off at school. If I wasn't playing ball, I was on the street with the Gaylords, or having fun with Henrietta. I didn't understand the value of education.

I turned the academic corner when the crew at Manhasset suggested I take an IQ test. Turns out I had a pretty decent IQ, and that encouraged me, exactly as my mentors had planned. By graduation, despite playing all that ball, I was a B— student.

When football ended my junior year, Ed called me to his office, shut the door. That summer he wanted me to work on a quicker start. Ed said all great runners get off quickly. I busted my ass that summer—start, run five yards, start, run five yards, for two hours at a time—so Ed would be proud. Not only did I have my finest high school season, but five years later as a NFL rookie, there wasn't a runner on the Browns who left the blocks quicker than I did. Not even Bobby Mitchell or Ray Renfro, and Bobby had been a Big Ten hurdle champ. Getting off the mark in a hurry was a trait shared by Walter Payton, Gale Sayers, Lenny Moore, Bobby Mitchell, many famous runners, and by me. I owe that to Ed. I did the physical work, Ed provided the inspiration.

When the scouts descended on Manhasset, Ed let me depend on him. With forty-some schools offering rides, I wasn't even sure where to start, neither did my mother, and things were still chilly between us anyway. Ed's first choice was Ohio State. Woody Hayes himself had called to say he wanted me.

"Jimmy, you've got a special talent," Ed told me. "Ohio State is a fine place to get an education. And it's in the Big Ten, which plays the best college football in the country. I think you ought to play with the best, and against the best."

Ed made good sense, but there were other voices. In my four years at Manhasset, the community had basically adopted me. They'd guided me, nurtured me, I was one of their own, and everyone wants their own to get out and succeed in the world. There ensued a great local debate: which university will Jimmy thrive at?

I wound up at Syracuse, where they almost ruined me.

5

WELCOME TO HIGHER LEARNING

SPRING, 1953. STALIN HAD died, Ike was a White House rookie, there would soon be an uneasy truce in Korea. In *The Invisible Man*, Ralph Ellison wrote about the black experience in America.

I was a senior in high school. My chief concern was fall, and where to go to college.

Enter Kenneth Molloy. Today he's Judge Kenneth Molloy, a New York State Supreme Court Justice, but anyone in Manhasset can still tell you all about him: little guy, Irish, steel-tough, starred in lacrosse at Manhasset High and later Syracuse, fought cancer and whipped it. A man who lives his life for others, especially kids. Kenny Molloy finds promising athletes who can't get into college—no money, no connections—somehow finds a way, the path often detouring through Kenny's own pocket. I love Kenneth, I'm proud to be his friend. When I was inducted into the Hall of Fame, I had Kenny introduce me.

My mentor at Manhasset, it was Kenny who suggested I go to Syracuse, his alma mater. It was a good school, Kenny said, the football team was working hard at going big-time, lacrosse was well established, and in case I had any problems, it was close to Manhasset, he could drive to the campus in hours. Money was not a factor, Kenny said. Syracuse was dangling a scholarship.

To me that sounded fine, even better than Ohio State, which sounded so far away. I told Kenny to call the Syracuse coaches, tell them I was coming. There was just one footnote to the story: there was no scholarship. Kenny only told me there was.

Kenny had tried, but Syracuse didn't bite. They hadn't scouted me, knew nothing about me. My gaudy high school stats, I imagine, were negated by the fact that I'd produced them on Long Island. Syracuse, and many Eastern schools, focused their recruiting on kids from the coal mines of Pennsylvania, not upper crust suburban New York. They told Kenny they couldn't spare the scholarship.

Kenny, being Kenny, wouldn't relent. He wrote a letter to forty-four of Manhasset's movers and shakers, asking for their contributions to a "Jimmy Brown fund" which would pay for my freshman tuition and expenses. When the people of Manhasset came through, Kenny went back to

Syracuse and offered a deal: the Manhasset crew would finance my freshman year and at the end of that year, if I proved my value on the field, I would be given a scholarship. Syracuse gave Kenny a muted yes. If I was *that* good, yes, a scholarship might later be made available. Kenny, certain that I'd get there and tear it up, struck the deal.

I was never told. I went to Syracuse believing I was on scholarship, when actually I was there on a trial basis. It wasn't until after I graduated that Kenny explained his actions. He didn't want me to feel indebted, wanted me to think I had gotten into college entirely on my own. He felt Syracuse, with its proximity, blend of academics and sports, would be excellent for me. He'd been treated well at Syracuse, thought that I would be too. He didn't know because they didn't tell him: Syracuse did not want black athletes.

I never considered that either, arrived at Syracuse with a typical college freshman's nervous optimism. I was shown to my new home, a row of converted barracks known as Skytop. It was up in the hills about three miles from campus, and I had to hitch to get to class. But I liked it up at Skytop. The rest of the students were non-athletic freshmen, and I had never envisioned myself as just a jock. I had a roommate named Gene Boshes, an intellectual, budding philosopher, and we'd stay up into the night discussing Life. My life at Skytop was wonderful because it was natural. I was just another freshman.

First day of freshman practice, I learned some things, though I didn't comprehend their significance. I was the only black on the freshman team, and the only player living at Skytop. All my freshman teammates lived in a dorm called Collendale, in the heart of the campus. I was so naive, I never even thought about race. I thought it was strange, left it at that.

My next discovery was also puzzling. All my teammates were given meal tickets that entitled them to eat at Slocum Hall. I was a big kid, always hungry, but my meal ticket was different—I was not to eat at Slocum, but at Sims, and my ticket provided for about half as much food. I decided to take matters into my own hands and the hands of a buddy: we started printing phony meal tickets. Terrified, we'd walk through the food line with our doctored tickets. Never got busted, though, and our stomachs got full.

Even when I had to hitch to school in the snow, at Syracuse it *snowed,* living at Skytop never lost its charm. Early on at Skytop I met Vinnie Cohen, who sounds Jewish, but he's a black dude from Boys' High in Brooklyn. One day Vinnie was leaving a barrack, I was shooting outdoor hoops.

I said, "Hey, man, you play basketball?"

Vinnie said, "Yeah, I play a little."

I was cocky, me and my 38-point average in high school. Already Vinnie had a minor gut, slumping posture, I figured I'd own him. Figured wrong. Vinnie was only 6'1", but he had fire in his belly. He could leap, also owned a murderous J. We played until exhaustion, and the beginning of friendship. Vinnie became my closest partner, and my idea of a great young American. Vinnie had no scholarship either, went on to graduate with honors, become a basketball All-American. Vinnie fell in love with the first girl he met in college, married her, they're still together today. After a stint at the State Department, Vinnie's now Managing Partner of a powerful D.C. law firm. And I had assumed he was just some funny-looking black cat. After Vinnie shaked me, baked me, popped his jumper in my face, I made a mental note: don't underestimate, dummy.

Living at Skytop, meeting Vinnie, many other bright young students, was nourishing. This college scene was fun! I even pledged a fraternity. I met a young black student, who explained all about pledging, and we pledged a frat together. It was Pi Lamda Phi, a Jewish fraternity, and it was pretty comical. All the brothers, as in fraternity brothers, were wearing their herringbone sports jackets, their button-down shirts from Brooks Brothers, their Florsheim shoes. I pledged in this funky gray suit and blue suede shoes. I looked like a very muscular pimp. The guys were cool, though, and knew I was an athlete, and they pledged me in. My freshman coach found out, told me to quit. He said it would take up too much time.

That was the first of many disappointments. At Skytop with Vinnie and the non-athletes, I was partying, learning, enjoying my new independence. Down the hill at practice I was largely ignored. When someone finally spoke more than two words to me, it was to tell me I couldn't be in a frat. Then I was issued a warning. The freshman quarterback walked over, said, whatever I did, I should not be like Vada Stone. I said, What? He smirked; I guess he thought I was playing innocent on purpose. In that week, two freshman coaches said the same thing. I said I didn't know any Vada Stone. Who was he?

Vada Stone, I was told, had played quarterback at Syracuse two years before. They said he had a cannon arm. He was articulate, flamboyant, and extremely good-looking. He had quit the team, dropped out of college, and went to Canada to play in the CFL. They said he was also a major force with the ladies. Girls would come to the stadium, sing to him while was practicing, and he had girls who would wash his clothes. Eventually he started dating the head majorette, who was white. And Vada was a black guy.

Very quickly, I got tired of hearing about Vada Stone. When another teammate brought him up, I cut him off.

"Wait. What does Vada Stone have to do with me?" I said. "I don't even know him. I'm not a quarterback, and I'm not dating any white girls. So what's the deal?"

"Well," he said, "you're a black guy."

"I'm a black guy, so you're hooking me up with Vada? Get out of my face. I'm just trying to play football."

That was it. Vada was black and flashy. He had messed around with the prettiest white girl in school, then left. Now, because I was black too, they were going to kick my ass, because they never got the chance to kick Vada's. I understood, now, why I was up on Skytop.

In a certain way, the people of Manhasset had set me up for this. I don't mean by sending me to Syracuse, which was done with every good intention. It was precisely that—their goodness—that had set me up. When I came to Manhasset High School, I was never denied an opportunity. I was living among all these white people, receiving all this warmth and support. It lulled me to sleep. I believed everyone would be as good as the people of Manhasset. I came to Syracuse with my guard down. At eighteen, I wasn't prepared for their venom.

I couldn't even fight back with my talent. I was the fastest back on the freshman team, probably the strongest, but if a coach addressed me at all, it was to needle me. One coach told me I had no future as a runner. He said I should think about playing line. One coach told me I should learn to punt. Punt? *Punt?*

When I realized what was happening, I recall thinking: *Okay, you racists. I know you're lying to me, because I know that I can play football. So fuck you.*

My anger was healthy, kept me strong. But each time I left Skytop and my friends, went down to suit up, my spirit shrank a little more. My anger got tired, doubt started creeping in. I went to practice one day, didn't want to be on a football field for the *first* time in my life. How perfect: they didn't want me there either. I was given nothing to do, but watch the other guys drill. I wanted to cry, but I said, No, fuck it, I won't. That night I went back to Skytop, Gene wasn't around. That was what I wanted. To be alone, to punish myself. I sat on my little bed, got right to it. *Maybe it isn't my race. Maybe it's me. Maybe I'm nothing. Maybe I don't have what it takes.*

I decided to quit. Give them what they wanted. I was no good anyway. Not like I'd be missed.

Dr. Raymond Collins saved me. The superintendent at Manhasset, he and his son had been my friends. I had called Ken Molloy, told him I was quitting the team, returning to Manhasset. Kenny told Dr. Collins, Dr. Collins drove right to Syracuse, found me at Skytop. I told Dr. Collins I was leaving. Didn't think I was good enough to play college ball. I wanted out.

Dr. Collins let my words spill. Then he told me I was wrong. I was more than good enough to play college football. If I stayed, I would prove that beyond any doubt. My heart hurt, I didn't know if I believed Dr. Collins, but it didn't matter: the fact that a high school administrator would drive to a college, try and help a kid, was awesome to me. No way, after that, could I tell Dr. Collins no. I promised to stay, at least for now.

Crucial moment? I believe it was. Had I dropped out of college then, I might have turned to anything. With my drive, I was going to be something, but I doubt if it would have been in sports, and I don't know if it would have been something good. Back in Manhasset the Gaylords were getting older and more dangerous, they might have looked best to a kid who'd just had his dream killed. I might have become one hell of a gangster. Might also be in jail or a corpse.

The last day of my freshman year, I was gone, right back to Manhasset. Before I left, I was summoned by the varsity coach, Ben Schwartzwalder. Ben called me into his office, told me he wanted me back as a sophomore, but he wanted me back as an end. I told Ben I didn't want to play end. Never played it, never wanted to. I was a runner. I wanted to carry the football. Ben persisted, so did I. Finally he shrugged, said he'd give me a try in the backfield. In retrospect, Ben wasn't a bad guy. He was just Schwartzwalder. The head coach.

And Ben kept his promise: at my first varsity practice, the coaches had posted a depth chart. I was at halfback. Fifth string, and I could live with that. My fate would now be determined by my running, all I'd been asking for.

Fourth game of the year, against Illinois, several of our backs were injured, they had no choice but to start me. I also got some time at cornerback, made a few rough tackles, a couple respectable runs. Illinois had an All-American back named J.C. Caroline. Once J.C. turned the corner, I rushed in and stuck him, they had to carry J.C. off the field. Next week, my coaches were more polite.

Game six was against Cornell. Our backs were still hurting, they'd moved me up to second team. None of our runners were doing much, and the fans started chanting my name. "We want Brown, we want Brown." Man, I got a chill in my body. Then the guy who started in front of me busted up his ankle. Coaches called my name, I *flew* into our huddle. I broke a TD for 54 yards, finished with about 150. That was my coming out party. I started every game the rest of my college career.

I received my scholarship, by graduation I was All-American. Senior year I averaged 6.2 yards per carry, nearly broke 1,000 yards in eight games. We were 7-1, won some trophy for being "best team" in the East. Final game of the season, I scored 43 points, we beat the toothpaste out of Colgate, 61-7. That clinched an invitation to the Cotton Bowl.

First I went to New York to appear with the All-American team on the Ed Sullivan show. Ed made us come on stage in football uniforms and sneakers, so we wouldn't scratch the stage. Bad look.

Being All-American, by the way, meant a lot to me. It was later that I frowned on most awards. In college, becoming an All-American was my dream. I used to hear it in my head: Jim Brown, All-American. It sounded so clean.

Meanwhile, it was 1957, the Cotton Bowl was in Dallas, Texas. It was the first time in my life that I would play football in the South. Up until then, whenever a black player went down South, his team would have to find a black family to house him. Some teams would leave their black players at home.

By the end of my senior year my coaches knew a little about me, enough to know I would not be *left* anywhere, nor would I be housed with any private family. Upon arriving in Dallas, our coaches took us to a small, nondescript hotel, on the outskirts of the city. One of our coaches made a quick speech before we left the bus.

He said, "We don't want you guys hanging out too much in the lobby. Just kinda stay in your rooms."

What he meant was: We don't want Jim Brown in the lobby. We're lucky to have him in this hotel. This is Texas. We don't want any trouble.

I understood their predicament, appreciated their extra effort. Typically, had I agreed, they would have found a nice black family for me to stay with. I would have practiced with my teammates, and when practice was done, they would go back to the hotel, I would return alone to the black folks. I would have been hurt and humiliated, because that's what racism does. And then my performance would suffer. See, if I'd played for money, prestige, I could get out there and fake it, go through the necessary motions. I always played for myself, and for my team and because I loved the game. To ensure I never lost that spirit, I vowed there were certain things I would never do, certain feelings dredged up by racism, I would have to avoid. I knew I could never play football with a broken heart.

Our week in Dallas went fine. We played heavily favored T.C.U.—Eastern football, even then, was suspect—and they beat us, 28-27. On to lacrosse.

At lacrosse I was also All-American. I played for Roy Simmons, the only coach at Syracuse who was good to me from the day I arrived. My size in lacrosse was uncommon, gave me a huge advantage. I was 225 by my senior year, playing midfield, where most guys were small. With my bulk, and able to match their speed, I could pretty much do what I wanted. We didn't lose a game my senior year. The starters would play a quarter, beat a team to death, Simmons would pull us, let the subs play. Roy Simmons is quite a man. Playing for him, playing lacrosse, was a fine way to say good-bye to college.

It took time, but today I've reconciled completely with the University of Syracuse. The process, as it usually is with these things, was gradual. After Syracuse accepted me, they asked me to help them recruit. We recruited the late, great Ernie Davis, John Mackey, Jim Manns—all exceptional black athletes—and Syracuse went on to win a national football title. In later years Syracuse earned a reputation for its abundant use of black athletes.

Two years ago I returned to Syracuse. With nine hundred other black alumni, people such as Dave Bing, Vinnie Cohen, Suzanne De Passe, the president of Motown's film division, I gave seminars to the students at Syracuse today. Seeing all those black professionals, graduates from a school that once had shunned blacks, was one of the richest experiences of my life.

Before that, the NCAA had a silver anniversary, decided to honor five outstanding student athletes of the past twenty-five years. They awarded Willie Davis, Ron Kramer, Jim Swink, who played at T.C.U. when we met them in the Cotton Bowl, and Jack Kemp. I was the other recipient, meaning that Syracuse had actively promoted me. Having me recruit black athletes had been one thing, beneficial for the athletes, also for Syracuse. Promoting me for this award seemed a more selfless message: the school was aware and regretful that it had once treated me badly, and was interested now in moving forward. I was honored and gratified, and that award from the NCAA, for what it represented on the part of Syracuse, is one that I'll always appreciate.

Just as I'll always appreciate and love Ed Walsh. And Ken Molloy. And Dr. Collins. And Roy Simmons. Those men literally changed my life, I can't thank them here the way they deserve to be thanked. Had it not been for them, going to college, which should be a privilege, might have been the most damaging time of my life. Instead, it was the most important. When I went from fifth string to All-American, earned my degree, I made myself a promise: for the rest of my life, I will never let anyone tell me what I can and cannot accomplish.

As a black man in America, I would draw on that credo again and again.

6

RACISM
IN CONTEXT

WHEN I TOLD MY best friend on this planet, Big
George Hughley, I was doing a chapter on racism
in my book, he and I sat down, reminisced. Today
Big George is the Chief Investigator for the Los
Angeles Police Department in the division that
combats fraud within city government. If he
doesn't have the goods on a suspect, Big George
won't prosecute. If he does decide to prosecute,
you're going away. Big George bats close to a thousand.

He's a fascinating man. He was born to a mon-
ied family in Santa Monica, came up surfing and
water skiing, chose to become a humanitarian. Big

George was a celebrated high school athlete, honors student. Some folks who knew him decided he would be perfect to integrate the University of Tulsa. George had never been to the South.

When he arrived in Tulsa, about 1955, there were signs reading: "Nigger, get your ass out of town before sunset." When George tells the story he laughs—he hadn't seen that shit in Santa Monica. And every season he played for Tulsa, there were two road games Big George was told he couldn't attend.

He said, "Damn, they got me down there to play seven games instead of nine!"

We laughed about that, too. You'll often find that people who've been in racist situations have a hell of a sense of humor about it, though the topic is serious. Laughter can scale a thing down to size, allow you to stare it in the eye.

One lady who has never lost her sense of humor, or her resolve, is Maggie Hathaway. In fighting discrimination, Maggie has been my mentor. She founded the Hollywood branch of the NAACP. She picketed Southern California golf courses to abolish segregation. She was the publicist for Ray Boots and Pete Brown, a pair of black golfers whom I financed on the Tour. Maggie helped me organize and clarify the agenda of the Black Economic Union. Whenever I've been in trouble, Maggie was always there, rapidly, at the risk of whatever she had going at the time. I could never write a book about my life, could never talk about the struggle, without giving my love to Maggie Hathaway.

Unlike Maggie, most people don't like discussing racism. It embarrasses many people. Others will say it doesn't exist, not in 1989. Some will hear that I'm writing a chapter on racism and they will be irritated. "Why does he have to do that? The guy is bitter."

It's not bitterness. It's far from bitterness. It's the desire to live a natural life.

What I want every day is to live my life with spontaneity. To live a *natural* life. That sounds elementary, but as a black American, I don't have that. As a black American, I monitor almost everything I do. I must be careful of how I look, where I look, my body language. If I don't act the way a black man is Supposed To, I'll make the people around me embarrassed, injure their feelings, or generate their anger. I will create a Racial Situation.

It's a terrible state to live in. And if you think because I'm famous, or tough, or outspoken, that I'm not affected by racism, then you don't understand. I am affected by it any time I see a black person who's not receiving an even shake. I don't have to go hungry to feel for the man with an empty belly.

Yes, I am relatively outspoken. And I will fight for my right to be free. If the scenario is right, I will die for that right. People say, Yes, the white man has his foot up your ass. Be patient, be understanding. He must adjust to not having his foot up your ass. Give him another two hundred years. Let him ease it out.

I say, No. Take it out. Now.

Does that mean I'm angry? Hell no. It means I'm a human being and I want to be treated as one. I don't want to go to Canada for that, or Russia.

Don't want to go back to mother Africa. America is my mother. When will I be accepted by my own family?

Unfortunately, the civil rights movement wasn't yet in full bloom when I first played pro football. I wanted mine, made no bones about it, people called me militant. On the football field they wanted me to be brave. Wanted me to take the ball when we were all backed up, our own one-yard-line, carry us out of there, where we could be safe. Away from football, they wanted me to be another guy. They wanted me to be docile. How could I have the courage to run that hard, then be so weak off the field that I'd succumb to inequity?

I'll tell you the biggest problem when people talk about racial issues: they're so damn confusing. If there's one thing I've learned in fifty-three years, it's that life is contradictory. In sitcoms and bad movies everything is tidy and simple. Life's not that absolute, neither is human behavior, and the subject of racism is *really* tricky. I remember when I was in my teens, I met all those loving white people at Manhasset. Then I went to Syracuse, ran chin first into overt racism. Someone had changed all the rules, forgotten to tell me.

I was lucky, or maybe smart: I never got so confused that I became a racist. I never thought every white man was the devil. Even before I understood it intellectually, I knew instinctively that categorizing people by skin color, then hating them in groups, was not what God intended for us.

When racism is not overt, it can be terribly elusive, as hard to define as it is to prove in court. It's a cliché, and a cliché even to call it a cliché, but

I'll bring it up anyway because I hear it a lot. White people say, "I'm not a racist, I have two black friends." Then I hear the black refrain: "That guy's a racist. He *said* he has two black friends." Now the white guy doesn't know what to think. Gee, maybe I am a racist.

Not so fast. Society has isolated him in such a way, brainwashed him really, that for a white guy to have two black friends, I think he's doing pretty well. Most white folks have no education when it comes to black folks, no meaningful exposure. What they have is TV. What they see there about blacks is ninety-five percent negative. Even when the rare exception, "The Cosby Show," debuted, some critics said "Hey, that's not a real black family. Black families aren't that way." Man, there are millions of black families like the Huxtables. And there are white folks in Appalachia who don't dress like "Dynasty."

But the brainwashing continues, and not just on TV. Maybe a person gets sick of TV, opens an encyclopedia. He reads about a guy named Shockley, an American physicist, who won a Nobel Prize for his study on blacks—why the structure of their brain makes them mentally inferior. Next the person finds a dictionary, looks up the word negro. I did that several times. In various references, it was said that a Negro was distinguished by a broad nose, large lips, arms that are unusually long, especially from the forearm, long legs, small calves, protruding heels, and hair that grows in an irregular manner.

No Kentucky Colonel? I loves dat fried food. It's not funny. TV, films, reference books, and authority figures still spew derogatory, stereotypical misinformation. That is powerful medicine. No wonder people get mixed up.

I think Jimmy the Greek got mixed up. A close friend of mine, a white insider who knows the Greek well, says Jimmy is basically a bigot. Put that aside, because it's only one man's opinion. My opinion is that the Greek simply got mixed up. I think he was high on booze. Anyone who knows booze knows it gets you talking some dumb, convoluted shit—and believing it. I think Jimmy was high, tried to combine some stuff he'd read in Webster's, few other sources, came out with some screwy hybrid.

I thought the Greek affair was insignificant. Having garbage in reference books, on the tube, is a million times more damaging than an oddsmaker getting buzzed and getting mixed up. I felt the same way about the deal with Al Campanis, another guy I thought was talking through his scotch. I know, they said Campanis hadn't been boozing. I think he was. Either way, the episode had no real meaning. Briefly it got people talking, even emotional, but after a week, maybe two, it was off the evening news, back to the old order. What happened with Campanis altered nothing, in society or even in baseball. Baseball has two black managers. In Bill White, its National League President, baseball has one top-level executive.

As meager as that sounds, and is, the NFL is even more exclusive. They asked former commissioner Pete Rozelle a few years ago why there were no black head coaches in the NFL. Essentially, Rozelle implied that none were qualified; they had to go through the system. Pete has retired now, but you still hear similar rationalizations. We could theorize on this one for weeks, but I'll use an actual example. At the time Rozelle made his statement, there were four NFL head coaches who I use to play with on the Browns: Walt Michaels, Paul Wiggin, Monte Clark and Chuck Noll. Walt Michaels was a hell of a linebacker, with an ordinary mind. Paul Wiggin was bashful, good mind for academics, ordinary mind for football. Monte Clark, also shy, great guy, very dedicated. Ordinary mind. Out of my four teammates, the only exceptional mind in that group is Chuck Noll. Chuck knows the game as few men ever have.

I also played on the Browns with John Wooten and Paul Warfield and Bobby Mitchell. All black, all respected, all bright. I think Wooten, a Dallas Cowboys scout, is more suited to coach than at least three of those guys I mentioned before. Bobby Mitchell, the assistant GM at Washington, definitely has the skills and everything else to be a head coach. Over the years, we had a *lot* of black Browns who could match intellect and football smarts with the other guys I mentioned. Had they gotten just a little encouragement, maybe they'd be head coaches today. Guys who have tried anyway haven't gotten any jobs. So please don't tell me the black guys today lack the experience. How can they obtain it if they can't get coaching jobs? That Catch-22 is getting old.

The issue here is power and leadership—a head coach has them both. In America and the NFL, that's a position that is still off-limits to blacks. Meaning you can have forty Jim Browns on your team, as long as Paul Brown is white. You can have ten blacks on offense, and as long as the quarterback is white, America still feels semi-comfortable. It used to be black guys couldn't play center, quarterback, and safety. Today, the black guy can't be The Man.

However, I don't run all over the NFL screaming "Racist!" every two seconds. I never called Pete Rozelle a racist, or any of the NFL owners, because I don't know that any of them are. In America, it doesn't always come down to how an individual feels about blackness. In America, actions often hinge on economics. That a white owner doesn't hire a black coach does not mean he's a racist. He may adore black people, but if ninety percent of the franchise's fans are white, he doesn't know how those ticket buyers would react to a black coach. A white coach might be better business. I can sit here and say, "Hey, hire a black coach," and you know I hope that someone does. But it's easy for me: I don't have millions of my own capital invested. You can't say to every businessman in America, "Protect your investment as you see fit," and not allow that right to the NFL owners.

I also believe if black folks are going to scream at white owners, they should first take a good look at their own. Check out the black superstars who largely ignore the black community. How different are the choices they make than those of the white owners? Both are more concerned with generating income, by projecting a certain image, than they are with effecting change.

I basically like O.J. Simpson. I do like Marcus

Allen. And I like Michael Jackson and Lionel Ritchie. If they don't care about black folks, that's one thing. If they do, then their contribution is lacking. I don't like saying that; I'm not saying it to try and hurt people. I'm saying it to try and help. Because if we don't help our own, who will? Until black folks take a stand, how can we expect white people to?

That's why I came out with this several years ago, began discussing the social consciousness, which I find negligible, of the modern-day athlete. That includes the modern black athlete. For years I never heard any black athletes complain that there was not one black head coach in the NFL. Where was everyone?

I can't tell anyone how to live their life. Every man has the right to look out for his own career, make a whole bunch of money. No one does that better than the Juice. He's popular, he's intelligent, he's commercial. On the other hand, O.J. cannot tell the truth to America. In order to stay popular, make the money, he can't say his black brothers are getting mistreated. That's why, among hardcore blacks, the Juice gets tremendous admiration as an athlete, and very little as a man. And that's why I never call O.J. if there's a black event that might be controversial, or I need guys to come down to South Central L.A. Even if he wanted to come and showed up, if someone took a photograph, and it went over the wire, the people at Hertz would be pissed. That's not the image they want Juice to represent to their consumers. I know it, Juice knows it, so I don't even put him in the position. I just don't ask. Here's the thing: white

America will never accept the Juice, wholesome image or not, as fully as it will a white guy.

When I look at the black stars today, I wonder if they ever study history. How do they think they got in the position they're in? Blacks who came before them paved the way, blacks who had to do more than just play good football, who had to endure some bitter cruelties. A lot of them did more than endure. They spoke out, provoked some thought, took some damn chances, instead of saying, "Hey, I've got mine. Everything is cool." If we had done that, the guys today would be starting from scratch.

And that is my crucial point: it's thirty years later, but everything is *not* cool. If blacks start taking their gains for granted, future generations will have serious trouble. I don't want the guys today to give *me* their damn time and money. I want them to wake up. To look around, realize the struggle is only beginning.

I look at athletes today, black and white, wonder if they watch anything but MTV. They're Very Nice, Very Rote, everyone says they're Wonderful. Maybe so. But I can't help thinking, They're not *that* wonderful. They won't say one word about South Africa. It's the worst country there is. They have apartheid. They're terrorists, killing people in the name of white superiority. These Wonderful Guys, particularly when they're at the peak of their visibility, are the ones who can get people's attention. Why don't they speak up?

All of that said, I want to be fair here. It is not easy making choices when you're a black American. Every black man isn't a revolutionary, and it's a *tough* decision: do I become active in black rights, risk losing jobs, or do I protect my own career? Is it possible for me, a black man in America, to find a compromise? To help a black man make *some* kind of choice, he can't even draw on his own tradition. He can't say, "Well, this how we've been doing it for five hundred years. This is my culture, this is my tradition, this is what I must fight to maintain." The black American came from many different tribes. Families were broken, sold into slavery, not only by whites, but by blacks selling other blacks. Masters were sleeping with slaves, having babies, bloodlines got mixed like crazy. Coming from so many tribes, after all of that fragmentation, the black American has no firm tradition. His only tradition is that of an American. Naturally he wants to move up. Become affluent, ride in limos, get on "Entertainment Tonight." Nothing's more American than that. And it's tempting, when your kids are in private school, your life is full, to get a little soft. That's not black. That's human.

And I *still* think we have to resist complacency. We're still black, too many black guys are still getting their asses kicked. We have to help to get that foot out of the other guy's butt. Any prominent black man who doesn't make some genuine attempt, and I really believe this, will someday wake up and feel remorse.

Me? I'll talk about racism with anyone, and I'll talk about racism in sports. But I get bored when that's all people want to talk about. By the time a guy arrives in the NFL, he's eating. He doesn't have to sleep on the sidewalk. Doesn't have to sell crack. The principle of equal opportunity should be applied to every man and woman, not just guys who drive Porsches. I wish them well, I'm glad they're playing quarterback, but I can't dwell too long on poor Warren Moon and Randall Cunningham. If that were my priority I'd be a fool.

Sometimes, all this talk about black quarterbacks makes me feel I've stepped into a time warp, landed in 1958. It's almost the 1990s, people still discuss a few black quarterbacks as if they represent some meaningful breakthrough for blacks. When Doug Williams played in the Super Bowl, I kept reading that the moment was proud and historical for blacks. Is that right? To me, it sounded more like the white media working out its own hangups. The story of that game wasn't Doug Williams's blackness. It was that Doug's career was nearly expired, he had the heart to keep coming back, to stay prepared, then excelled in the most pressure-filled game of his life. That had nothing to do with his blackness, and I don't buy its profundity for other black people. Blacks in the 1990s don't need any more symbols. They need equal rights. What Doug Williams did in the Super Bowl won't do shit for a cat who can't throw a football.

When I was a child, the two main people in my life, Mama and Myrtle, were gentle and loving. But they accepted racism. They had lived their lives in the South, knew there were worlds forbidden to blacks, and if they tried to enter, they could be arrested, and their lives would be endangered. When did I first feel racism? I felt it when I was a baby. I sensed the apprehension of the women in my family. By the way they held me, whispered to me, they seemed to be saying, Son, you have to be careful.

Even as a little boy I was . . . different. I didn't use the word racism, but I knew when I didn't like something. On St. Simons Island, we weren't allowed to enter the only theater to see a movie. Our water fountains were trickly. I was never allowed to swim at Port Allen where the dock was, and all the nice little shops. Blacks would have to go down about three or four miles, walk a narrow path through the brush to the negro beach. That bothered the hell out of me. I didn't want to go to any negro beach.

Our black school sat in the backwoods. It was basically a shack divided into two rooms. I had two little white buddies, and sometimes I'd see them on their school bus. Once they took me by their school on a weekend—it was big and bright and new. I wondered, How come? Why is it so much better than my school? I knew I wasn't inferior. I could run fast, shoot marbles, roll tires, climb trees, and talk about lots of stuff. What was inferior about me? I couldn't see it. I wouldn't accept it.

Beginning at home, I questioned old habits. My grandmother had a white Jesus on her wall, this blond, handsome, blue-eyed, pink-skinned Jesus. And I got into it with her over that.

I said, "Jesus don't look like that. Why is he blond and blue-eyed? Nobody knows what he looked like. Why don't you take that off your wall?"

Before my senior year at college, I returned to the island to see Myrtle. Usually I spent summers in Manhasset, but I missed my people at home.

Myrtle was doing housework, her employer had asked to meet me. We went to his house, knocked on his door. He looked out his window, stepped out on his porch. He said he loved football, wanted to shake my hand. We talked for a few minutes longer, Myrtle and I went home. She was proud and pleased. I was upset. Myrtle wanted to know why.

I said, "We go to his house, he doesn't have the decency to ask us inside. Grandma, that's just common courtesy."

She understood what I meant, but she had reconciled herself. She would fear God, love all people.

Grandma said, "He's a nice man. At least he wanted to meet you."

And she had a point. But my instinct was screaming, NO! I don't like it like that.

The 1950s, the South, it was a strange trip. Back then, it was wise to avoid entire states. Stay the fuck away from Mississippi. In the South you had to worry for your life, and you worried not about so-called criminals, but the government. Driving from town to town, it was horrible knowing that the sheriff or the police chief might also be Grand Dragon of the Ku Klux Klan, and that he could bait you, kill you, in the name of the law.

I once had an encounter that easily could have turned violent. As a freshman at Syracuse I had enlisted in ROTC; by graduation I was a second lieutenant at Fort Benning, Georgia. One summer, I would drive over the Alabama border to the Tuskegee Institute to visit my girlfriend. I made friends with a couple of black guys my age, locals.

One day we were taking a ride in my red convertible, top down, when we passed another car on a hard dirt road. Moments later, two sheriffs waved us down, pulled us over, approached my car. They were in regular suits, not uniforms, one guy looked about thirty, the other maybe fifty. The younger guy told me to get out of the car, so I did.

He said, "Boy, why did you throw dust up on those white people? Huh, nigger?"

I said, "What are you talking about, man? I'm no nigger."

My friend in the back said, "Oh my God."

My other friend got on his knees right in the car. He said, "Sir, he's not from here. He doesn't understand. Don't shoot him, please. He just got out of Syracuse, that's way up North."

On "Syracuse," the older cop looked harder at me.

He said, "Yeah, I recognize that boy. He's the boy who played up there at Syracuse, played that football. They give you this car?"

I said, "Yeah, going to school got me this car."

The young guy was fuming, but the old guy was calling the shots now.

He said, "Look. We weren't gonna bother you, but you were getting kind of arrogant, the way you were driving. I'll tell you what you do, boy. You get back in the car and get on outta here. Don't be throwing dust up on white people no more."

We left, me breathing deeply, my friends talking a mile a minute. Other than drive a red convertible, we had done nothing. And that was the life you lived in the South.

That also got confusing. You'd start to feel

paranoid, some white guy would befriend you. As blatant as Southern whites could be in their hatred, there were other Southern whites, if they liked you, who were just as straight-out, would stand up for you against any man. In the huge middle, there were all those white folks who didn't know how to act. They were also affected by racists. How do you be a good guy in Mississippi? You invite three black co-workers for dinner, the Klan might torch your home. You might love those black guys, but not enough to risk the lives of your family.

To try and stay sane, I had to measure each situation individually, and every person. I had to remind myself that in matters of race, very little is absolutely clear, and many factors are interwoven. I took the same attitude to the NFL. The NFL of the 1950s did not exist in a vacuum. Was there racism? Yes. To the same extent that there was racism in America.

When I entered the NFL—1957—there was a quota for blacks. I doubt it was written, you probably couldn't prove it in court, every owner would deny it, but it was there. We always knew each team would have six, perhaps eight, blacks on a roster. Never seven though: it was always an even number, so none of the white guys would have to share a room with a black. Once we went on the road, had an odd number of black guys and an odd number of white guys; one of the black players was back in Cleveland with an injury. Rather than pair off the extra black with the extra white, management bought each player a separate room. They were willing to pay for an additional room in order to preserve the color line.

I never had to worry about making the team, but I still hated final cuts. The last few days of cuts I'd walk around the locker room, silently counting the remaining brothers. I knew they'd get paired down to six or eight. I knew some great black ballplayers would lose their jobs.

There were even restrictions within the quotas. Some teams would stack up three or four of their black guys at the same position. If a team had three black receivers, they'd stack them at one particular spot—typically flanker—so blacks wouldn't occupy all the receiver spots. We'd see guys who were second and third string, running back punts and kickoffs, know they should be starting across the board.

The NFL was not an island: The owners were acting in concert with society. Each franchise wanted predominantly white teams, sprinkled with blacks, so the predominantly white fans wouldn't have collective seizures. Not just any black athletes were wanted. They wanted nice guy blacks, humble blacks, just-glad-to-be-there blacks, lower-pay, work-hard, say-the-sky-was-blue, the-sun-was-shining blacks. Blacks who wouldn't rock the status quo.

In that respect, I'm not certain how far we've progressed. America still prefers its black athletes to keep on smiling. I remember when Magic joined the NBA. His smile was as luminous as his game. He was a Nice Guy, everyone adored him. Then he stopped smiling, blamed Paul Westhead for screwing up the Lakers offense. Man, they ripped him. First of all, if Jerry Buss was happy with Westhead, ten Magic Johnsons couldn't get Westhead fired.

Jerry fired Westhead, not Magic. And not only was he dead right about the offense, Magic was only verbalizing what many Lakers people, and not just athletes, were already discussing off the record. Magic's the one who spoke out; he got condemned from Boston to Seattle. You think what you think. I think he was a black athlete, criticizing his white boss, and white fans resented it. I think if Magic had been white, no way people would have been that mean to him. White folks speak out all the time.

When I joined the Browns, the status quo held no interest for me. If I felt management was out of line, I would say so, but I would tell management, not the press. I'd talk to the press about the plight of blacks in America, but if it was specific Cleveland Browns business, I'd try and work it out within the group. Inside the organization, I became the spokesman for my black teammates. As a star, it was hard for management to ignore me. Right after that trip when management bought the extra hotel room, I went to see the young owner of our team, Art Modell. I told Art I didn't mind rooming with black guys, I was very comfortable with it. I got along with all my black teammates, and I didn't want to room with a guy only because he was white. I told Art we didn't want to hang out with white folks. We also didn't want to be told we aren't good enough to be with white folks.

Art got mad at me. He said, "Jim, I'm not prejudiced. I give more money to the NAACP than you do!"

I said, "Look, Art, I like you. I'm not saying you're prejudiced. But you can't room a black guy

94

by himself to keep him from rooming with a white guy. We can't accept that. If you want to talk to the players yourself, tell them your response to the problem is that you give money to the NAACP, then go ahead. Tell me how they react to *that.*"

I think Art understood why we were upset. And I never considered him racist. Yes, he was discriminatory in some of his actions. Every owner in the NFL was. And it would have been very hard for Art Modell to defy what was happening in America in 1960. I was coming from one place, Art from another.

Of course I don't give up very easily, and things changed when I came to the Browns. I organized the black cats. If the brothers were going to be separated, I wanted us separated on our own terms, not the team's. I told my teammates we had to maintain our pride and dignity. We couldn't roll over for every double standard.

I said, "Look. They don't invite us to the parties and events with the pretty white girls, then we won't go to those community functions, that boring, political shit, where they want to make us look like one big happy family. If we can't go to all the stuff, the fun stuff, then we won't do the fake stuff. They room us together, we'll stay together. We'll play hard, dress right, carry ourselves with class, and be team people. But we don't have to kiss any ass, or take any attitude, to pacify some redneck from Mississippi."

The message got around: If you were black and you played for Cleveland, you had support. We took every rookie in, explained how we did things on the Browns. We had one kid named Sidney Williams, still a good friend of mine. Sidney was a strong-willed individual, who came out of a Southern black school. His rookie year we beat Unitas and the Baltimore Colts, won the NFL championship. They showed the title game on national TV, when the cameras panned to Sidney, he started making silly faces. It was 1963.

We said, Sid, we don't do that. We're on a mission here, we're being scrutinized, and we carry ourselves in a certain way. We're not clowns, shuffling, or uneducated. We're together, we play hard, and we want to be treated like professionals. So don't make faces on national TV!

I have to say it because it's true: we were ahead of our time. The Cleveland Browns had the best organized blacks in all of sports. We partied, chased women, but we also discussed economics, and talked about life after football. Our influence spread across the league: our guys would get traded, then they'd organize their new teams. When Cleveland traded Bobby Mitchell, he became the first black Washington Redskin. There were no Falcons then, no Saints, Washington was as close to a Southern team as we had in the NFL. The Redskins' owner, George Preston Marshall, said as long as he lived, there would not be a black on his team. As I understand it, the Kennedys intervened, impressed upon Marshall that the stadium was public property, and discrimination wasn't lawful. Marshall bowed to the pressure, traded for Bobby, he became All-Pro, now he's their assistant GM. We still keep in touch, as I do with most of the blacks from the Browns. Everyone is still alive, doing well. That's pretty damn good.

The most meaningful thing I did with the Browns was to help create the Black Industrial and Economic Union. In the middle 1960s, we opened eight offices across the country, most offices headed by a professional athlete. We were totally black, had cats working for us who were brilliant, with MBAs from schools like Cornell, University of Chicago. Our motto was "Produce, Achieve, and Prosper." It wasn't an exciting concept, I wasn't up there being outrageous, making wild speeches. And it worked. The whole purpose was to take a young black guy who was bright, had a good idea, help him get financing for that idea, then supply him with the technical knowledge to turn that idea into a business. The result was wonderful: we started businesses across America owned and operated by blacks. Eventually we received a grant from the Ford Foundation for $520,000. Then they upped it to over $1 million.

No one ever talks about it, but it was something I took real pride in. I've always worked for the advancement of black people, always within the system, always preaching the American way. But while I was being discussed in many other ways—playing football, making movies, being prosecuted —my main work was rarely mentioned. That didn't reduce its power: we helped introduce many blacks into the world of business. Our organization was the first in the last thirty years to emphasize economic development for black people.

Economic development is the only way to move up in this country. Big problem is, most black leaders don't emphasize economics. Because most black leaders come from the clergy, black leadership in America has rarely been elected. It's been designated, by the church. If a black minister has a following of two thousand people, he becomes a leader in the community. In today's world, more than ever, you want your leaders to be expert at economics. For that you need experience, but ministers have their backgrounds in theology, not economics. Their approach is emotional, not pragmatic. Uplifting speeches are great, when you need them. When black Americans thought black was bad, Stokely Carmichael and H. Rap Brown started saying Black is Beautiful. I needed that. After I have that, what I need is education: what capitalist techniques do I need to know to make money? Because once I have money in America, if I work with *other* blacks who have money, I can get power. Then I don't have to run around asking anyone for anything.

It's true. I've never seen any white American who didn't want to make some money. Even the racist, if he can make enough money, will deal with black folks. You can go into the baddest black neighborhoods in America, you'll find white entrepreneurs, risking their lives to make that green. Money is America's God. The stock market crashed, there were men jumping out of windows.

Black leaders need to push that capitalist message. Even a man as great as Dr. King, who moved the nation and did effect change, did not quite understand economics and political clout. I loved Dr. King, but he never told us how to utilize our earnings. He told us to integrate. He even went into Cicero, Illinois to integrate there. Encouraged black folks to do the same. Economically, that type of thinking wasn't sound. Why should a black family pay five times what a house would normally cost just so they can live next to white people? Black people don't have that type of money to throw around.

I loved Dr. King, but near the end I think he lost his way. It isn't about integration, it's about discrimination. Nobody wants to live by anyone because they're white, or black. They just don't want to be kicked in the ass. In fact, a lot of people said so-called integration was the worst thing that ever happened to blacks. We became dispersed into the general economy, rather than having an economy of our own that could flourish, and then become a very powerful part of the general economy. That's what the Koreans and the Jews and the Japanese did. They kept their monies among themselves, poured it back into their own communities. They fixed up their stores, cleaned up their neighborhoods. Now they're an integral part of the economy, meaning they have political clout. Our monies, on the other hand, went to other merchants, other races. Our monies went largely to brand-name products. Blacks are the best consumers in the world.

That's history, now is now. And it isn't too late to copy those other guys. It's a great time to do it. It's perfectly obvious we can't rely on the government, not in a capitalist society, not with a government that's ninety-nine percent white. I think black folks are starting to see that.

I wonder if the black guys playing today know anything about Otto Graham. Now that Otto has turned himself around, I don't like to talk about his past, but you can't deny people their history. Whenever blacks in the NFL talk about the struggle, one of the key figures is Otto Graham.

This is not hype: Otto Graham was one of the finest all-around athletes in the history of the NFL. He excelled at golf, basketball, any game he wanted to. Otto went to the Hall of Fame for his quarterbacking. He played for the Browns in the old AAFC, then in the NFL, led them to a series of championships. He was a brilliant two-minute passer, a relentless competitor. There are old-timers who swear that Otto was the best ever at his position.

Otto was also a racist. I first met him in 1957, at the College All-Star Game in Chicago. Otto was an assistant coach under Curley Lambeau, I was coming out of Syracuse, on my way to the Browns. Otto walked up to me one day during drills.

He said, "Brown, you'll never make it in the NFL."

First I was startled. Then I thought, *Well, that's bullshit. Of course I'll make it in the NFL. Why is this guy picking on me?*

As more blacks came into the league, guys started talking, Otto became famous. As a perennial coach on the All-Star staff, Otto had the chance to encounter many great black athletes, used that opportunity to try and discourage them. Otto told Bobby Mitchell that he'd never make it to the NFL. He told Gale Sayers he'd never make it to the NFL. He told Duane Thomas he'd never make it to the NFL. Bobby, Gale and I are in the Hall of Fame. Duane was All-Pro. Otto wasn't blind or stupid. It was purely racism.

When Charley Taylor came to the NFL after a spectacular run at Arizona State, he also played for Otto in Chicago. Though Charley was a phenomenal athlete, Otto told him he had no future in the NFL. Charley went on to win Rookie of the Year for the Redskins, retired as the leading pass catcher of all time, is another Hall of Famer. In his second season, Charley and the Redskins were playing in the Hall of Fame game. Otto was there, too, for his induction into the Hall of Fame. Driving to the ceremony in a convertible, Otto passed several guys on the Redskins. Several players put their hands to their mouths, shouted to Otto: "Hey Otto, Charley Taylor will never make it in the NFL!"

Had they owned a crystal ball, I think those guys would have kept their mouths shut: one season later, Otto was named coach of the Redskins. I knew the black Redskins, every one of them said Otto was terrible. Big George was there, right out of the Canadian Football League. He told me about the time Otto walked into a meeting, said he didn't want to hear one more word about dissension between white players and black players. When one of the Redskins asked Otto what he meant, Otto didn't explain. That pissed off everyone, white and black. A bunch of the white guys got together, went to speak with Edward Bennett Williams, the famous attorney who had purchased the Redskins. They told Williams there *was* no dissension, Otto was stirring up trouble that didn't exist, and it wasn't the first time.

Toward the end of my own career, I had played in the same golf tournament as Otto. Otto hooked a drive, the ball struck a spectator in the head. A year later, Otto's lawyer came to see me in training camp, said Otto was being sued by the guy he hit with the golf ball. Did I recall the incident, could I give him some information?

I said, "Yeah, I remember. Otto hooked one and it hit a spectator. I didn't see anything though, just heard about it. There's nothing I can testify to."

The attorney went back to Otto, apparently told him I wouldn't cooperate. Otto got angry. Why do I think that? A few months later, out of nowhere, Otto ripped me in public, not the last time, but the first. He said the Browns had never won a championship with Jim Brown. He said as long as I was there, the Browns would never win one.

I thought those were pretty strong words, but I didn't respond. Just as I'd let go his crack that I wouldn't make the NFL. Even when we won the NFL title, I didn't rub it in Otto's face. I knew where Otto was coming from, didn't want to join him on that level.

I forgot about Otto until two years later. I was retired, had business in Washington. The Redskins were losing, the Otto stories coming out of Washington were getting uglier. A Washington beat writer asked me what I thought was wrong with the team. I thought, the hell with it. I'm telling the truth.

I said, "You have to get a new head coach."

The next day there was a headline. A few months later Otto was fired. Obviously it wasn't my statement, but I have to admit it felt good to nail a guy who'd been so detrimental to blacks, and to me, for so many years. I can't say I was disappointed when Otto got fired.

I don't want to jump on a man, not tell the good part of the story. Later in life, Otto contracted cancer, and he whipped it. I started hearing from people that Otto had changed. He didn't have it out for blacks, didn't have it out for anyone. I was curious as hell to see if it was true. Joe DiMaggio and I used to host the Joe DiMaggio-Jim Brown golf tournament in Las Vegas, for athletes who were in the Hall of Fame. We invited Otto, he accepted, and I swear to you, he was a different individual. He was gracious and kind to everyone, and it was real. In my opinion, Otto took a look inside after facing his mortality, came out with a new way of looking at life. I recently went back to Cleveland for another golf tournament, and Otto was one of the reasons I did. When a man wants to get himself right, I will never hold a grudge. Otto came back to be great. I'm glad for him.

As Walter Payton zoomed in on my all-time record for yards, the *Chicago Tribune* ran a story about us. Sam Smith, the writer, wrote, "But there may be one principal reason why no runner can compare with Jim Brown. He played when there were few blacks in the league, and as a black and the biggest offensive threat on his team, he was the target of every opposing defense."

Smith included interviews with many of my peers, including my old teammate Gary Collins. He quoted Gary:

"I remember we went to Dallas in '63 and we're at a motel at the airport and I'm thinkin', 'What are we doing at the airport listening to jet engines when we should be downtown?' It was because they wouldn't let blacks in the downtown hotels. Jim went out the next day and ran for 232 yards in 20 carries. He responded to those challenges."

Good story or what? I kind of wish it was true.

I remember the game and I did have a bunch of yards. But I didn't know we had stayed at the airport because of me. I wasn't responding to any racial challenge. I was out there playing football.

What do I think? As a black man in the NFL of the 1950s and early 1960s, was I a special target?

Not really.

I'm sure there were guys in the league who wanted to hit me harder, did it a little later, because I was black. But I'm not here to sing the blues. And when I reminisce about my opponents, my memories are not of being mistreated because I was black. Yeah, guys would try and grind my face into the dirt. They'd leap on me during pile-ups. They'd scratch me and twist me. They did that to *every* good runner. That's the NFL. If you were good they wanted to hurt you.

There was not a lot of name-calling. My entire career, I think I heard two racial slurs. One was my rookie year, in a game against the Detroit Lions. I don't remember the guy and I don't remember if I responded. That's how insignificant it was.

I remember the other time only because it was funny. We were playing an exhibition game against the Pittsburgh Steelers and they had a guy named Lou Michaels. Lou was one of the dirtiest players in the NFL, he pulled some shit on me, I told him to back off.

Lou said, "Why don't you go back to the Mafia where you came from?"

I guess he wanted to call me a nigger, or tell me to go back to niggerland, but he messed it up.

Rocket scientist.

Typically, the verbalization of something racial doesn't bother me. Let me qualify that. It depends on the situation. If I'm sitting in a restaurant with my lady and a crazy man comes to my table and says—"Hey, nigger, what are you doing sitting at this table?"—I will whip his ass. Quickly. It's not so much the "nigger," it's the audacity of laying *his* cancer on *me* when I'm having a private moment. If his body language and manner are a particular way, he could never mention the word and I'd still jump him. Whereas with "nigger," I'd jump on him twice.

Even in high school and college, during games I never concerned myself with racial epithets. I knew they were trying to enrage me, so I'd start a fight, be ejected, and that made their words seem almost impersonal. And I noticed something: very few guys who were winning the war bothered to call me names. It was the frustrated guys, the ones who couldn't handle my game, who'd talk their trash. I looked at it as a backhanded compliment.

In the NFL, what concerned me far more was my immediate family—the Browns. I didn't know most of my opponents. I knew my coaches, my owners, my teammates. So they had the real power to hurt me. When Eric Dickerson left the Rams he said it wrong, but his bottom line was right: it's hard to run a football when you don't feel wanted. Had tempers flared at practice, one of my own called me a name, it would have struck a tender nerve.

That never happened, and I never felt bad about my teammates who were white. I didn't party with them. Sometimes I felt they had more of a bond with the white Detroit Lions than the black Cleveland Browns. But I liked a lot of them, and those of whom I didn't, it had nothing to do with race. I never ever considered them my enemy.

What I felt from the white guys on the Browns was additional pressure. Higher expectations. It was very subtle but this is the vibe I sensed from my teammates who were white: You're a black man and we're allowing you to be the star of the Cleveland Browns. That's not a position we grant readily. Which means, Jim, you'd better perform.

If you asked the guys today, one by one, I'm sure they'd say they never felt that way. Perhaps it was subconscious, they don't *think* they felt that way, or maybe I'm wrong. It's all in the vision of the individual. I'm sure the white guys have a different view of the past than I do. They weren't black, weren't inside my head. From where I was, the pressure was strong and real.

Black or white, it's not as if we could strap on our helmets, shut our minds. America was in turmoil, that was evident every night on the evening news. First year in the league I led the NFL in rushing, established myself as a star. I wondered what might happen if we got a white rookie from the deep South. Would he accept a black star, or poison our team?

I got my answer right away. My second year, the Browns drafted Gene Hickerson. University of Mississippi. That was one rookie the black guys checked *out*. We knew he could be important to us: we were a running team, he was a big young guard with speed. More than any group, the guys on the offensive line must function as a unit, and we knew Hickerson would have to block in tandem with our other guard, John Wooten, who was black. And Hickerson would have to block for me.

I noticed something immediately: the entire time we studied Gene, he was studying us. The kid was fascinated. He hadn't been around blacks, I believe we didn't represent what he had heard about blacks. We were into business and civil rights and dignity. Not only was he taken aback, Gene began to appreciate us. At practice, he saw Wooten and the other linemen busting open holes, me crashing through them, and he got off on our performance, excited that he could be a part of it. Gene wanted in.

We used to play the Cardinals twice a year. Because of Hickerson I'll never forget one of those games. We were looking at defeat. It was something like fourth and twenty, ten seconds left, on the Cardinals 25-yard line, and we had one time-out remaining. Frank Ryan, our quarterback, found Gary Collins on the *one*. It was masterful, by two tough players. Frank stuck in the pocket, took punishment, as bravely as any good passer I've ever seen. Collins was always making critical catches. And Gary could hit.

Time out. We're on the one-yard line. Time for one play. Every person in that stadium knew who was getting the ball. And I'm thinking, *Here it comes. They're giving me the ball. And I want it. It's fucking mine. But the big play has already been accomplished. Fourth and twenty, Ryan and Collins came through. Everyone thinks it's easy now, means it isn't easy at all. All that's left for me is to fuck this up!*

And here comes Hickerson, this boy from Mississippi. He was tired. His big old face was redder than usual.

Gene said, "Jim, you got to do it for us man. This is it. We're counting on you. This is *it*."

I just looked at him. Thinking, *Look at this motherfucker. Boy from Mississippi is up in my face, putting his life in my hands. Goddamn.*

So I went to talk to Ryan. I told him I wanted to call my own play. Not something right up the middle, where there might be two thousand pounds of human gridlock. I didn't want to jump right into the line, get stopped, and say, Oh, I didn't make it. I wanted a play where I started off-tackle, but if that was closed, I could sweep around the end, use my athleticism, stop and reverse my field, run backwards for fifty damn yards if I had to, *anything*, before I would get tackled on that play.

Frank agreed. I scored the TD, rammed it in hard, straight off-tackle, we beat the Cards. Ryans and Collins had made the huge play but that one yard felt like ninety. Damn Hickerson had me all emotional.

I always liked Gene. I don't know how many guys he called nigger back in his hometown, and I didn't give a damn. By the time he got with us he transcended any Mississippi bullshit. I don't think he ever said so, but I think Gene liked me, too. The respect was there.

My relationship with football fans was more complex. When I was playing in the NFL, something made me very strange in the minds of most Americans. They felt if a black guy was playing pro football, winning, driving a Cadillac, he should be satisfied.

Satisfied? With the dichotomy of my life, I'm lucky I didn't crack up.

Fans in Cleveland knew pro football. Blue collar town, no-nonsense fans. On the field I was dominant, they couldn't get enough. I'd score a TD, 80,000 people would chant my name.

Cleveland also had a place called Little Italy. Cleveland was a city divided, East Side and West Side, black and white. Blacks who went to Little Italy were often attacked. I could have scored twenty touchdowns Sunday afternoon; if I walked through Little Italy that evening I'd have been jumped. I'd have no 32 on my back, all they'd see was black.

I didn't mind living and socializing with black folks. Black society was fun. What I wanted was the choice. I knew whatever discrimination was doing to me, what it did to my insides, it was many times worse for blacks who didn't play football, blacks on the East Side of Cleveland, who were being treated as less than human for the color of their skin. Press some dollars into my hand, you expect me to forget that?

America loved my performance, yet I couldn't check into certain hotels, drink from any water fountain when I was thirsty. If that's not strange you tell me what is. I didn't want to give up football, did not want to close my eyes. I tried to find a way I could live with the contradiction, still feel decently about myself. I accepted trophies, never displayed them in my home. I liked the cheers, didn't allow them to fool me. I never forgot who I was, and from where I came. Throughout my career I'd drive to the bleakest neighborhoods in Cleveland, spend time with the lowliest brothers.

7

HELLO, BROWNS

I Look Back On my career in pro football much the way a fan views the athletes and teams he cheered as a child: I prefer to recall the triumphs and good times, banish the disappointments to regions of my brain where they can't disturb me. I am fifty-three years old. Today when I think of Paul Brown, I remember the good times.

In a certain sense, Paul and I will always be married. We'll always be linked to each other, the history of the Cleveland Browns, and the history of the NFL. We had clashes, but they can't diminish our shared accomplishments. Not for me.

Dealing with a sports legend did get complicated. In Paul's case that isn't hyperbolic. To the public, Paul *was* the Cleveland Browns. Paul formed the team. He gave the Browns its name, his name, the Browns being the only NFL team ever named for their coach. For seventeen years Paul was the Browns' head coach and general manager, for most of that period one of its owners. In 1950, the Browns, San Francisco 49ers and Baltimore Colts were absorbed by the NFL. The cocky NFL thought the trio from the AAFC would be out-classed. Paul won the whole damn thing his first year. The Browns won Eastern Division titles the next five seasons, and two more NFL champion-ships. Cleveland faltered when Otto Graham re-tired, revived when I appeared one year later. The bridge from past to present was Paul.

Paul literally invented much of modern coach-ing. Among his innovations: studying games on film, weekly grading of players from those films, utilizing playbooks, IQ tests for athletes. Paul started calling the plays for Otto Graham in 1946. Now it's standard. As players or assistants, Paul taught Don Shula, Chuck Noll, Weeb Ewbank and Bill Walsh. They've coached ten Super Bowl win-ners.

Paul was a contained, chilly, brilliant, fanati-cally organized man, who once taught high school English. At the first team meeting of every season, Paul would give his trademark speech: "You are a member of the Cleveland Browns. You are the New York Yankees of football. You will conduct yourself in a proper manner. I expect you to watch your language, your dress, your deportment. If you're a drinker or a chaser, you weaken the team and we don't want you. We're here for one thing—to win the championship. Let's get to work."

By the time that I arrived, the face of the

Browns had changed. The brawlers from the past had mostly retired, leaving Lenny Ford, Don Colo and Bobby Gain as our only genuine thugs. Lenny was on his way out, even Paul couldn't control him. My rookie year, Lenny drank so heavily his arms were swollen. Next season, Paul banished Lenny to frozen Green Bay.

Once we lost Colo and Lenny, I felt we became the straightest team in football. The old Browns had the maniacs, we got the model citizens. We had Mike McCormack, good blocker, company man, whose lips probably never touched a drink in his life. We had Bill Glass, a preacher playing defensive end, and our other defensive end was Paul Wiggin, a mild-mannered grad from Stanford. Later we got Frank Ryan, a professorial type, and Ernie Green, who was pure Establishment. They were all fine players, all nice guys. And they were all goody-goody. It worked against us at times. Pro football is *not* nice. And you're not going to win a lot of championships with goody-goodies because goody-goody guys try and *be* goody-goody. You get up against a bunch of thugs, you can't retaliate, they'll run you off the field. It happened my rookie year, when we played Detroit in the NFL championship. They stomped us, 59–14. We had some injured players on offense, but I think it made no difference. It was like cats off the street playing guys from Beverly Hills.

But that's what Paul Brown wanted, and what Paul Brown wanted he got. His trademark as a coach was fear. He was a small, omnipotent man who could make people do things. Paul was all about performance and winning and organization, and Paul. He never spoke loudly because he didn't have to. He could reduce you with The Look, and a cutting one-liner.

Paul was famous for his one-liners. We used to have a chubby, jolly, left-handed halfback named Charley Scales. In a game against the Steelers our quarterback fumbled. Trying to salvage the play, Charley picked up the ball, decided he would throw me this little lefty pass. I was prepared—improvisation was one of my strong points—but Charley wobbled it, the pass was intercepted. Charley knew he was fucked and he was. As Charley ran off the field, Paul one-lined him: "You'll never have a chance to throw another one." True enough. Paul got rid of Charley a short time later.

Since our fear revolved around Paul, so did our humor. Our collective terror of a man half our size became a nervous, good-humored joke among the black Cleveland Browns. We kidded about the way Paul pronounced Unitas, stressing the U, so it came out Johnny *U*-nitas. Our favorite line was "Just so you know." Paul would always use it to punctuate a statement. When we'd get by ourselves, when a guy did something dumbass, everyone would dog him. Then you'd hear one final voice: "Just so you know."

Just so you know, Paul even frightened Gain and Colo, our wildmen defensive tackles. A vigorous man, Paul would lecture us about tradition and pride and winning, run out the door to practice, and we'd storm out right behind him, then Paul would lead us in calisthenics. One day Paul ran out and *braked*—he'd forgotten something. Gain and

Colo froze, damn near fell like tenpins. When Paul was leading His Guys, you didn't pass him.

Among former Cleveland Browns, the mention of Paul Brown's name still inspires damp palms. I was recently playing golf with Sid Williams, a former teammate. Sid used to be a linebacker, was reminding me of that fact as he lined up his tee shot.

"Hey, man, you're talking all this shit," I said. "How tough you are. Big linebacker. You were scared of Paul Brown, too!"

Sid said, "Well . . . *Every*one was scared of Paul."

We started laughing—Sid confessing fear, any fear, was grounds for a press conference. Then Sid looked back up from his tee.

He said, "Hey, I didn't even play for Paul."

It was true—he'd played for Blanton Collier. But he'd heard so much about Paul, Sid was afraid of him, too.

It wasn't a physical matter, that's never why football coaches frighten their athletes. It's Power —to play you, bench you, trade you, keep you. On the Browns the Power was Paul's. Though he hired some excellent assistants, allowed them their say, there was no question who was Little Caesar. And there was no doubt the man had given his style of ruling some thought. At team meetings we each had our own chair with our name tags taped to the back. If a guy's tag was showing Paul knew he was late. The guy would come sheepishly in, Paul would say nothing, everyone knew that man was fined fifty bucks. No questions asked, no wasted seconds. Paul was that organized.

I didn't mind all the rules. In one important way I liked them. In the 1950s there was widespread racism, in the nation and in professional football. Paul's dicatatorship discouraged cliques, and that discouraged racial prejudice. His rules were not to be questioned, by anyone. We all had to abide by them equally. That was very pleasing to me.

The players made light of Paul's stiff ways but we also recognized his talent. Paul was the first NFL coach to administer tests to his athletes. At the onset of camp he would hand out written exams, long and impossibly hard. If you played offense, the play was a sweep, you had to know what you did, as well as the tackles, flanker, quarterback, every position. Forget about it. Except for the quarterback, who has to tell guys what to do when they get hit in the head, can't remember, no one gives a shit what the other positions do. Even if they did, they couldn't learn all that and still know their own job. Yet on the Browns it was ritual. Lou Groza had been there seventeen years and was still taking the test, though his offensive tackle days were long over. Lou was just the kicker.

We'd laugh about those tests, never take them seriously, but we knew Paul wasn't crazy. Crazy? Man was smart. We cheated on those tests. Eighty degrees outside in Palo Alto, guys were wearing long-sleeve shirts and sweaters. Had to hide those crib sheets. But after years of cheating, laughing at ourselves and at Paul, we drew a conclusion: Paul knew we were cheating. And didn't care. He knew in the process of cribbing, writing our plays on our sheets, we'd learn more than we would have otherwise. We said, "Damn, this guy is brilliant."

At the beginning, I loved playing for Paul. I was a runner. Paul wanted me to have the ball. I loved him for that. It was that simple.

Paul also planted a very nice one-liner on me that's now a part of football lore. When people said Paul was working me too heavily, Paul didn't hesitate. He said, "When you've got a big gun, why not fire it as often as possible?" How can I *not* like a guy who says that?

I never wanted to be traded. Being a Cleveland Brown was more important to me than going to another town and making more money. I didn't sit around and wonder, What if I played for this team or that team. People said to me, "Man, if you played behind that line in Green Bay, behind Kramer and Thurston, you'd gain so many more yards." I never quite believed that. I had Ray Renfro and Paul Warfield and Gary Collins, receivers who would run downfield, block their butts off. I had Dick Schafrath, a lineman who would block at the line of scrimmage, hustle downfield and look for someone else. Gene Hickerson would work with me. John Wooten would work with me. And they'd work together: Hickerson and Wooten were one of the finest pulling-guard tandems in NFL history. We didn't have the most talented line in football, but what we had was more important: a perfect blend. I never wanted to leave that. I respected Jerry Kramer and Fuzzy Thurston, had no desire to play in Green Bay.

I also think I would have had problems with Vince Lombardi. Lombardi was a fascinating, complex man. Without him the Packers would have been nothing. They used to call Green Bay the Siberia of the NFL. Whenever a coach wanted to mess with you in the old days, he'd say, "Look, I can send you to Green Bay." Nobody wanted to play there. It was cold. There were no girls. It was a small community and a lousy team. Lombardi came in, changed everything. He picked up guys who were sitting on other teams' benches, resurrected their careers. He took a team of losers, in a town known for meat packing and toilet paper, turned it into a dynasty. He was tough and his players were tough. The Packers believed in blocking and tackling and they played football the way it should be played. A lot of guys loved Lombardi, said his presence changed their lives. And a lot of guys didn't.

The anti-Lombardi sentiment was underground—he was not an American to criticize publicly—but it was there. Some guys didn't care for the screaming and intimidation. The story goes that Jim Ringo once came into Lombardi's office, said he wanted an agent to negotiate a contract. And that Lombardi told Ringo to wait outside, went into his office, traded Ringo to the Eagles. I believe that story is true and I think it's terrible. No one should ever advise anyone to sign a contract without some counsel, and certainly no one should forbid it. Yet here was the great Vince Lombardi, refusing to recognize basic players' rights. Within the confines of the league, the review on Lombardi was always mixed. It all depended on whom you spoke to.

I couldn't see myself playing for Lombardi.

Unlike Paul, Lombardi was a hollerer and a name caller. I don't respond to that. I would have done one of two things—totally withdrawn, or gotten right in Lombardi's face—and neither would have been good for the team. Paul might have been a tyrant, but he was my tyrant.

Paul's system, at the start, was fantastic for me. Even then, I never accepted it as gospel. Some men are born to be obsequious, some are not. I was not, nor was I that type of athlete. Most champions are not conformists. They're unorthodox, and they defy being catalogued. What I tried to do was work within Paul's system, yet retain my individuality. If what we needed was a yard, I'd put on my blue collar, crash into that hole. If the situation was looser—say third and seven, or first and ten—I'd alter my mindset. If the coaches called for me to go one inch off the center's left hip, and I saw daylight elsewhere, a chance to stomp my opponent's back with a long exciting run, I'd turn into an artist. I knew greatness only came through sometimes stretching the rules.

When certain coaches, particularly in the NFL or college basketball, accumulate unusual power and respect, it's assumed their systems are exalted, Beyond Questioning. In reality the process of developing a system is patchwork: steal a little from that guy, borrow a lot from this guy, then hope you get some athletes who are studs. Paul Brown, one of the winningest coaches ever, traded Willie Davis to the Packers. Willie is now in the Hall of Fame. Paul traded Bobby Mitchell to the Washington Redskins, Bobby's in the Hall of Fame. Paul sent Bill Quinlan and Henry Jordan to the Packers, Jim

Marshall to the Minnesota Vikings. All went on to be All-Pro. Even Paul Brown is human.

But Paul didn't want you to think so. He used his mystique with his employees as effectively as I utilized mine on Sundays. I never felt I could talk to Paul, not about anything intimate, so I never did. We were on the same side, but there was a distance, and I never knew quite how he felt toward me, except that he wanted me to have the ball. After he left the Browns, took over Cincinnati, Paul made some pointed comments about many of the people from Cleveland, and some of those statements regarded me. I found out things about Paul, his attitude toward me, that I never knew as one of his players.

Paul said my performance in games had been excellent, that second effort was my trademark, but I was lackadaisical in my approach to practice. He attributed this to my overall "attitude problem." Both interesting statements. I'll start with practice.

The fact is, practice was extremely important to me. But it was not about making the coaches love me. It was not about Rah-Rah. Not about symbols. Once the regular season started, practice was about one thing: Preparing for Sunday. If we weren't prepared, every Sunday, not only would we lose, but a Night Train Lane or a Jimmy Hill could maim us. There was no coach on this earth who knew *my* body better than I did, and no coach who could tell me what *I* had to do to get it ready. Let me use an analogy: When I first entered the league, I met a lot of fans who'd give me that firm, hearty handshake—the type that male fans like to give football players. And I learned that it was no good for me. When I played football, guys would try and rip the ball from me, miss and rip my skin. I'd bang my hands on guys' helmets, guys would step on them with their cleats. My hands were gouged and scabbed and crooked, my fingers chronically jammed. So when a fan would go for the power handshake, I quickly learned to say, No. My hands are sore and swollen. I need my hands for Sunday.

Some fans would think I was lying or arrogant. Others would say, Gee, I never thought of that. Take care of those hands. Man, we need you Sunday.

I had similar experiences with *my own coaches*. Football coaches are freaks for structure. It's the nature of the beast. Teams need structure. I happen to think structure is essential, but not at the expense of common sense. If my forearms are bruised and scraped, painfully tender, don't ask me to do a million damn pushups. The ability to throw my forearm on Sunday is one hundred times more important to me than impressing coaches.

I suppose it's all in your point of view. Some of my coaches questioned my work habits, implying that I was living off my ability. Yet Bill Russell once wrote that I was the most competitive human being he had ever met. To me, competitive doesn't mean "hating to lose," it doesn't mean doing a bunch of talking. Being competitive means working your ass off. If you're saying you're competitive, and you don't work, you're just talking. The first year I picked up golf, I ended the summer shooting 77. I played five, six, seven times a week, practiced before and after every round. I played so much golf my hands would bleed. People told me, "Jim, that's great. Shooting 77 your first summer." I didn't think it was so great. I put enough damn work in.

Those people who criticized my work habits didn't realize I love to work. But I don't work blindly. I was a master at what I did, and masters have a deeper understanding. When I was in high school, I built a high jump pit in my backyard. I'd spend hours there, alone, without any coaches, working and working and working. I'd challenge the fastest kids in the neighborhood to races. It wasn't fun for me—it was serious. People who knew me then would sometimes get scared. I had an intensity they had never seen in a kid my age.

On Sundays in the NFL no one questioned my intensity. Yet Paul didn't like the way I practiced. What Paul didn't understand is that I worked at playing football 365 days a year. I'm not talking about jive calisthenics. I mean focus, so severe sometimes that people think you're living inside your own head. The offseason that Paul Brown left Cleveland, I wanted to come back and have a monstrous year, prove that Paul, his system, was not the only reason for my success. That summer I'd be driving down the street, thinking about running a play, imagining the contact, CRACK, I'd smash the steering wheel. People on the street thought I was crazy, I could tell by their looks. Come fall, I had the best season of my life.

Some of the coaches complained that I did my own calisthenics. I couldn't believe they'd waste their energy. To me it was not complex: you do not give the same exercises to every man. I don't think Edwin Moses works out for the hurdles the same way a shot putter does for the shot. And whether it was me or Leroy Kelly or Ernie Green, I never believed a back should do the same calisthenics as a 275-pound lineman, or a quarterback. The demands of our jobs were entirely different.

Today specialized training is standard, but in 1958 you had coaches who were saying, "Hey, this is right for you. Just do it." Because a lot of coaches, unless your leg is broken, your ankle sprained, think you should get out there and play some football. And if you wanted to be prepared mentally and physically to bring blood to people's noses every Sunday, you had to resist those coaches. You had to say, No it's not really good for *me*. I'm gonna try and get you what you want, but not the way you want me to. Please, do not fuck with my process. I will give you results but not my soul.

I thought the Cleveland Browns had a decent coaching staff. I was not in awe of their collective brainpower, and I didn't think they were all nice people. Two of my favorite people in the organization were Leo and Morrie, the guys who worked in our dressing room. I loved those guys, and I respected them for the men they were. I don't measure people by their titles. And I don't give my respect to authority figures unless they earn it. The coaches on the Browns seemed to believe, simply because they were coaches, they were mentally superior to the Cleveland players. Well, I didn't know how bright the staff really was. I don't know how bright any football staff is. If my knee is hurt, and a man wants me to run forty yards ten times, how intelligent is that? If I don't take care of my leg, how am I going to give him his yards that week, help him keep his job? A miracle? Grind that knee all week and Sunday it will be ready?

These guys definitely weren't building any spaceships, and it wasn't worth my time or concentration to debate every point. I'd usually keep it to myself, but I often thought, too, they were way off the mark in assessing our practices. They'd say we'd practiced poorly, I'd be thinking, *Not really. Not if you look at it. The guys are beat up and tired. It's good they didn't try and impress the coach. It's good the guys with pain took it easy. Let them heal. We got New York Sunday.*

I've heard it a lot over the years: Paul and the other coaches didn't like this about my attitude, didn't like that. But they loved the damn performance. They were right about one thing: I did have an attitude. And my attitude, and this is what my coaches could never see, was not shaped only by the game of football. If my mind was limited to football, per the desires of the Cleveland Browns staff, which would later be fired by Art Modell, what type of man would that make me? My attitude was shaped by personal conviction. It was shaped by society, and my role in that society. It was shaped by being black in America in the 1950s. And if it wasn't for that "attitude" that people spoke of, I never would have made it to the Cleveland Browns. I would have been stopped in Syracuse, the first place they tried to change me. They never knew it, but my attitude was a blessing for the Cleveland Browns. Without it they never would have gotten the yards. What happened on Sunday *was* my attitude.

124

Most of Paul's criticisms surfaced after he left the Browns. While I was playing for him, Paul was pretty nice to me. In his comments, his manner, I thought the three guys Paul rode gentlest were Mike McCormack, Ray Renfro, and me. Mike and Ray because Paul liked them personally, me because I was his star. Paul would fine me if I was late, no doubt, but he didn't want to mess with me too much. Forgetting race or personal friendship, the greater your value to the franchise, the more preferential the treatment. Believe me, Don Shula does not speak to Dan Marino as he does Marino's teammates. Typically, quarterbacks are the most privileged people in football.

I was also in a skill position, producing those points, even Paul Brown made exceptions for me. Before I came to the Browns, none of the players owned Cadillacs. Paul had a rule: No big, flashy cars. But I was not a Ford Fairlane type of guy. Rookie year I purchased a Cadillac convertible. It was light purple and white and I'd park it right outside League Park, where we used to practice. I knew the rule, guys told me, but it was my money, my car. Though I knew Paul was irritated, he never mentioned the car. Even Paul wouldn't cut his first round draft choice over a car.

I was Cleveland's first choice in the 1957 draft. Chosen before me were Lenny Dawson, Ron Kramer, John Brodie, Jon Arnett, and Paul Horning. The week before camp, I'd been in Evanston, Illinois, at the college all-star game, where Otto Graham told me I'd never make it in the NFL.

Later that week, in the game against the New York Giants, Curley Lambeau left me sitting on the bench. And I thought I was going to start! The only action I got was kicking off, and catching a couple passes late in the game. I was humiliated. After the game I left Soldier Field, drove to our dorm at Northwestern, grabbed my stuff, drove all night long to Hiram, Ohio, where the Browns had camp. I was the first rookie in camp, and I couldn't wait to begin pro ball.

Paul was equally anxious to get me started: our second exhibition game, he started me at fullback. We were in Akron, against the Pittsburgh Steelers, in the Rubber Bowl. Third quarter, I drove into the secondary, guys didn't know my speed, took the wrong angle, I broke a forty-yard TD. Paul pulled me out of the game. As I ran over the sideline, Paul called me over.

Paul said, "You're my fullback."

Then he walked away. I started grinning like a goddamn clown. It was a huge moment. This guy was businesslike, his organization was tight, and he wanted to *use* me. I was never satisfied with my career at Syracuse. Though I'd overcome many things, *my* thing is constant performance, from day one to the end of the line. I wasn't allowed that at Syracuse, and it gnawed at me. Coming to Cleveland, Paul Brown, I felt like I'd died and gone to football heaven. I've never told anyone this, but when Paul said I was his fullback, it was the greatest moment I ever had in pro football.

It wasn't all touchdowns my rookie camp. First time I walked into our dressing room, saw the size of the defensive linemen, I was aghast. These cats

126

were humongous. I thought, *Damn, how am I going to deal with these guys every day?* As I went to practice, I began to see that my quickness nullified their size. It was tough for them to hit me square. I could dip a shoulder, guys would get only a piece of me, or go flying right by me. I had also had some power of my own: if they were back on their heels, I had momentum, I could strike *them* a blow.

My rookie year was also painful: I still had a dangerous college habit. I would get into the secondary, stop, then start again—I was getting flattened by the pursuit. In college, a guy would get blocked, he'd lie on the ground like the play was over. Pros don't lie on the ground. They get back up, come after you. So the game was now three or four times faster. After I was freight-trained several times, I learned that my running had to be continuous. Had to make those cuts on the run.

The veterans on the Browns were good to their rookies. They didn't humiliate them for their personal entertainment. I didn't believe in that tired football bullshit, so I was thankful. If the veterans had tried to haze me, I think I would have pulled a Mike Ditka. When Ditka arrived at his rookie camp, Chicago's veterans told him, "Look boy, you gotta sing your school song." Ditka said, "I'm not singing shit. And no one is going to make me." And no one made him. The old Bears were lunatics, but they knew Ditka was one of those motherfuckers who would fight. So was I. I didn't want to, but I was not going to play the chump rookie for anyone.

Where the veterans tested the rookies was on the field. They tried to see if you could handle punishment, see if you were going to help them. To complicate my case, I was trying to take the job of our veteran fullback, Ed Modzelewski. Ed was popular, tight with a lot of the veterans. His boys put me to the test, but the test was fair. It was only discrimination I hated, and I didn't get that from them. Any test that took place on the field, I had a forearm, too. So it was a good set of circumstances.

Though I managed to lead the league in rushing, I did not have a spectacular rookie year. I did give the league a glimpse of who I could be in game nine, against the Rams at home. I carried the ball thirty-one times for 237 yards, including a sixty-nine yard TD after one of the Rams smashed me so hard my helmet flew off. People around the league started talking about this kid in Cleveland. Another coach, Sid Gillman, took a poke at Paul. Sid said, "If he carries the ball that much in many more games, he'll wind up either punch drunk or a basket case."

But I loved being the fulcrum of the offense. And my success didn't surprise me. Except for that dark period as a Syracuse freshman, I'd been confident since the day I'd left high school. That was largely because I always felt I was an all-around athlete, not only a guy who could run a football. I played lacrosse, baseball, football, basketball, bowled, and golfed, excelled to some degree in all of them. It seemed logical that I would be good right away in the NFL. There was no isolated anecdote, no single morning when I woke up, said, "Hey, I am good. I can play with these guys." But I knew what I wanted. I didn't want to have three years of apprenticeship and then move into the starting lineup. I wanted to start my rookie year. I wanted to play a good game every single Sunday. I wanted to satisfy myself and help my team win games. Those were my goals my rookie year.

I didn't reach those goals. I had some good games, didn't play well every week, did not feel fulfilled about my performance. Though the Browns went from 5–7 to 9–2, won the Eastern Conference title, even that was imperfect: Detroit dismantled us in the championship game. Still, not a bad rookie year, and Paul and I had no substantial problems. He still fit my ideal for a professional coach. Then we drafted Bobby Mitchell.

Paul Brown has used black athletes for as long as I can remember. He coached them during World War II at the Great Lakes Naval Academy, in the AAFC, then in the National Football League. I don't think Paul was consciously trying to create opportunities for blacks. I think Paul was trying to win football games. For me that's fair enough.

While Paul gave black players NFL citizenship, he didn't give them full citizenship. Blacks were roomed together, we had a team quota. We all had the same rules, yet we didn't all have the same rules. And Paul was the man who ran our organization. Later, when Paul wrote a book, he made some statements regarding my childhood, regarding blacks, that I felt showed a lack of sensitivity. He also said he never had a "racial problem" until I came to the Browns. Apparently Paul thought everything was OK for the black Cleveland Browns in 1958. It wasn't. I don't want to belabor the point, but one man's racial problem is another man's equal rights.

If I sound a little confused about Paul, what transpired in Cleveland, I am. It *was* confusing. And complex, and contradictory, not only for me, or my black teammates, but for white Cleveland Browns, and that includes Paul Brown. People who think American life in the 1950s was clean and simple were not there, or else they were watching a lot of TV. I know it got confusing for Bobby Mitchell.

Since Detroit beat us for the NFL title in 1957, they played the college all-stars the following summer. I watched on TV. What I saw was the Bobby Mitchell show. Bobby scored two spectacular TDs, made a couple of Lions look feeble. I saw the future. It was a black kid from Hot Springs, Arkansas.

I was also glimpsing my future teammate. Paul had drafted Bobby out of Illinois. After watching Bobby that first time I had no illusions: I knew if I didn't hump, Bobby would overshadow me.

Bobby arrived, turned out to be bashful. He was also outrageously in love with his new wife, had no desire whatsoever to go out and chase women with us. First day of camp, we knew Bobby would change the complexion of our offense. With his speed and talent, they couldn't ignore him, stack all their men on me. After five games, I was leading the league in rushing. Bobby was second. The team was 5–0, and we were loose. Bobby and I would kid in the huddle, tell the guys how much we would gain on that play, go out, with their help, and gain it. Bobby and I were young and ascending, backs get lots of attention to begin with, and the writers responded. We started dominating Cleveland's headlines.

It unraveled in New York. We had the Giants by ten at halftime, blew the game, absorbed our first loss. Bobby fumbled three times in the second half. Although he hadn't fumbled all year, and we recovered all three, Paul yanked him. He replaced him with a back named Lou Carpenter. Lou was a nice man, but it made me heartsick playing next to Lou with Bobby Mitchell sitting on the bench. Paul froze out Bobby the remainder of the season, using him only to run back kickoffs and punts. Even there, Bobby was running back punts for TDs. He set up several others with exciting runs. The man was winning games coming off the bench.

I understood football talent, so did Paul Brown, and what happened to Bobby didn't smell right. If an NFL coach has ever dominated a city, it was Paul Brown in Cleveland. I think Paul was jealous that Bobby and I were stealing all the press in his town. I also think Paul was looking for a reason to bench Bobby. He was hard on Bobby from the day Bobby arrived, even rougher than he was on most guys. When Bobby showed without any doubt he could play, Paul put him in the starting lineup, but he continued to make every practice a drag for him. Ultimately, I think Paul became uncomfortable having two black stars on the 1958 Cleveland Browns. That thinking certainly would not be unusual in other cities, and I believe that's what happened in Cleveland. When Bobby fumbled three times against the Giants, I think Paul used the moment to return our team to the status quo, meaning one black star was plenty. Paul was

131

running a business, he may have been motivated by economics. Whatever, I hated what Paul did to Bobby.

The best thing for Bobby would be leaving Cleveland, and Paul made it happen. Paul traded him two years later to Washington, where Bobby played the rest of his career, before moving on to the Hall of Fame. His first season in Washington, we played against Bobby. We had a rookie linebacker, Sam Tidmore, from Ohio State. Sam was fast, not Bobby Mitchell fast.

I warned Sam. I said, "Look, Sam, you're a young kid. You can outrun people, but Bobby is kind of special. Whenever you see him, think twice about the angle you take. Take a deeper angle, try and run him out of bounds. Give him some yards, ten if you have to. *Don't* give him a TD."

Though I was only twenty-six, I felt like the old fox talking to the young fox. Sam was a rookie, starting at linebacker in the NFL. And rookies who are fast are even cockier. Sam said yes, he'd take the angle. His eyes were saying, Shit, I'll own Bobby Mitchell's ass. Worry about yourself, Mr. Brown.

Late in the game we led, 16–10. Bobby hadn't done much. Then Norm Snead hit Bobby with a little curl pass over the middle.

I said, "Oh my goodness."

Bobby went up, brought down the ball, put some nasty shimmy on our first guy, started heading toward our bench. Tidmore was in good position to get him . . . if he took the right angle. Bobby stopped, as if to make this sharp cut. When Tidmore stopped too, Bobby, who hadn't really stopped, just looked like he did, kept right on flying toward our bench. Tidmore lunged, almost broke his leg, Bobby shot untouched around the corner, danced into the end zone. No shit, Bobby *danced* in there, *sideways,* saying hello, I'd have to guess, to his former coach. We lost 17–16 and I was happy and sad; distressed that we had lost, pleased that my man had done well.

I still root for Bobby, which is why I was astonished when I read that Paul said I resented Bobby Mitchell. I think Paul is the only one who resented Bobby—*he* benched him. I've been around a lot of years, I'm controversial, there are 9 million misconceptions about my life, but this is one I can't let slide. I loved Bobby Mitchell's talent, admired him as a man. Bobby is not a self-promoter and for many years he was overlooked by the Hall of Fame committee. Big George and I went out and lobbied, simply gave a little push to a movement that was long overdue. When Bobby was inducted in 1983, I was elated.

I have to admit the Bobby Mitchell trade always bothered me, but it's not as if Paul and I were constantly at war. At the end of Paul's reign with the Browns, we clearly had some problems. They were football problems, disagreements on technique, strategy, winning. Man to man, though, in the six years I played for Paul he only disappointed me once.

It happened in New York, 1959, my third season. First quarter, in a pileup, I was kicked in the head. Though I didn't black out, I was lying under the Giants, not knowing where I was. Instinctively I stood up, walked back toward the huddle. My head began to clear, and I recognized my teammates. But I couldn't remember our plays. I thought, *Wait, try and remember how you got to the stadium. Get your mind working again. Then figure out the plays.*

I had no idea how I got to the stadium. I didn't want to go out, so I pulled aside Milt Plum. Milt was our quarterback.

I said, "Milt. I can't remember my assignments. Tell me where to go and I'll go do it."

Next several downs, Milt would call Paul's play, also tell me where to go. Then he got tired of that shit, decided it was not going to work. He called time, walked to the sidelines, asked that I be taken out. Paul pulled me. For most of the second quarter, I sat on the bench.

At halftime, I was sitting on a bench in the visitor's dressing room. I was sitting perfectly still. I was fighting with myself. I wanted to remember the goddamn plays, I couldn't, and I was livid. Then Paul walked up. He said one of my teammates had gotten hurt. And *he* was back in the game.

It was vintage Paul: drop that one-liner, walk off, let it work on a player's mind. I watched him walk away, didn't say a word. Thinking: Fucking Paul. You think I'm playing this game for you? I want to play this game worse than *you* want me to play it. I don't know what's happening, but I'm trying to get back. I don't want to miss no fuckin' playing time, this is what I fucking *do*. You insult me, you take my spirit. Don't you know me by now? I thought you knew me.

I went back in the second half, made Milt tell me the plays the first time we got the ball, and then they started coming back to me. But I was still dreamy, not really there, and get this: Sam Huff told me Paul was crazy. He said there was no way I should still be in the game. I wasn't sure how to take that. I didn't know a whole bunch of guys in the NFL who cared if a sucker got his head rung. I didn't know if Sam was concerned, or was trying to plant some garbage in my head, psych me out and get my ass back on the bench. When Sam started to say it again, I stopped listening.

And that was the deal. New York killed us that day. And in the six years I played for Paul, that was the low point.

One area in which we rarely warred was contract negotiations. As far as I know, I was the first man in the NFL to be represented during negotiations. Kenny Molloy did my first contract. Kenny got me $10,000 in salary, and a $5,000 bonus. I was planning on asking for a total of ten grand, so I felt pretty damn shrewd, having Kenny on my side. My next jump was to $22,000. At the height of my career, I earned $65,000 a year.

The reason Paul and I never fought over money was me—I didn't want to fight over money. I knew you could hurt your own performance if you got too heavy into the money. I wanted constant production, not to wallow in negotiations, maybe have to miss practice. I also didn't battle too hard because I didn't want to dislike my owners. I was a professional and all that shit, but not a corpse: if I liked the men I worked for, I knew I'd play better football. If I arrived at a stalemate with the Browns, where all it could get was ugly, I just gave in.

I also knew that money only had the value of

how you used it, if you used a million dollars wrong, it didn't have the value of $100,000. Knew that when people died, they never called for some money or some things. They called for some*body*. Knew all the things in life with real value, anybody can attain.

I was not a money man, but I wasn't dumb. After I saw how things worked, I knew exactly what the Browns were doing—business. They would urge us not to discuss our contracts with other players, teammates or opponents. That way they could fool people. All the teams did it. And all the owners would talk. In the middle 1960s, Johnny Unitas and I were the two highest earners in the NFL. My owner, Art Modell, and Johnny's owner, Carroll Rosenbloom, were buddies. And they would talk. Then Carroll would get Johnny into his office. Carroll would tell Johnny, Jim Brown is only getting such and such, and he's the greatest player in the game. Then Art would get me into his office. Art would tell me, Johnny Unitas is only getting such and such, and he's the top player in the game.

Just because Art and Carroll were smart did not mean Johnny and I were a pair of fools. Me and Johnny did some talking, too.

8

SOME RUNNERS

GREAT RUNNING IS AN art so intensely personal, no two men do it quite alike. When a cat makes a beautiful run, it's poetry and jazz. That's why no coach can "make" a great runner. Great runners are works of God.

Because they're judged by a higher standard, great runners must think, I Am Superior. By the time I walked on the field, I thought *I* was God. I was the back who would lead the league in rushing. Period. Any Sunday, all I needed was a break, maybe two, and I felt that I would run wild. Don't let anybody kid you: Walter Payton, Gale Sayers, Earl Campbell—all the top runners have felt the same way.

That includes O.J. Simpson. The Juice likes to pretend he's modest, but that's just the Juice, *being* the Juice. O.J. is extremely smart, man knows how to make a buck, and his "aw shucks" image is his meal ticket. He's not about to jeopardize it by being honest. I was watching the Juice announce a game once, he said the guy down on the field was probably a finer runner than he'd been. What a bunch of bullshit! I know O.J. Simpson. He doesn't think there's a runner, dead or alive, who was a better back than he was.

I basically like the Juice, but I never look at him the way I do a Bill Russell, or a Walter Payton. I talk to those guys, see them speak, I know what I'm hearing is the real man. Too often, I can't say the same about O.J.

However phony the guy, O.J. the runner was the genuine item. The Juice was fantastic. You have to see the Juice out of uniform to appreciate the strength he has in his shoulders. Combined with his world class speed, precise sense of when to accelerate, O.J. was a bitch. He also had a few nice moves, but he wasn't pretty like he says he was. Gale Sayers was pretty, the Juice was not. O.J. had this strange little humpback style of running. I'm telling you, Juice, that shit was not pretty.

The Juice didn't have to be pretty. His ability to run the football matched anyone's. It's not what he's noted for, but O.J. ran with great determination. Though he wasn't punishing, the Juice *was* going forward, and there would be no hesitation before a hit. At his best, O.J. had a lot of heart.

When I talk about backs, I talk about heart a lot. When you're running the football, you better at least have some. Some backs lack talent yet they're brave. Others have gifts but not the courage. The man with great skill and great heart is devastating. He will kick your ass, a lot.

In Cleveland, we once drafted a guy named Milt Campbell. Milt could run, literally, as fast as anyone in the NFL. In college, he was a champion in the decathlon, and the high hurdles. Milt was no coward, but he didn't have the heart of a football player. Without it, every one of his skills was nullified. He never made it.

Everyone prefers a certain style of runner. I've always favored the hardnosed backs. The guys who were purest of heart. Larry Brown will not be remembered by a lot of people, but he'll always be loved by me. Larry didn't have all the skills, but concession was not part of his package.

I also came to love John Riggins, but not until his last few years in the NFL. At first Riggins's game left me disappointed. I knew he had talent, thought he was screwing around to a certain degree. I don't know how he got his head right, but his final two or three years, Riggins was running like a psycho, carrying people three more yards, making them look like punks. When Riggins ran like that, behind those killer Hogs, I was jumping all over my living room.

I've always admired Walter Payton. Walter had the skills, and the ultimate heart, a mix that can take a man anywhere. His energy and athleticism and determination were awesome. He had a dynamic first step. He had striking power—Walter went about 195, struck like 220. He never ran out of bounds except to stop the clock, missed one game his entire career.

The only quality Walter lacked, in my opinion,

was what runners call a fourth gear. It's the ability to get one step on a defender, be *gone*, for seventy, eighty yards. Within the fraternity of runners, that extra dimension is something we take special pride in. The Juice had it, Sayers, myself, but not Walter. Walter is as gutsy a runner as I've ever seen. But he didn't have that fourth gear.

People get offended when I say things like that. They don't like to break a player down, look at his particulars. That involves details. Most people get bored with details. Not glamorous enough. For me, details are what's happening. I think any person, in any field, has a good chance to succeed if he looks at the details. Because in order to look at the details, you have to love what you're doing, and you have to be highly motivated. I loved playing football. I relished the details.

I used to study my teammate Bobby Mitchell at practice. When Bobby ran, he appeared to skim right over the ground, his feet barely touching the field. I'd walk over after one of Bobby's runs, there were almost no cleat marks! I knew I could never use that; with the power of my stride, when my feet hit the ground they would almost become implanted. Still, it was fascinating to watch Bobby run in that style no one quite understood. And it's details like those that stay vivid in my mind.

But whenever I talk to people about football, they're not into that. All they want to know is Who Had How Many Yards, and Who Was The Greatest. If I mention a detail, not even the fine detail, just dissect an athlete trait by trait, if anything sounds remotely negative, people get mad. They say I'm mean or hypercritical.

Let me say something right now about pointed observation, or criticism, or dissent, or whatever you want to call it. I've been saying what was on my mind since I was a kid. I wasn't about to stop just because I got famous. I won't stop now. When I form an opinion, I'm not careless. I do my research. I study history. I look hard, particularly as I get older and wiser, more tolerant, at the other side's point of view. Sometimes I'm still wrong. Sometimes I don't do enough research, get sucked in, then biased, by image, instead of discovering a man or an institution for myself. I don't particularly like myself when I do that, but it happens, and those moments are not enough to silence me. I've always felt it took courage to speak out, particularly if the object of your scrutiny is something or someone you care for. It's easy to nod your head and conform. And if everyone did it, we'd be fucked. That would mean we had no more patriots. It's the patriot, not the conformist, who takes the unpopular stand. I won't bullshit you: I haven't always been noble or patriotic in my criticism. But I have criticized this country, the NFL, certain individuals, because I loved them, felt they needed to be reminded, by someone, of something they had lost.

I happen to like Walter Payton, as an athlete and a man. Walter, when you get to know him, has a very agile wit. He also has good taste in friends: Mary Dee, a broadcaster in Chicago, a wonderful human being, is close to both of us. I also have strong feelings about superstar athletes and retirement. I don't like to see a superstar stay too long,

141

get pushed out by management, his retirement become a national issue, *everyone* starts feeling bad.

When Walter was nearing the end, I said he wasn't himself anymore, should probably retire unless he needed the money. Rushing to Walter's defense, as if he needed it, was Mike Ditka. That struck me as more than a little hypocritical. Many people on the inside feel that Walter's retirement was essentially forced. The Bears had those frisky young runners, Neal Anderson and Dennis Gentry and Thomas Sanders, needed room to let them grow, wanted Walter to step aside. It was clear that the Bears were easing Walter out of their offense, out of their plans. You don't think Iron Mike called that shot?

Writers often ask me if Walter was the "greatest back of all time." Or was I the "greatest back of all time?" As if Walter and I are the only two backs who ever kicked ass. Man, I don't even know if Walter was the "greatest" Chicago Bear of all time. They used to have a man named Gale Sayers.

The Juice loves to talk about Gale. So do I. Every runner I know, deep down, would like to run the way Gale Sayers did. No one has ever run prettier.

Gale's was a pure, pure performance. Gale's cuts were electric. His moves were embarrassing: they lunged here, Gale was there. He was tough, had the fourth gear, could glide through Chicago's snow and mud. Gale was what I call a true runner. A true runner is as dangerous when he's trapped behind the line of scrimmage as he is in the open field. He's energetic and crazy and always, always wants more. That's how Gale was. He'd double back, twist in the air, do anything to steal that daylight. I'd marvel when I'd watch Gale. I'd marvel when I'd watch Bobby Mitchell. I considered myself a master at running with a football. Here were two other masters, doing things I never could. They lifted me.

If he hadn't gotten injured, if he could have played ten or eleven years, Gale might hold every legitimate record there is. His talent was that unique. I know, in Gale's mind, he *was* the best, and that he feels he never got a chance to prove it. Since no one will ever know, Gale and all of us fans will just have to settle for what he did do, which means no one is settling for anything. Gale was magic. His performance will never be forgotten by anyone who understands football.

Another one of my all-time favorites is Earl Campbell. Earl's career could have been even greater. Earl got messed up in the minor leagues at Houston. His first three years he played for Bum Phillips, and Earl was brutal. Then Bum left, they had a parade of coaches, and Earl got switched all over the backfield. But no matter where he played, Earl was frightening. I saw him in a college all-star game and I didn't think Earl had speed. I was way off. Earl's *football* speed was tremendous. And Earl would crunch people. He'd come surging through about two inches off the ground with those gargantuan thighs and that Mt. Rushmore head—Earl once hit Isiah Robertson so hard I thought he might kill him. I have played and observed a lot of football. That may be the hardest hit I've ever seen.

A lot of folks thought Earl was strictly a bruiser. He was a bruiser, but Earl could also cut.

No question about it. Earl could cut, or cut you in half.

Usually Earl opted to pulverize. That's what made him famous, that's the way it should be. Those announcers on TV can rhapsodize all they want about the intricacies of the game. Football *is* hitting. You can't play football if you don't enjoy the physicality. If you don't want to give a man a blow, keep on running while he falls, you have to get out of the game. And no one in the NFL had to be told to hit. People ask me, Did coaches ever tell players to put men out of the game? No. That's amateur time in Dixie. It's not the NFL. Back when I played, guys were afraid *not* to hit: there were only fourteen teams, no one wanted to lose his job, go back to the coal mines or the streets. If you look at old films, sometimes you'll see nervous rookies, slamming into guys from behind, clipping the shit out of 'em.

There were some non-violent players, and their reputations preceded them. Runners knew exactly which guys would wait until the ball carrier was past them, then dive at their legs, or jump on their back. We used to call those guys Directors of Traffic—as you breezed by, they'd sorta wave at you like a crossing guard. That was the worst insult of all, except for Arm Tackler. Those guys would reach out and grab, you'd run right through their "tackle." Coaches despise arm tacklers, even if they used to be one.

If a guy was a hitter, he was called just that—a Hitter. "That guy's a hitter. He'll break your neck. He'll stick his head and his shoulders right in there."

"That guy is a non-hitter. He's gonna try and find a better way."

I once conversed with John Mackey, the fantastic tight end, about the physicality of football. John was noted for his powers of persuasion. I asked him about it.

John said, "Shit, when I used to play against certain guys I knew were scared, first play I'd pop them upside their head. That was the end. I didn't have to worry about them the rest of the game."

John was right. Football is not about tricky plays. It's about dominance. Physical and mental dominance. And the best way to dominate is to *run the football.* If you can run on a team, shove it up and down the field, it means you're kicking ass (that's physical), and both of you know it (that's mental). Running is power. Give me a team that can run and play tough defense, *I* can take them to the Super Bowl.

There are all styles of running though. It's not just, "Okay, I'm dropping my shoulder now, running everyone over." And you don't blast full-speed into every hole. Take a sweep, for example. I liked to get off quickly, take some hard steps, so at least I'd get a few yards, but then I might have to float, wait for my blocks, then accelerate around the end, drop it down again, into third, then slam it into overdrive, escape from the rabble.

The general public thought I was a Bruiser. Big, strong, woodchoppin' motherfucker. You know, thighs as big as telephone poles. I was once watching a TV show, they started showing my clips. I knocked over an opponent, announcer said, "Jim Brown was not a beautiful runner. He was a *power* runner." Next clip, I see myself cutting and spinning, making moves I used to do in the playground. I was thinking, "See? I'm no bruiser. I'm a runner."

Even if I was only a bruiser, I'd never admit it. Not to myself anyway. All of us runners like to think of ourselves as nifty. *Gimme an inch and I'll break it on you. Go ninety damn yards.* Breaking a long one is a runner's dream, especially if he ducks two or three tacklers, knocks over another, outsprints the last few. That's when a runner puts down his stamp.

That's why I never wore a lot of extra pads: didn't want to be weighted down, so I could break the long ones. I wore big shoulder pads and a secure helmet—my shoulders were my weapons, I liked having a head—but I never wore hip pads, and I would take my thigh guards, cut out all the padding, just use the inner cardboard. I learned that from a little guy, about 165, a runner named Leroy Bolden. My second year in the league, Leroy came to camp from Michigan State, starting shaving down his pads. I said, "Damn, if that little guy can do it, I bet I can, too. I'll be quicker, more able to maneuver." To me it made all the sense in the world. Can't be nifty with too many pads.

Hey. I wasn't *that* nifty. I would always look for the least amount of resistance, and if that meant not getting touched, that was perfectly cool. If I had a choice of running around you, or over you, I'd go around you. I wanted the yards, not to prove my manhood.

Now, if I couldn't run around you, then we'd have to deal. Then I wanted to hit you as hard as you hit me. No, I wanted to hit you harder. I wanted your nose stinging, bleeding was okay, too. I wanted you flinching and demoralized. The next time you saw me coming, I wanted you to say, Oh shit.

If we had to deal, you'd probably meet my forearm. Some backs throw it better than others. Guys began to talk about mine in the papers, so I guess I threw them pretty good. I used mine scientifically, depending on how close to me the tackler was, and how rapidly he was moving in. If I had a lot of time, could see the tackler coming beneath me, I would bring my forearm down on his head, try and hammer him like a nail into the field. If I had less time, a guy was on me before I saw him coming, I'd *flick* out the straight arm in his face, try and make him blink, get him off me. If I had no time, the tackler was right in front of me, force against force, I would deliver The Blow. That was a forearm, thrown hard and up, into a tackler's chest. At least I'd aim at the chest. Then I'd settle for what I could hit, try and make it count. The Blow was my favorite.

Normally, I didn't throw the forearm until I'd broken through the line. Meaning sometimes I'd use it on a linebacker, more often on a safety or cornerback. With those little guys, I'd come through with the forearm cocked, *really* threaten them. Why not? They were usually small, I went about 228, by the time I rushed toward them, I had built up steam. For a little guy, that was not a peaceful sight.

I threw my forearms a lot, now I have the fingers to show for it. They're crooked and scarred.

When I played, my arms and hands were pretty much sore my entire career. I always figured it was better to have mangled arms and hands than mangled ribs. Just saying "sore ribs" is painful. Guys love to hit runners in the ribs, and the forearm, sometimes, foiled their wishes.

I threw a lot of forearms, actually knocked some people down. But it's very seldom, at the level of the NFL, that you run a man right over, leave cleat marks on his jersey. That is cartoon shit. What you hope to do is get the man off you, so you can keep moving toward the goal line. And always keep those legs moving. Always.

Another myth is the "perfect back." There is no such creature. The bottom line is, Did he dominate? When I think of domination, I think of Gale and Walter and Earl and O.J., in no particular order. Give me Gale's cuts, Earl's power, O.J.'s speed, and Walter's heart. That would be the perfect back.

In 1984, *Sport* magazine asked me to rate the running backs. Five being best, I gave Eric Dickerson a 5 for rushing. I gave him a 5 for speed. For heart I gave him a 1.

Now?

Eric's talent for running the football is still superb. He can cut, he's got that pretty track man's stride, microwave acceleration, fine natural instincts. He's the most skilled runner in football.

I'm still unsure of his heart. To me it's not quite right, and I'll give you an example. It was late in the season, the Colts needed a win to make the playoffs, the game appeared to be lost. Dickerson apparently hurt his wrist. He kind of got out of the game, I guess they looked at his wrist. Next time I saw him he had his hands in his pockets. He was finished for the day. To me, Eric was saying, Screw it. I'm done. I'm making some money, the season's over, I don't want to mess around out here and get hurt.

Maybe that isn't wrong. Maybe some guys today are just smarter. I still prefer the pure of heart, and theirs are the performances I'll always remember. I know in the same situation, Walter Payton would have been out there banging right until the end.

This made me more uneasy: when the Rams traded Eric to the Colts, before the transaction Eric was talking about holding back, not playing hard, unless the Rams came through with the money he wanted. That's death. A sportsman doesn't do that. The whole trade, from beginning to end, was handled gracelessly by Eric. I know he wanted out, but his comments were ridiculous. Whether someone was feeding Eric his quotes, or they were his own, they were terribly unappealing. Even I'm better at public relations than that.

That's not to say I was pulling for the Rams in that dispute. I thought both sides acted poorly. I hated Eric's means, but I admired his results: he exposed the Rams as a jive organization. When I say that, it has nothing whatsoever to do with John Robinson. And it was not John Robinson who engineered Eric's trade. It was John Shaw, Georgia Frontiere's financial right arm. He's a robot, he treats his players like robots. The man doesn't have

149

an ounce of human compassion and you need human compassion, even in the NFL. It's robots like John Shaw who hurt the game.

This is what I would have said to Eric if I were Shaw. "Look, you're one of us, not the enemy. Yes, we outfoxed you on your contract. You weren't smart enough, we kinda clipped your ass, but we're going to give you a raise, at least come close to giving you what you want. All we ask is that you play football as hard as you can. And next time, when we negotiate a contract, understand that you better get the best business people. And once you sign the motherfucker, don't be reneging, and don't be crying the goddamn blues. And don't *ever* threaten not to give your all on the field." That's what I would have said to Eric.

I talk about him a lot, but I like old Eric. He's a nice kid. Once he invited me to a publicity party for him. Eric's boys were all there, and a bunch of pretty girls. Someone was running around with a camera, filming the party. Eric and his boys surrounded me, talked me into saying Eric was the greatest runner of all time. They turned on the camera, I said, "Yes, Eric Dickerson is the greatest runner who ever lived." Those boys were happy!

And you never know about Eric. If he does some growing up, he can be unstoppable. Even now, because I also do like talent, he's my favorite runner in the game.

Eric also had the benefit of running in a system, John Robinson's, that showcased his talent. I think Tony Dorsett, in comparison, might have enjoyed much greater success had he played for another team. At times I'd watch Tony during games and he'd be off in a private world. As a fellow runner, I didn't care much for that. When I looked at Tony's eyes, I wanted to see the fire every time.

Yet I also had an idea why it wasn't there. Tony was a God-gifted runner. Instead of turning him loose, featuring him, the Cowboys perennially made him bow to their game plan. Tony, like any great back, wanted to be The Man. When the Cowboys failed to do that, some games Tony looked frustrated.

Look at Super Bowl XIV, when the Cowboys lost to the Steelers in Miami. I was at the game, and I could see that Tony was hot. He was running extremely low, dashing and scooting, seven, ten yards at a pop. When they're hot, backs can score a TD on anything. To me, Tony was ready to tear it up.

And then they went away from him. Because the game plan called for something else.

Well damn! I understand that you must have a game plan. But when a great back is ripe, ready to perform, stay with him. It's not logical, it's not intellectual, it's not your game plan. Stay with him anyway: he'll create things you could never write up on any blackboard. People don't realize it, but backs don't necessarily gain yards because of well-designed plays, or even great blocking. Some days a back runs crazy just because he's special.

After that Super Bowl I was down in Dallas for a benefit basketball game against several Cowboys. I saw Tony in the dressing room, went and sat beside him.

I said, "Hey man, I picked up on what happened at the Super Bowl. The man went away from you and you were hot, weren't you?"

Tony said, "You saw that?"

"Yeah, I saw it."

He said, "Wow. Yeah, I was ready."

We let it go at that but I think he appreciated it. And the reality is, if the Browns had shared the attitude of the Cowboys, I would not have gained half the yards I did.

Now Tony's with the Broncos. The Cowboys moved him out for Herschel Walker. Herschel is not the type of player I particularly like. He frustrates me. I see a guy with incredible physical gifts. I also see a guy who's always so contained. It's not healthy for a runner to be that inhibited. Just once, I want to see Herschel's socks roll down. I'd like to see him jump up and scream. Put an elbow on someone. I want to see *something,* in his body language that tells me he's playing all out. People say Herschel "doesn't know how to make a tackler miss." I don't think it's that at all. What the man needs to do is get loose. You have to be a little strange to be the best.

Bo Jackson's another guy whose heart still bears examining. The report on Bo by the players on the Raiders is that the man is an awesome physical specimen, and an unbelievable athlete. Does things in practice and guys just say *"What?"* And Bo can scald a baseball. For that I have admiration, having played baseball, and not very well.

What I don't admire someone for is potential. Potential puts me to sleep. Get out and execute, then we'll talk. I'm just not a fan of this two-way career stuff, not the way Bo's treating football. To me playing half a football season is ragged and incomplete and I can't get behind it. Apparently I'm in the minority: when Bo came to the Raiders, ran over Brian Bosworth, it got more coverage than the Second Coming, as if knocking guys down was something Bo just introduced to the NFL. It didn't make the news, but I thought something else involving Bo was far more telling. I was watching him on national TV when he hurt an ankle, then they showed him running to the dressing room with a trainer. What? Any time you can run to the dressing room you can stay on the field and run the football. I know this country is starved for heroes but I think the hype about Bo is premature, and I don't think it's helpful to Bo. The kid is twenty-five, already speaks of himself in the third person, as if he's a prophet.

Marcus Allen, the Raiders' other runner, seems to be mentally tougher. Marcus is a nice young man, an intelligent football player, though not a great pure runner. For one thing Marcus lacks striking power. This isn't scientific but I think it's his body: Marcus is light in his butt. However, Marcus catches passes. He can throw the option pass. At USC he blocked for Charles White the year Charles won the Heisman, and Marcus is still an angry blocker. And he still has that attitude: I'll do whatever I have to do to help my club win games. Since he's called on to do many things, Marcus will never have gaudy statistics, so he might be overlooked by history. That would be unfair. He's a sound ballplayer.

If Marcus was more in tune with his owner, I think his career might benefit. I don't know exactly what the deal is, but Marcus and Al Davis can't seem to get along. As a friend of both men, I think that's too bad. One man's the boss, one's the player, but they need each other. No one asked me, but I think they should be pals.

Jimmy Taylor would have made a vintage Raider. Jimmy and I had an interesting relationship. I admired him a lot, and I still like him. Jimmy got smart. Most old guys marry old women. Jimmy found himself a pretty young wife. He stays in shape, plays a lot of different sports. He's still a bulldog.

I think all purists loved Jimmy Taylor. He didn't have special size, speed, or moves, yet football in his hand, Jimmy Taylor was Defiance.

They were always comparing Jimmy to me. It was almost like I was the heavyweight champion, they were trying to find a replacement. I don't believe it was racial, don't think they were looking for a Great White Hope. My successor could have been mauve, as long as he was a Good Guy. Because I was a Bad Guy. Nonconformist. Malcontent. Locker Room Lawyer. Militant. Image isn't everything, but it's a lot, and Jimmy's was easier to digest.

People would say that Jimmy was the superior back. Others would counter, No, Jim Brown is the best. I loved Jimmy, but sometimes I got annoyed, having to answer the same tired questions. I didn't think Jimmy was the runner that I was. I was faster, quicker, at least as strong, at least as smart, and more productive. My actions spoke louder than my manner. I wasn't as visibly emotional, but no one, even Jimmy, wanted to win more than I did.

By the way he was quoted in the press, it seemed Jimmy had some animosity toward me. He probably thought the Packers were better than the Browns, he was better than me, yet I was still getting most of the ink. On the other hand, I don't even know if Jimmy was being quoted correctly. As I'll get to later, most Sports Feuds are more hot air than substantial. Take a few writers, specifically those who don't lose a lot of sleep if they punch up a quote, make it juicier, have those writers *initiate* the rivalry in the first place, mix in a few prideful guys like me and Jimmy, not exactly shy, you've got yourself a Sports Feud.

Jimmy's genuine fight was with the New York Giants. One game the Giants defense decided they were going to get Jimmy Taylor, beat him up. Jimmy was an excellent target—he'd never run around you. And Jimmy got trashed. He had internal bleeding, had to leave the stadium, go to a hospital. I always felt that game was the beginning of the end for Jimmy. He finished up with New Orleans, never was the same runner. I really felt for Jimmy that afternoon against New York. He was this gladiator, and they finally broke him.

Years later, in the early 1980s, one of the networks put on a bowling show in Las Vegas. They wanted two-man teams, recognizable guys who could jack up the ratings. They chose two players from various sports—Oscar Robertson and Wilt Chamberlain, Arnold Palmer and Ray Floyd, Willie Arcaro and Bill Shoemaker. They wanted me for football, hadn't chosen my partner yet. They showed me a list of ten former pros, asked me who I wanted to bowl with.

I said, "I don't know how any of these guys bowl, but I'll take this guy here, Jim Taylor."

I knew the cat was tenacious. I also knew in any contest with me he would break his ass to try and look better. And there was no way I was going to let him do that. That alone, I surmised, gave us a fighting chance.

The networks brought in this bowling coach. He was trying to teach us how to throw a hook. I didn't throw a hook. I threw a backup ball. It went the wrong way, like a screwball. I told the bowling coach, "No, no, no. I don't have time to learn a hook. I'll just use this little backup ball I have. At least I can be consistent with it."

Taylor, meanwhile, had gotten his hook down pretty well. Somehow we got into the finals, against Ray Floyd and Arnold Palmer. All day I'd been watching Palmer. He'd impressed the hell out of me. He had a backup ball, too, but he picked up all his spares, got a few strikes, sheerly through the force of his will. In fact, Arnold bowled a little bit the way he golfed: Don't Look Cute or Refined. Do What the Fuck You Have To. And Win.

As the games continued, me and Palmer and Taylor were hanging in, mostly on guts. I began to view us as three of a kind. Wilt Chamberlain, on the other hand, who I like as a person, had a chance to move his team into the finals. He needed three pins, threw his ball in the gutter.

So we're in the finals, $40,000 to the winning team. Now it's not just pride. Now that I am this close, now I want the money. So did Jimmy. It was a time in our lives when both of us really needed it.

It appeared the golfers were going to beat the

football players. Jimmy and I entered the tenth frame needing two strikes, and a few extra pins. I got up, threw my little backup ball, was lucky enough to get my strike. Here comes Taylor. Either he'll prove my theory, or he won't. Taylor threw a little hook for a perfect strike.

Now I'm the crucial man. I need three pins. That scares me a little, don't like the easy stuff. I think to myself, *Damn, if I do what Wilt did, throw the ball in the goddamn gutter, they'll know I'm not much of a competitor. I better get this.*

I threw it nice and easy. Knocked down five pins. We each won $20,000.

I am now going to pat myself on the back. Not for the way I bowled, which was not that great. I'm patting myself for being perfectly objective, recognizing Jimmy Taylor's special talent, maximizing my opportunity to win twenty large. And that's my favorite story about Jim Taylor.

Jimmy's partner in the Packers' backfield was Paul Hornung. Paul is a textbook example of a player who found the right system. Before Paul played for Vince Lombardi, his career was essentially over. He was a quarterback then, and he wasn't getting it done. Lombardi realized Paul's talents were multi-dimensional. Lombardi transformed Paul into a kicker, a runner, and a receiver. From a career with little hope, Paul went on to win a MVP. Lombardi saved Paul Hornung. When Paul was inducted into the Hall of Fame, I believe he mentioned that fact himself.

Paul was also good on his own terms. Smart, soft hands, could throw that option pass, played hard. As for Paul "smelling the goal line," the phrase they attached to his name, I credit a lot of that to Jimmy Taylor. Taylor usually carried the ball down the field. Once you get the near goal line the defense will key on the guy they think is toughest. That was Taylor. While the defense swarmed around Jim, Paul's job was made easier.

I've always liked Paul. I enjoyed the swagger and the attitude. He was anything but dull. Paul loved to be seen with his women—the Golden Boy. I don't think Paul was quite as handsome as he thought. He was kind of chunky and his hair was going thin. I know none of the players thought Paul was king when it came to women. Paul was publicized as the great NFL lover, yet he was no more a lover than ninety percent of the players. Getting women wasn't real difficult.

To some of the black guys, Paul's sexual rep was funny. First off, we thought we were the great lovers. With women, with life, the white guys got all the breaks; as black dudes, we had to be power smooth. And when we'd watch a white guy who was highly acclaimed as a lover, they'd often look a little bit Square. It was like watching people dance. Most black guys stay just in back of the beat, no rush. Most white guys stay just in front of it. They want to get there so fast, they get there before the beat does.

Me and my partners all liked Paul. We just thought he was a little ahead of the beat.

9

NEW REGIME

THERE WAS NOTHING DEEP about Paul Brown's demise as a coach. Paul enjoyed so much success, his way, he refused to acknowledge the future. Green Bay had hired Lombardi, New York had Allie Sherman and Tom Landry, and they and others were evolving defensive strategy. Paul couldn't or wouldn't adapt. His last few seasons, we felt Paul was stifling our team. There were games when we'd come in at halftime, have to reassure our teammates.

We'd say, "Come on, we can win this despite Paul. Don't let Paul get us down."

Our offense became severely conservative. As he had in the past, Paul sent in all our plays by messenger. But now, defenses were changing formations just before the snap of the ball. Paul would not let our quarterbacks call any audibles. Even if half the defense was partying in the hole, we'd have to run the play.

As Paul became decreasingly creative, the messenger would often come in with a play we knew wouldn't work. The quarterback would have to call it anyway, so we'd be faced with a decision in the huddle: do we run this fucked-up play, or do we change it? The quarterbacks were understandably afraid of angering Paul, so we rarely changed plays. When we did convince the quarterback to change a play, we all agreed, if the play should not work, to tell Paul it had not been intentionally changed, but had gotten screwed up in the translation from the messenger. If the new play did work, no explanation was needed. Most coaches don't complain if the result is positive. Even when Bobby Mitchell was with us, our messenger once came in with a pitch-out for Bobby. He was tired from a long sprint, so I lined up at halfback while he took my spot at fullback. I went twenty-five yards for a touchdown, the coaches never mentioned the obvious switch.

I don't want to overstate the importance of Paul's refusal to let us audible. At times it did hurt us, but it wasn't the key issue. Much more critical was the closing down of our offense. Even as a runner who loved having the ball, I knew we had to diversify the offense to beat the top teams. Especially against the Giants, our nemesis, we needed to pass more often. Paul would get up against the Giants, we'd run maybe four different plays! We'd be thinking, *Is Paul scared of the Giants? Let's open things up and go for broke.* The analytical Giants knew our offense cold, yet we never designed new plays for them. The Giants would stand across the line, call out our plays before we ran them. "32 Trap. Here he comes!" I'm not kidding. Robustelli would sometimes tell our messenger what play Paul had just sent in.

Against New York Paul became a defeatist. He thought so highly of Robustelli, Svede Svare, other guys depending on how they were playing at the time, he would tell us we had to run the ball away for them. He would tell us they were too tough to try and attack. We were proud men, did not want to back down to anyone. And by the time Paul finished telling us where we couldn't run, no wonder we had four plays. It was conservatism through fear. And it was one of the crucial breakdowns between Paul and his players. Though the Giants mostly beat us, I don't think there was a man on our team who felt they had our number. Against the Giants, we thought Paul had our number.

I was also concerned about myself, as an individual. The last few years, Paul started running me tackle to tackle. Suddenly I had no sweeps. Started thinking, *Whoa! These guys are gonna kill me, they know where I'm coming. Don't sell me short because I'm big. I'm a sweeps man, too! I'll run inside, but let me outside, out there I can break some. Make all our lives easier.* I think every one of my opponents knew I was a bitch on sweeps. And was probably very happy that I wasn't running them.

In 1962 we finished the season 7-6-1. We felt we had lost some games, considering our personnel, we didn't need to lose. In December, several of the veterans decided things had gotten too strange. We designated several team leaders—Bernie Parrish, Mark McCormack, John Wooten, and me—to represent our point of view to Paul. Guys had individual complaints about Paul, always had, but that was not what this was about. We wanted Paul to open up the offense. The guys on defense felt stilted, too.

We planned to visit Paul at his home. Our new owner, Art Modell, found out about our plan.

Art said, "You don't have to do that. I have a solution."

I guess his solution was that he would handle Paul. The first week of January, Art called Paul into his office and fired him. There have been many stories about the players on the Cleveland Browns firing Paul Brown. There were accusations and rumors and gossip of Byzantine plots. I think it's ridiculous to believe that NFL players wield the clout to fire a coach, but people should believe what they want to. This is what I know: we did not want to play another season in seat belts. We definitely wanted Paul to open the offense. But we wanted *Paul* to do something about it.

In pursuit of the Team Fires Paul Brown storyline, I think the press may have been, let's say, encouraged, by Art Modell. You have to know a little bit about Art, and his relationship with Paul. Art came to Cleveland from New York. He was thirty-six years old, an executive in advertising and TV. In 1961, Art did something I thought impossible: he purchased the Cleveland Browns. For Art, an outsider, to arrive in Cleveland, have the audacity to even *think* about buying Paul Brown's team, was astonishing to the players. Here came this young, slick Turk from New York to challenge Paul Brown. To us, it was the shootout at OK Corral.

Before Paul sold the team, he was coach, general manager, vice president, major stockholder. When the rumors began circulating that Art was after the Browns, Paul told us it would never happen. It happened. Paul stayed, but Art established his presence quickly and dramatically. Paul had a stadium-front office. Art moved him out of there, put him in back. NO ONE moves Paul Brown to a back office. When practices began, immediately Art started coming down, standing behind the offensive huddle. I guarantee you Paul did not dig that.

When Art bought the team I was shocked. I never thought Paul would sell in a million years. His position was perfect: he was a coach who could not be fired. However, when Paul sold the team, and Art fired him, I was not shocked. By then I knew Art and his audacity. Anyone with any kind of mind could see that Paul Brown and Art Modell would not co-exist for long. You had a Hertz and Hertz, and no Avis.

Those who said the players fired Paul weren't true insiders, didn't see what went on in the front office. I don't particularly care about all the stories that came out, but I understand why they did. Art was extremely shrewd about this whole deal. After he left, Paul took a harsher stance. Paul said Art used me and my teammates to help Art dump Paul.

It is true that Art was very nice to me, courted me in a sense. I figured he was simply doing business, being intelligent. I was important to the success of his new acquisition, regardless of what would evolve between him and Paul. Do I think Art "used" us? I would say that Art manipulated us. If Art came in, summarily fired Paul, the local response would be outrage. I think Art wanted to run the Browns himself, waited for a fertile situation. Art didn't create the situation, he didn't tell us to be unhappy with the offense, but he utilized it, from a business standpoint, beautifully. When Art fired Paul he knew there was player unrest, as did everyone else. Art took that fact, used it skillfully with the media, diverted the glare from himself onto us, and smoothed his transition into power.

When Paul left Cleveland he was hurt and angry. And he bounced back. In 1970 he created the Cincinnati Bengals. Already, Paul has taken them twice to the Super Bowl. Paul Brown is a force.

So is Art Modell. In their awe of Paul, a lot of folks failed to see that. Art understood business and money, had the ego to take on Paul Brown. When Art came to Cleveland, he was after three things: to create the TV doubleheader, bring a dose of Manhattan to the NFL, and rule the Cleveland Browns. He accomplished all three.

When Paul left the Browns my emotions ran the gamut. The image of him leaving, actually cleaning out his office, was disturbing. But I couldn't help but be pleased for Paul's successor, Blanton Collier. Blanton was the kind of man who makes you wonder how God decides who should die young and who should live to old age. When Blanton passed away it saddened the entire organization. He was a sweetheart of a human being.

As a coach Blanton was quiet, emotional, actually hugged a few guys as they ran to the sideline.

The players loved him, knew they were fortunate to have him: Blanton had been one of Paul's assistants. Out of loyalty to Paul, Blanton almost told Art no, refused the job.

For myself, I felt invigorated when we made the change. I had a need for self-expression. When Blanton came in I saw a chance to fulfill it again. I also knew the football world would be watching me. Not only because we'd stuck out our necks, complained about the offense. A lot of people believe that a runner can only excel in one system. Without Paul, there was some question as to how effective I might be. When I showed up at camp, I could run ninety yards without breathing hard. I *always* took pains to be in excellent shape, that was my thing, but this was a higher peak. I wanted to run the football the way no one had ever run it.

Blanton brought in Dub Jones, a former star receiver with the Browns, to help revamp the offense. Dub and Blanton were big hits with the guys on offense. They would consult us, listen to us, let us participate in devising plays. Blanton started running me around the ends. He let me catch passes. I even threw some, and if you don't think that was a blast, then you've never played running back. Blanton worked closely with our quarterback, Frank Ryan. And Frank began to emerge as a passer. Frank had always been long on brains and courage, but he'd been dealt a rough hand. We were a running team, I dominated the press, Frank was always overlooked. Wounded pride can hurt, not as much as a broken body: under Paul, when Frank threw at all, it was often third and long, and Frank got roughed up. I never wanted to give him the ball, say, Here man, you be the meat of the offense. Yet I felt for him. On another team, I knew he'd be more appreciated.

Blanton also instituted an option play. The offensive linemen would take their men wherever they wanted to. I would read their blocks, and go. I had good peripheral vision, I could pick, and this was ideal for me. Though we only had one option play, and as the up man in the I formation, I didn't have a lot of room to play with, the option was a godsend. It was instinctual football and I averaged about nine yards on that sucker. And if I'd had that option play from day one, my career might have been unbelievable.

As it was, for the first time in years, I was free to roam the entire field and to use all the skills I brought to the game. It was a good year. Though the Giants won the division at 11–3, we went 10–4, split our series with them, and had some fun. Liberated by Blanton, with my boys on the line doing some blasting, I was a running fool. I rushed for 1,863 yards, averaged 6.3 yards a carry. Had games of 162, 232, 175, 123, 144, 223, 154, 179, and 125. I was twenty-seven years old. I never ran better in my life.

In 1964, we played the Baltimore Colts for the NFL championship. We'd beaten the Giants twice, finished 10–3–1, but the Colts were stacked, had gone 12–2. Supposedly, they were going to whip us. We beat them 27–0. I played well, Frank Ryan threw three TDs to Gary Collins, who won the game MVP. And the defense was magnificent. To shut out Johnny Unitas and Ray Berry and Lenny

Moore, anytime, was almost inconceivable. To do it in a game that big *was* inconceivable. We had a tough undersized linebacker named Vince Costello, who'd been there ever since I had, and Vince kicked some ass. Also fantastic was Bernie Parrish. Bernie and the rest of our defensive backs did something revolutionary for 1964: they moved up to the line of scrimmage, started popping Baltimore's receivers. It screwed up Baltimore's timing, played a large role in our victory.

I've always loved how that game unfolded. Team Victory is an overworked phrase, but this was it. I knew there were guys on the team who must have felt slighted all those years, watching the reporters always question me, and if they did question them, it was often for a quote about me. It wasn't the way it is today, with 90 million reporters for every player. But after we beat the Colts, reporters were bouncing from guy to guy, and those guys were *yapping*. I knew they could take that feeling home, have a championship in their life, no matter what happened after that day.

My first NFL championship. What the hell do you know. I have a list of words I don't prefer, and "thrill" is one of them. I was a warrior. I didn't go around getting "thrilled." That shit sounds like a girl who goes to the prom, they name her Queen. I felt . . . potent. Sentimental. Grateful. Whole. My goddamn melon hurt from smiling. I also felt intense relief. Unless he wins a championship, even a superstar is never fully accepted. Some people use the absence of a title to criticize a successful individual. They say a team *can't* win a championship with him. He's too much of a soloist. Otto Graham announced it to the world about me.

So it felt GOOD to get that primate off my back. I said, Self, breathe this in, and don't be in any rush. You got exactly where you wanted to go. In life that is rare.

So is repeating and we couldn't pull it off. We went all the way back to the title game, but Lombardi's Packers denied us, 23–12. Those guys were rough and skilled, but I think they received an assist from the elements. The game was in Green Bay, the field was ice, and we couldn't run. They'll hate me for this: I think we would have won in normal conditions.

I retired after that season, and I retired happy. Those last three years were a romp.

No one probably knows this, outside of me, but in 1982 when the 49ers played the Bengals in Super Bowl XVI, I was the game's Grand Marshal. The game was in Pontiac, the Detroit Chamber of Commerce was in charge, the Chamber guys were mostly black, wanted to do something different, so they made me the Grand Marshal. I'd say that's different.

The Chamber guys had a suite in the Silverdome, that's where I was before the game. In the suite to our left was the Pete Rozelle group. In the suite to our right was a group led by Paul Brown. I peeked around, through the glass, saw Paul's son, Mike. Mike is Cincinnati's General Manager. He was a boy when I played for the

Browns and we'd always been cool. Mike spotted me, smiled.

He said, "Jim, how are you? Hey, come on over."

I knocked on the door, Paul stepped out. I hadn't seen him in a lot of years. He seemed glad to see me, and I was happy to see him, I guess that's why I went there in the first place. It was noisy inside their suite so we stayed in the hall. We chatted a couple minutes. It was easy and nice, no awkwardness or animosity. We were just two guys who'd shared some wars. No one saw us, and we didn't have to strike any poses. It was a quiet meeting, and before we left we wished each other well. I thought it was perfect.

Paul has a golf tournament back in Dayton, called Paul's Guys. I attended it last year because Paul asked me to. I knew it would be a lot of old Browns people—players, coaches, front office guys. It had been awhile since I'd been back, but now the vibration felt right. I realized a lot of organizations, a lot of people, have learned over the years, as I have. That's the attitude I went back with, and I was right.

I was teamed on a foursome with Paul, and two businessmen. I was the anchorman for our foursome, and three or four times I made a clutch putt. I knew Paul enjoyed the hell out of that. And I did. It was this sweet crazy deal, Paul and Jim back together. Paul was still the General, deciding how to play the holes, and I was the guy coming through for him. Christ, what a day.

I flew back home on this lovely high. I also took back a memento. The tournament guys had snapped photographs of each foursome, copied the photos, put one on each man's golf bag. Paul's on my bag right now. If we're gonna be married, I figure it might as well be happily.

10

GOOD—BYE, NFL

AT THE AGE OF twenty-nine I retired from pro football. Originally I planned on leaving after the 1964 season, but when we won the NFL championship, I decided to return, attempt to help us repeat. After we lost to Green Bay for the title, I told Art Modell that was it. Art heard my voice, didn't really hear my words. That was not unusual: Art always had his own vision of when I would quit, was always trying to make it my own.

Art wanted me to play a minimum of one more year. I said no. It was summer, 1966. I had already done my first movie—*Rio Conchos*—had a film agent, and a three-movie deal with Paramount Pictures. That summer I had a prominent role in *The Dirty Dozen*, on which filming was beginning in London. Prior to leaving, I told Art I was not coming back. Art was characteristically persuasive in his argument. I compromised: I told Art I wanted to quit but might reconsider while in London. If I did come back, and I was not promising, it would only be to help the team.

I received word in London: in Cleveland, Art was telling the press I would definitely play for the Browns that year. Reporters began calling me for comment. I said I wouldn't be playing. I wasn't planning on playing. The chance of me playing another year, at that point, was perhaps thirty percent.

Rain began falling in London. It delayed production, cost thousands, the filmmakers fell behind schedule. Training camp was approaching. As the London sky grew dimmer, so did the prospects for my return to football. Then Art turned out the lights.

Art issued a public ultimatum. He told the press if I didn't show up on time for camp, I would be fined $100 for each day I missed. Had Art not done that, I still might have returned; at the least, I may have reached the point where I felt substantially torn. Art's edict removed that possibility. I couldn't help an organization that played that particular game on me. I said, "Fuck it. Now I won't even consider it."

Art should have known, intimidation does not work with me. It was a bad move by a smart man. As for Art fining me, he couldn't. I didn't have a guaranteed contract. I had what we used to call a one-way contract. If I broke my leg in camp and was out for the season, I'd never earn a cent. My contract started, I began getting paid, when I played my first game. Then I'd functionally be paid game by game. Threatening to fine me at the start of camp was threatening to fine me invisible money. Until I showed up to play football, I was a free man, could live as I pleased. If the Browns wanted me back, they had to treat me like a free man. They didn't.

Carroll Rosenbloom, Art's confidant and fellow owner, apparently had business in England. At Art's request, Carroll appeared on the set to discuss my return to football. Carroll, being extremely bright, knew after two minutes I wasn't coming back. He didn't belabor the point, we spoke of other things, and Carroll left.

I wrote a letter to Blanton Collier. I told him I was going to retire, but not to worry. He had an excellent runner in Leroy Kelly, a fine blocker in Ernie Green, and they would be a real good team even without me. I wished Blanton all the luck in the world. Simultaneously, I mailed a copy of the letter to Hal Leibovitz. Hal was a columnist in Cleveland, an honest man and a scrupulous writer. I wanted people to know I was actually retiring, so they could move on. I wanted the story to break with Hal so it would be printed correctly.

Then I issued a brief statement on the film set. I said I was quitting with regret, but no sorrow. I answered a few questions, returned to my work as an actor. My football career was complete.

There is no single, tidy explanation for why I left football when I did. There were several factors.

Least of all, retiring made economic sense. I had the three movie deal with Paramount. With the Browns I had a consulting contract, an addendum to my playing contract, which ran for three more years. I had deferred payments coming for five more years (I was one of the first guys who asked for deferred money). Straight out of football, I earned more than I did in it. And no one tried to bust my head.

I wasn't retiring, I was retiring from football, to go into acting. I was fortunate and I knew it. I knew if you went from stardom to something obscure, the descent was too radical, knew a lot of guys freaked when the adulation screeched to a stop. I was too hardened for that. I remember when I was still playing, I'd go out to Beverly Hills during the offseason, big shots couldn't pamper me enough if I let them, and sometimes I did. It was good to be the King. Then I retired, the Juice came along, they bowed to him. I saw it coming, I wasn't deflated.

I don't want to get too bleak here: going into acting had some monumental perks. I knew when you went from Sam Huff to Raquel Welch it wasn't exactly bad shit. I saw the chance to parlay what I had, while I was still hot, into something sultry. I said, "Man, this movie business looks good. I can make more money, work with those sexy girls, see the world. I can move into that, not even miss football. Time for me to get OUT."

Acting was a challenge unmet and that intrigued me. In football I knew I was running out of goals, knew for me that was hazardous. What else was left? Win another rushing title? Another MVP? We had filled my largest void, won an NFL championship. The next year we had another shot. All that was left was to imitate myself, compete with my

174

own legacy. The moment felt right, perfect, to move forward. It was 1966. Change was in the air.

Though Art's ultimatum clinched it, my retirement was anything but a rash decision. I always had thoughtful convictions about athletes and retirement. Two things I always knew about my league, the NFL: you don't ask for favors, you don't hang around. A man might love the game, but the game loves no one. The game will use what he has, discard him. The shit isn't personal. Game needs new blood. A ninety-year-old woman can't be on the cover of *Playboy*. A washed-up athlete can't play football.

I was not washed up. That's the beauty. I never *wanted* to stick around. You kidding? I wanted to leave before my retirement even became an issue. I knew once they're talking, it's an issue, you've stayed too long. The owner who loved you now has to find a way to get rid of you. If you're a journeyman, milk it and milk it some more. Hang on until they won't pay you any more. If you're a star, you have the money, you have the choice, why wait until they stick you on the bench, until you're begging for one more year? My thing was to leave before it got sad for everyone, deal with it before *they* deal with it. Everyone comes out smelling like a rose.

I wanted to depart in style, on my own set of terms. I wanted a career so consistent, production so constant, no one could fuck with me, the way they always do with an athlete who has lingered too long. My first year in the NFL I led the league in rushing. My last year I was MVP. Bench *that* motherfucker.

I know a lot of guys hang on because they need the money. If that's why they have to stay, they should stay. Play until they're second string, third string, until their legs fall off. It's a good living, it's legal. There's no loss of dignity in that.

What I did was look ahead, made sure X and O were not the only letters in my life. My entire career I worked for Pepsi in the offseason, in public relations. I worked, didn't rest on my name, and my offseasons were always crammed. It was the survivor in me: I knew I needed financial options, wider knowledge. I looked at football as a waterhole when you're crossing the desert. You stop, enjoy the scenery, sip a little water, get your ass out of there. Knew if you stayed too long, it would turn on you.

I saw it turn on the best and the brightest. Saw the Colts try and retire Johnny Unitas against his will. Johnny did not want to leave the game. They practically had to rip him out. I despised that. Such a melancholy finish to a gorgeous career.

I thought Joe Namath played too long. It hurt to see him on TV playing with the Rams, standing on the sideline in the mud and the rain, knees shot, accomplishments behind him. I thought Joe Louis stayed too long, though I know he needed the money, and Frazier and Ali. And Walter Payton.

Every man must make his own choices. I've been asked if I have any regrets about the way that I left football. No. I'm proud as hell. By leaving when I did, still satisfied with my ability to perform, I felt good about myself. That allowed me to feel good about the game. Since my leaving never got ugly, neither did my feelings toward the NFL. I could have done some things better, but I never prostituted myself for money. I hate it when people are in just for the money. I played the game pure, as pure as I knew how.

A lot of athletes turned actor don't like to talk about football. I don't mind people coming up to talk about football, because I understand. Though football was only one part of my life, though I don't talk about it much, I never make it less than what it was. Football set the foundation for the rest of my existence. I know now that I can withstand pressure. I can survive racial politics, and those knocks were harder than any knocks I absorbed on the field. For nine years I competed, man to man, and I competed well. I don't think I can ever compete again, at anything, that ferociously. Having competed on that level, I'm released from having that need.

I guess it's no surprise that what I loved most about playing football was playing football. What gave me the sharpest jolt was running with the ball. When I was clutching the football my instincts were so acute it made no sense. Any movement, any sound, didn't matter where, how slight, I seemed to be aware of. I don't think my senses have ever felt that ridiculously heightened. Physically, I don't know that I've ever felt more vital.

And I love certain friendships. I love the friendship of the linemen, John Wooten, Gene Hickerson, Dick Schafrath, Monte Clark, Jim Ray Smith. Ray Renfro was a wonderful person, who transcended race, whose desire to block, his ability to run and cut, inspired me. I admired Frank Ryan's courage. I respected Ernie Green for doing the dirty work of blocking. I remember Gary Collins and feel remiss, realize he was much greater than I knew at the time. For their acceptance of me as an athlete, I love the fans of Cleveland. Playing for the Cleveland Browns was a rich time in my life.

I don't *miss* playing football. I never missed it, not for one second. And just as I understand when people want to talk about football, when I tell them football was only part of my life, I want them to understand that. I was never only a football player. I'm not even sure football was my favorite sport. I also loved track and golf and basketball and lacrosse. And before anyone put a football in my hand, I had my social consciousness. I run into guys whose whole world was football, all they want to do is tell me ninety football stories, forty-five about them, forty-five about me. That brand of masturbation is boring. Man, we already *did* it.

People come up, ask me what I'm into now, I don't segue to the time I ran over sixteen guys, in eight feet of snow, with three broken ankles. Today, I explain that I'm Executive Director and Chairman of the Board of Vital Issues. It's an extension of everything I've done since the 1960s—trying to find a way to help black people and society as a whole. I got involved about eight years ago when I met a fellow named Jim Kress, who invented a program called Personal Development and Life Management. You develop yourself and you manage your life correctly. I was excited as soon as I heard the details. This wasn't abstract psychobabble. It was pragmatic and accessible. I took a lot of courses in college, enjoyed college, yet it never taught me much about life—goal setting, problem solving, decision making, family relationships, financial stability, emotional self-control, seeking jobs. Those were the areas Vital Issues worked in. I told Jim I wanted to help. I helped him win a contract in Houston for $900,000, he was on his way.

Three years ago Jim returned to me, said he needed someone he could work with. I became the Executive Director. We now have a contract with the state of California to work in five California prisons. What I've learned is that alcoholism, unemployment, drug abuse, street crime, are not the problems. They're symptoms of a deeper problem —a people problem. Before a person can reorganize his life, regain control of it, he must first change his way of *thinking*. Vital Issues helps him try and make that change. Whatever a person's situation, we try and give him the mental equipment to make it better. It's not a "Jim Brown" thing. I do it for the community.

As Executive Director of Vital Issues, I've worked with the top men in California government: Governor, Speaker of the House, Director of Corrections, Director of Education. We've worked with some of the roughest prisoners at Soledad, and gotten letters from them, and the staff, thanking us for Vital Issues, offering to fight for our program, saying our work was important and good. When I read a letter of hope, return address Soledad, how can I miss football?

That doesn't mean I never think about the people. Some of my closest partners used to play in the NFL. I still see Art Modell. Today we're close. Time and events have brought us back together.

Art was decent about my retirement. He didn't like it mostly, I believe, because he didn't get his way, and Art wasn't the kind of man who was used to that happening. He has a big ego, and I say that with respect. A man with a large ego isn't a parasite, doesn't ride on the back of others. He creates and accomplishes.

Art didn't like it, but he accepted it, never did anything to hurt me. I retired, we went our separate ways. There was nothing else for me to do, I wasn't into hanging around the locker room. I didn't see Art for a number of years. When we spoke publicly of one another, there was a subtle but aggressive edge to our tone. The mutual respect was still intact, but the summer of my retirement, the emotions it evoked, was still nibbling at my relationship with Art.

By the late 1970s, Art and I began speaking on the phone, and it was clear that we never really stopped liking each other. When Art would come to Southern California, I would try and see him. He and his wife were always nice to me. Six years ago the bond pulled tighter. I think two things made that happen.

In 1984 Art suffered a heart attack. After he recovered he made a trip west. I went to see him at his hotel and it was a beautiful coming together. I think that heart attack changed some things for Art. I would never say he mellowed. I don't like that word either. To me, mellow sounds like your head's going soft, you're lying in some state of limbo. Art wouldn't know limbo if it bit him. Man is tough, will still get down to business. I just think Art took a look at some of his relationships from a new angle. All I know for certain is that I've felt love between us ever since.

Next time I saw Art was when the Browns played the Rams in exhibition. He came out with Paul Warfield, we drove to Anaheim, where the three of us sat in Art's box. Watching the game, Art leaned over toward me.

He said, "Jim, I really had fun when you guys were playing. I loved those days. Now . . . the damn game is no fun. A kid signs for a million dollars, and if I want him to change positions, I can't even talk to him. I have to talk to his agent! This shit is no more fun."

And that's the second thing: I think when Art looked at the modern ballplayer, he felt a lot closer to me.

It was nice for both of us, up in Art's box. And it illustrates the way that life spins to its own mystical beat. After I retired from the Browns, I only went back to the Stadium once, and the owner's box was not where I sat. The old veterans were supposed to get tickets that day. I didn't receive mine. I suppose the circumstance of my retirement had something to do with it. I purchased a seat, intentionally, way up high in the bleachers. I sat down, fans started going nuts. "Oh Jim! Look at you! What are *you* doing in the bleachers?"

I said, "Man, when it's over it's over. I don't play any more, they don't give me good tickets. Now I'm up here, with you straggly-ass suckers."

But you know, I liked it.

11

SOME GIRLS

I WALKED OUT OF football into the sexual revolution.

Actually, I already had a pretty good start. Sexually, I have chosen to live a free life. That's part of who I am. Some people don't care for that, they talk about me as they might a dog. Others respect the hell out of me.

What else is new? Most people don't know who I am. I'm not exactly your standard Sports Hero. I'm also no Puritan, and I don't believe any man is pure. When it comes to sex, sometimes it's the chumps who preach the loudest who are most full of shit. And I don't like being told what I'm supposed to want. For instance, I prefer girls who are young. My lady right now is nineteen. Even one of my friends tells me I should find a woman who's "more sophisticated." He knows sophistication and age have little correlation. What my friend means is that I should find a woman who is older. Hey, I have what I want. If I wake up in the morning, I hunger for crab, then I don't want steak. Do I?

So people look at me funny. They say, "Man, you like *what?*" Then I start thinking about it. *Hmmm. Maybe they have a point. You get a woman with all that experience and*—and I just stop. I know who I am, I know what I like. When I eat a peach, I don't want it overripe. I want that peach when it's peaking.

I use that analogy because it involves nature, and I think the study of nature can tell you an awful lot about man. Physically, from the standpoint of nature, a young woman is fabulous. Everything is peaking. The breasts are firm, the thighs are taut, the buttocks are tight. Physically, between a young girl and an old one, there is no contest. I used to drive down to the California state beach, see the bodies on seventeen, eighteen, nineteen, twenty, twenty-one, twenty-two, twenty-three, twenty-four-year-old girls. They were the prettiest bodies on earth.

A lot of people don't want to hear that. They'll read this and say I'm fucked-up. Maybe I am, but I don't think I'm going to change. I'm highly selective in what I want and it isn't always what someone else wants.

Even when I used to hang out in clubs, I was always a little different. A lot of guys would talk about the girls who they heard were hot, had the big rep, and when those girls would appear, the

cats would be pushing and rushing, didn't matter if **she** was overrated, they had to score that prize. I **never** played that. All I wanted was the girl who was pretty to me.

Usually that meant a woman who was small. I don't mean mousy small. I mean tight. Petite. Delicate. No excess. Thin legs, nice butt . . . small. When I get into the bedroom, I don't want to see anything that's big like me. That includes big breasts. I don't want big breasts anywhere around me. Keep those big breasts away.

My boys would see me enter a club, they'd be pleased: they knew I'd never chase the same chicks they were, the ones who were all stacked up. They knew I'd be after that wispy little girl in the corner. Those guys still tell me my women all look like clones. Uh-huh. Once I lose my touch, that's when you'll see me with someone different.

It's not only young bodies I like, although I like them a lot. For me, the most wonderful emotional qualities in a female are innocence and spontaneity. You take a girl who's nineteen years old. She's not bitter toward men, or bored with their bullshit, or jaded by society. She's excited by new people and ideas; when she looks at you, there's hope in her eyes. Mix that young body with that young spirit, and for me it's damn near irresistible.

I've gotten ripped many times for my attitude, yet in Hollywood, where I live, I don't see any guys with old women. My friend Hugh Hefner's got a young woman. My friend Berry Gordy's got a young woman. Clint Eastwood and Crocodile Dundee both have young women. Jerry Buss, owner of the Lakers, has a thousand young women.

It's not that women who are thirty or forty or fifty or sixty aren't part of my life. I interact with women of all ages every day, as an activist and an entrepreneur and an occasional actor and just a guy. I'm fortunate enough to converse with some of the brightest people in the world and of course a lot of them are women. That's the other side of my life, trying to help black people, trying to do some work that has worth, trying to make a living. It stimulates me, and the women I meet in those capacities stimulate me. But that's one facet of my life; for the sex and companionship I still prefer youth.

I've been asked by writers if I considered myself a womanizer. I'm not sure what "womanizer" means. I do know I have a great appreciation for women, think I have some understanding of them. Yeah, I'm a sexual person. If a fine woman offers me her sexual charms, chances are I'll accept. I don't want to be lying on my death bed, doing the big summation, thinking about all those women I *didn't* get to have.

Some people think that makes me all zipper. Truth is, some of my tightest friends are women and they're often women I used to make love with, but now the sex has run out. I happen to be a good listener, which is why I still have old lovers who call me when they're having problems, want a male point of view. A lot of those women call me Daddy, because a lot of them are black, don't have a real daddy. That type of bond is much more powerful than sex.

Though she calls me Jim, I have one of those timeless relationships, at least I hope I do, with

Mary Dee. Mary makes her cash in radio and TV, but her passion is people. For the community work she's done in Chicago, Mary's a local hero. She's also beautiful, bright, in her forties. I can recognize Mary's greatness, and in many ways she'd be ideal for me. And Mary's body looks *good.* Yet it still can't compare to the body of a girl who's twenty years old. If I do look at one body the rest of my life, that body will have to be young.

As promiscuous as I have been, I've always looked for relationships of value. Just to fuck every night with no meaning, with a blank face, gets hollow quickly, and I find I want to do some fucking with meaning. I don't mean I want to marry the girl I fuck, but I want something happening that's spontaneous and alive and makes us both feel somehow special.

I have no desire to get married. I look at the practice of marriage two ways: it's designed by society to keep emphasis on the family, which is good. Marriage is also designed to give the woman the lawful right to take most of your shit when she gets rid of you. If a woman lives with me for a significant period, gives me everything on earth I want from a woman, totally backs me up, even sometimes when I'm wrong, then maybe I'll get married. If she does that, she deserves all my stuff when I die, and I'll marry her to make sure she gets it, and to show my appreciation, if that's what she needs to perceive it. To me, though, the piece of paper means nothing. You're married when you're married in the mind and heart and soul, not by government decree.

People are brainwashed to expect so much out

of marriage. When no one can deliver, they get disillusioned, confused, get a divorce. I've been married once and divorced once. If I ever marry again, or hang with one woman, she'll have to be young and pretty, with an exceptional and curious mind. She'll have to be committed to helping black people. Most likely, she'll have to be black.

I have had relationships, sexual and otherwise, with many women, black and white. I've dated a lot more black girls than white girls. Generally, I am more comfortable with black women. I'm also an activist. If you're going to be my lady, for real, you're going to hear a lot of talk about freedom. Even if a white girl is sensitive and intelligent, she can't truly understand how it feels, what problems are encountered, when you're black and you're living in America. It's not a part of her life experience. If a woman and I are going to connect, on every level, I need that passion. Not every black girl has it: a lot of black folks, male and female, don't want to be black folks, would prefer that they were white. But many more blacks have the passion, and most of the women in my life have been black.

Some constipated white dudes just gave a large sigh of relief. Actually, I have never known too many white guys, plugged up or otherwise, who have been joyous at the sight of a black guy with a white girl. If she's butt ugly it's cool. But black guys know the greatest evil they can perpetrate on a white guy is to have a white girl who is fine. If he can find a white chick who's beautiful and rich, that's Lotto.

Look at Wilt Chamberlain. You think most

white folks in Hollywood get uneasy seeing Wilt because they're still haunted by the fact that he couldn't make a free throw? Wilt is up there in his Bel Air mansion, 360° view, dealing only with young, rich, pretty white girls. Wilt is death to a white guy. When white guys see Wilt with a pretty white girl, they may be smiling and nodding, but you know what they're thinking: Do *Not* Fuck With Any White Chicks. We Will Kick Your Seven-Foot Ass.

I never hungered after a woman in my life because she was white. If a woman is pretty, especially if she's thin with small breasts, I might hunger like a wolf. The best way to get me to date white girls is to tell me not to. Then I'll do it just to make fun of your ass. When I arrived in Syracuse, immediately I was warned about dating white girls. There weren't any white girls I wanted to date, so I didn't. When I was a senior, I started dating a pretty white coed. White folks didn't care for that, made no attempt to mask their disdain. I said, Oh yeah? So one afternoon we hopped in my convertible, big red Pontiac. I put down the top, drove to Archbold Stadium where I had a lacrosse game. All the fans were out on the road. We drove real slow, parked my car. I walked my girl to her seat in the bleachers, gave her a kiss, went down to change. Stands were so quiet you could hear time crawl.

When I played in Cleveland, I rarely dated white girls. The black players lived in black neighborhoods and the neighborhood girls were *cute*. They were right down the block, why go cruising somewhere else? People who make fun of Cleveland spend too much time looking at lakes. Some

189

of the sexiest girls in the world live in Cleveland. Go Cleveland.

When I chased women with the Browns, I chased them with the other black guys. My partners started calling me Hawk. In a crowd, anywhere, Snap, I could pinpoint the superior women. They'd send me out on Hawk missions.

In Cleveland, the black guys rented a house, called it Headquarters. Good times, brother. We used to throw a party for our Main Girlfriends. Those were the chicks we loved or liked a lot, who we'd hang out with when we felt elegant or romantic, the same chicks we'd hide like a motherfucker when we'd have a freak party. For the Main Girlfriend Party, we invited our Main Girlfriends to Headquarters. The men all wore tuxedos, the women long evening gowns. Everyone arrived by limo. We ate fine food. Danced real slow. Had a ball.

We had another party called the Night of a Thousand Fingers. No Main Girlfriends, no way. The party was named for the fact that we all had a thousand fingers, and those fingers were going to touch every warm little girl in the house. We'd all bring two or three girls. You couldn't lock any doors, couldn't hold any chicks back. Those pretty girls from Cleveland were allowed to express themselves freely and creatively.

Once at training camp, I dated a white girl who worked in our lunch line. I was in my early twenties, she was maybe eighteen, fine, and every white guy on the team, and yours truly, was trying to hit on her. I happened to be the one who succeeded. Maybe she dug fullbacks.

We used to sneak away at lunch and go for drives, rendezvous at night, do a lot of dreaming. This girl was not only pretty, she was bold. She didn't give a damn about the other players. They might glare at her, but she had too much spirit to care. We were both young. For us it was all just bright and breezy.

Not so for others. I walked into camp one day, Eddie Ulinski, an assistant coach, asked to speak with me. According to Eddie, my girl's father and uncle were planning an ambush. If they saw me with her again, they were going to shoot me. I told Eddie those were big words. Then I thanked him. My girl said she wasn't worried about her family, we maintained what we had. No one got shot.

I'm not sure attitudes have changed much. A black man who messes with white women, especially if that black man has no economic power, still takes a gamble in this country. O.J. Simpson did it. He left his first wife, Marguerite, who is black, later married the lady he's with now, who is white. As image-oriented as the Juice is, that surprised me. Now in those corporate boardrooms, the Juice isn't quite so All-American. They didn't blackball him, didn't take away his commercials, but you can bet he heard about it, or felt it, on some scale, in one guise or another.

Then again, we're living in a retrograde decade. It was so much different in the late 1960s. That was the height of interracial romance. I saw a lot of mixed couples out here in Southern California where we had that huge influx of flower children, and in the South, among black locals and the young white civil rights workers. It was the fumes from the Revolution. A lot of white kids looked at black folks, saw, or at least perceived, a more natural existence. And once different peoples mix, become exposed to each other, they'll do what comes naturally, and that includes making love.

Of course you'll always have people who go overboard, and some of my black friends stopped going out with black girls altogether. One guy I used to run with was Freddy Williamson. The Hammer was suave and built and handsome, you know he was cocky. I'd go to a club with Freddy, he'd instantly recruit four or five white girls, be surrounded by them at his table. At the time I was dating a woman named Jessie. Jessie was one of the lead singers for the Friends of Distinction, the R&B group I helped discover, then managed. Jessie was black, and one day Freddy started in on me.

He said, "Goddamn, Jim, you always stay with those black girls. Black girls, man, they're too mean. They don't treat you right. They're mean."

I said, "Man, that's not true. You have to move around. There's all *kinds* of black girls. You want some tough black girls, go to South Central L.A. You want them bourgeois, you go to Baldwin Hills and View Park and get some light-skinned, curly-haired black girls. You have to look, Freddy, but there's every kind of black girl you can imagine. There's even some virgins."

Freddy laughed, considered that. He said, "Look, man, I'll tell you what. I know this black girl. I'll take her with us to Vegas and try this out."

We went to Vegas. Freddy had neglected to mention that this black girl he knew was breathtakingly beautiful. We partied. We gambled. Night crept into morning. Next groggy afternoon I saw Freddy. Alone.

I said, "Hey, where's your pretty lady?"

Freddy said, "I sent her home. Too mean."

I thought that was funny as hell. I liked Freddy but his rap was ridiculous.

I would cut out my tongue before I'd say black girls are mean. And while I hung with Freddie and his women down on Sunset, I also hit the great black clubs on Crenshaw Boulevard. I dove right in, became part owner of a club named Maverick Flats. John Daniels, our manager, was a bad motherfucker, knew his music cold. Before they were famous, John booked the Temptations, The Fifth Dimension, and Jessie and her Friends of Distinction. Pretty soon, we had the hottest black chicks in the city. Once the word drifted out about the music, the Hollywood crowd filtered in, led by Mia Farrow. And we were snooty, as snooty as any club on the Strip. If you weren't looking sharp, you could not come in to Maverick Flats.

It was roughly that time, 1968, when I bought my first home, the one I still live in today. It sits high in the Hollywood Hills, several winding miles above Sunset. My house sits on the edge of a peak, the view is spectacular. From my pool deck, when the sun burns through the haze, I can see the skyscrapers downtown, all the way to the beaches of Santa Monica. I love this house. It's my castle and my sanctuary and because so many people like to stop by, cool out, I find myself spending more and more time here.

I've had every type of party there is here. One week I might have three hundred black people up from South Central, which you don't see a lot in these hills. I've had two hundred white kids from Pacific Palisades. My parties for kids are always straight. There may be sexual undercurrents, when teenagers get together there usually are, but no sex.

I'll always remember one particular party, the most meaningful one I believe I ever threw. During the same period of time, I was golfing a lot with some black gang-types, I had promised the Miss Black California pageant I would let the girls come down to my pool and rehearse, and I was friends with a crew of affluent white kids who I'd see at the beach. The same night, I invited all of them over: about twenty black gangsters, forty black beauty contestants, sixty white beach kids. On the surface, I had three groups who didn't want a thing to do with one another. I had my speakers up on my roof, the house was jammed with all these different look-ing people, and on the stereo I blasted "Family Affair," by Sly Stone. Everybody started mixing. Everybody started dancing. It was the funniest looking shit on earth. Young white girls from the beach were dancing with black gangster guys, and white beach boys were dancing with these pretty, poised black girls. There was no sex, no drugs, just the most harmonious, outgoing party I've ever had. End of the night, these people were beaming, saying it was the finest party they'd ever been to. To this day, some of them stop by around Christ-mas, get sentimental about that evening.

I've also hosted many political parties and fundraisers. Malcolm X, Jesse Jackson, Minister Louis Farrakhan, Mayor Tom Bradley and the Hollywood branch of the NAACP have been to parties at my home. Being about power, on one scale or another, those parties were Ultra Straight.

I've also had what most people call orgies. For us it was a way of life. They started in the 1960s, which have now become fashionable to bash. I know there were unfulfilled dreams and harsh disappointments, but I loved the 1960s. America met Rebellion, got its pompous ass woken up. We had the war movement, the women's movement, the civil rights movement, Dylan, and Motown and miniskirts. The culture flipped upside down, got a heady new sense of freedom.

Especially sexual freedom. California led the parade, I was right in there marching. Back then the parties never stopped. We had what we called Creative Orgies. A standard orgy to us meant something outlandish, haphazard, everyone screwing everyone, an ugly, convoluted pile. What we provided was a setting, very controlled and very sensuous. You might make love to three girls in one night, and you might see others making love around you. But it was never vulgar or done with disrespect.

It was our way of life and we had certain rules. Never invite women who were noted swingers. No prostitutes. The main reason we called them Creative Orgies was that we'd look for women who normally would never even consider going to an orgy. That was our particular quirk. We'd find women who were sweet and seemingly innocent. That's when I started learning about appearances: some of these sweet little innocents turned out to be total freaks!

Those girls didn't just walk into the house, have a sexual transformation. Their sexuality had to be caressed to the surface. We would seduce them with mood and atmosphere. Man, we had technique and a half. If we met the girls at night, we would bring them to the house, drive them down my driveway, first sight they'd see was the lights of the city. We'd bypass the front door, walk along the path on the side, through the trees and the flowers, they'd be drinking in the scent, the view, when they'd see the pool. It's cool at night in the hills, the water in the pool would be steaming. The girls would feel the pool, its warmth, ask to get in. Once a girl got her body warm and wet, you didn't have to touch her. In time, she'd swim over and touch you.

Those parties were successful because all the guys worked together. We knew if everyone was cool, no one was rushed, we'd have a nice night. We'd play Serious Guy, Funny Guy. I was always the Serious Guy, the Philosopher, I'd let the other guys get the laughs, and the girls would gravitate according to their preference.

I started to become famous for my parties. Guys would fly in from the East, couldn't get here from LAX fast enough. These Easterners who hadn't spent much time in California would walk in the house, there might be four or five girls, nude, lying out by the pool. The girls might walk into the kitchen, get a glass of wine, some pop, go back out and laze in the sun. None of us would think twice, but the guys from the East got real big eyes and some other stuff. They didn't see that shit in Boston.

Finding women was never a dilemma. I hung out with two of the smoothest operators who ever lived, couple guys named Boom Boom and J.D. As Mac Men—cats who could pick up women cold, just with their rap—they were considered the best in all of Hollywood. They knew the way to a woman's heart and regions below was by making her laugh. Boom Boom and J.D. were so damn funny, so non-threatening, chicks found them irresistible. At times I didn't leave my living room. I'd straighten up the house while Boom Boom and J.D. drove down the hill to Sunset. That's when Sunset was glamorous—The Strip—there were women cruising on the street and in their cars, or having lunch, maybe a drink, at those sunny outdoor cafes. It was all very social, and no one was more social than Boom Boom and J.D. They'd tell women, "Come with us, we're going to see the Master." I'm sure the girls were thinking, What the hell is the Master? But they were also intrigued: in two hours, Boom Boom and J.D. would hook six or seven chicks.

They'd caravan to the house, Boom Boom and J.D. would begin their performance. They'd play some Marvin Gaye, start cracking jokes, tell stories about celebrities they knew. Then Boom Boom, the joker, would strip off all his clothes. He'd run all over the house, dancing some funky dance, anything silly. The girls would start laughing, pretty soon the nudity was no big deal. If it was making someone nervous, she said so, Boom Boom would get dressed. That was the rule.

Another rule was no watching TV. We didn't want Mister fucking Ed killing the mood. The ultimate rule was that you could not single off with a girl, lock the door, and refuse to share. We were always messing up though. When we found a girl we thought was just right, we didn't want to share her with anyone, not for backgammon, let alone sex. I know I was that way. I wanted to shut down the house, send everyone home, say my head hurt, my aunt was due in, goddamn if I hadn't forgotten. I'd meet a girl who was cute and demure, be thinking, *This pretty little thing? Don't do it baby! Don't go for it!* I wasn't alone. Cats would be ducking into crannies in my house, trying to deal with that girl alone. Couldn't do it too often though. Guys would start to look at you funny.

No one was allowed to lock a door. In my house, all three upstairs bedrooms are connected. Men and women would be moving around the house, finding that body or that spirit that intrigued them. Some people got off on watching. There was one kid who was an unusual freak: he only wanted to watch me fuck. He wanted to stare into the woman's eyes while I was making love to her.

The only guy exempt from the rules was Big George. George would bring over his current lady, take her upstairs, and lock the door. I never knew if they were napping or playing around or what. George and his ladies would never join the party.

One day several of us were naked in the pool, Big George came by in his suit, stood over us in the deck, looking like a damn policeman. I noticed the girls stopped splashing, started looking jittery. They'd been fine when no one was dressed, now a man in a suit was standing over them. And *he* was getting nervous.

Big George gave me his trademark greeting: "Hey, Jim, what it is?"

I said, "Hey, man, get in the pool. It's hot. Take off your clothes and have some fun with us."

"What it is?"

By now the girls were squatting in the water, covering their breasts.

I said, "Come *on*, Big George, go change."

"What it is?"

"Man, get your what-it-is ass out of here, before you fuck up the party."

Big George cracked up, the girls eased up, the party resumed, though he never did get in. He's a hell of a man, solid proof that everyone you revere doesn't have to be the way you are. We don't party the same way, accept that, love each other regardless. I just don't want him locking too many doors, messing up my lifestyle.

I was never one of those hosts whose parties abruptly ceased when the host ran out of steam. If by two in the morning, I'd had everything I wanted, was tired, I'd lock the door in my bedroom, go to sleep, let the others carry the torch. Some mornings I'd inch out of my bedroom, the living room would be strewn with bras and panties, their owners still on the premises. Once, after a party that had started at noon down on Sunset, migrated to my house, ran well into the night, I was startled from my sleep at five a.m. The big tree outside my bedroom window was moving. In the darkness, me just out of a dream, it was spooky. I collected my faculties, peered outside. It was the girls from the party, wrapped around the tree, naked. They'd been partying for seventeen hours.

My lifestyle was unorthodox, the scope of my friends wildly diverse. It led to some unique situations.

I had one friend named Jimmy Toback. Toback lived in New York, wrote books and screenplays. He wrote *The Gambler* with James Caan. I believe his last produced film was *The Pickup Artist,* with Robert Downey Jr. and Molly Ringwald. Toback was a multitalented, erudite madman. He was a rich kid from Harvard who would go down to Harlem with his cane, in his cane he'd keep a sword, in case someone messed with him. I have no doubt where Toback got the inspiration for *The Pickup Artist:* He was an *extremely* persuasive lover. Toback would talk to any woman who was fine, seduce her, convince her to screw him in daring, public places. I kid you not, Toback once had sex in the Harvard library.

Toback used to spend a lot of time at my house when he was working in Hollywood, once brought over an actress who was due to be in one of his films. They started, full throttle, having sex on the couch. In the wild days that was everyday stuff for my partners and I, especially when Toback was in town, and there was only mild amusement.

In walks Bill Russell.

Russ and I were friends, not nearly as close as we are now. But I knew Russ was worldly, figured he was like the rest of us, had been to all kinds of parties, seen all types of sex. When Russ walked in the rest of us were playing it cool, I figured Russ would. Wrong. When Russ saw Toback, the actress, fucking on the couch, his eyes got BIG. He didn't say anything, though, and then he left. I received a call from Bill that next morning.

He said, "Hey, Jim, it's Bill . . . I've never seen *anything* like that!"

Sexually, it turned out Bill was relatively strait-laced. And that day was the birth of his sexual re-education. He was single at the time, he'd come over, I'd tell him about parties in the pool, having two or three girls in my bedroom all to myself. Bill was shocked and fascinated. A short time later he called me again. He was hemming and hawing, unlike him, about something he'd done.

I said, "Bill, what's up?"

"Jim," he said, "I did it. I had two girls with me. I like it!"

What's not to like? If I'm in my castle and I'm surrounded by a few pretty girls, I'm what you might call A Happy Motherfucker. And I'm comfortable enough with my sexuality that I don't have to do a lot of fucking. I simply enjoy having women in my presence. I like to watch them walk, the way they smile when they laugh. Even when I used to meet unfamiliar girls in clubs, we'd do the one-night thing, they knew they could always come back the next day to sit in the sun or just talk. My house was always open.

It was also open to my male friends, and one day I was paid a visit by Kareem Abdul-Jabbar. I'd known Kareem for many years but we hadn't hooked up for quite a while. It was nice to get reacquainted, I could tell Kareem was glad to see me. He was gladder when he spotted my two houseguests. Two lovely girls were staying over.

They were natural creatures, didn't care much about clothes, would glide around the house naked, check out the icebox, put on some lotion . . . and here's Kareem.

In those days Kareem was often usually serious, almost dour. It seemed he was searching so hard, spiritually and intellectually, he forgot how to be loose. But as those girls kept moving around the house, Kareem became flat-out chatty. He was buying time, I knew it, and I thought it was cute: the great and imperial Kareem had finally turned into one of us. He got after those two girls, and they got after him.

When Kareem left that night I told him to come back any time. Next morning, ding dong, standing on my step was my man, Kareem. He wasn't there to shoot hoops.

I like a ménage à trois myself. Only one kind though: me and two ladies. I want nothing to do with two men having one chick. I don't do that. If it's two women making love to one another and to me, I find that very sensuous. It's difficult for a lot of guys to accomplish unless they get two prostitutes, who will do anything if the price tag is right. I never dealt with prostitutes, yet was considered a master at ménage à trois. I knew many women could and would make love to another woman without having any homosexual tendencies, and not only enjoy the act, but feel no remorse when it was over. Sexually, emotionally, women have a much finer sensitivity than men. In a ménage à trois with two sensitive women, they would take care of each other, make sure neither of their feelings got injured, and no one got left out. For me, there was nothing I could possibly find sexier than watching two pretty women discovering each other, then looking up, wanting me.

Just between you, me, and the tabloids, I've had up to eight girls in my room, maybe four on my couch and four on my bed. I might have sex in one night with four or five of them. But only if Jim Junior was feeling exceptional.

Some people think that makes me a pervert. I think it makes me lucky. Having more than one woman is a fantasy for a lot of guys. Ever read *Penthouse*? Ever see a guy in bed with two men? And you don't want to.

If you're gay that's your business. If you're a man who likes women, what's unnatural about wanting more than one? This is how I figure it: The more women in my bedroom the better. If one girl is wonderful, two girls is wonderful, three or four gotta be wonderful. Who's kidding who?

There are times when I have no interest in sex. I have a non-physical life that has nothing to do with sex. But I'm also a product of nature: there are moments, I'm seized by an urge, I just want to fuck. I think it's innate, I think it's true of all God's creatures. At times I desire two girls, or three girls, or one girl—as long as it's new pussy. Sometimes I get the urge when I'm in a "relationship." I may love my woman, but I see another girl, I feel that heat. To avoid being a cheat, if I begin to have something emotionally substantial with a woman, I will tell her upfront what kind of man I am. I'll say, "I care about you. You're my baby. But there are times when I'm like a freak. It's a physical need that I have. I won't lie to you or run around behind your back. This is who I am. Can you accept that?"

Most women can't, another reason I don't have many long relationships. Most women, I've found, can't separate love from sex, feel it's one and the same. I don't feel that way. Sex is part of love, can enhance love, but it is also separate. If love and sex are the same, how do you account for masturbation? When a man or woman masturbates, what are they getting? They're getting a thrill. They're not falling in love with their hand. They're not taking their hand to any damn movie.

I *know* my lifestyle isn't for everyone. That's why I get so tired of people telling others what is and isn't moral. I am a philosophical person. I became interested in philosophy while at Syracuse, when I took a course in Logic with a strong professor. I received an A, my buddy, Vinnie Cohen— Mr. A—only got a B, and has never forgotten it, because I won't let him. Ever since I took that course I've suspected *all* dogma. My philosophy on sex is that God equipped man and animals with sex organs to ensure reproduction, and the future of a species. After reproduction, who's gonna tell me what sex is for? Some punk who's cheating on his wife?

I'm not saying that I am not sexually hypocritical—I am—just don't tell me if you're a man, that you aren't. Most guys I know are so hypocritical about sex, it's scary. Their double standard is stiffer than any hard-on. I'm a double standard man myself. I want to be truly liberated. It's logical. It's fair. And I'm not. I want to freak when I want to, but I don't want my woman to. I want her to be something I'm not willing to be. Even when I was at one of our crazy parties, sometimes I'd stop, get depressed. I'd think about my main girlfriend, how she might react to a party like this. Would the mood make her do things? I'd get so insecure I'd lose my desire to party.

I think most men, particularly those who've had sex lives like mine, are insecure about their women, are hypocritical. Liberated Male looks good on paper, but I don't think it exists. Still, we lie about it. "No man, I'm cool. I'm modern. My woman can do whatever I do." Bullshit! The double standard is a weakness in almost all men. It's definitely a weakness in me.

At times, my reputation as a prolific lover has also been a negative. It caused other men to act strangely in my presence. Even my own friends found themselves trying to compete with me. At pleasing women, they thought I was Superman. I was never Superman. I had the same doubts about performing up to expectations that they did. Yet I was hyped as this macho man. "Jim Brown? His dick never lets him down."

That was bullshit, too. Every dick, including mine, has a mind of its own. I never felt like I could fuck any woman, any time. My sexuality hinged on the woman and the situation. If the atmosphere was erotic, if the girl pushed my particular buttons, then maybe I would screw all night. Other times, even if the girl was pretty, but the mood was incorrect, my mind wasn't quite there, I might look down, Jim Junior might be asleep. Or maybe just groggy. Then, if I fucked at all, I'd do the best I could, know there's always morning. Any man who says his dick gets hard any time he wills it to, is a liar. Any man who says he's never insecure about sex might be terrified.

I still don't know why all these guys would want to try and out-fuck me. Intelligent guys, too, like Jimmy Toback. Toback wrote an entire book devoted to our comparative sexuality. He called it "Jim."

I never competed with my friends for women. When I used to partner with Freddy Williamson, we'd spend a lot of time with Timmy Brown, who used to play for the Philadelphia Eagles. Timmy was amazingly handsome, could get any woman in town, used to date Diana Ross. When Timmy, Freddy, and I rolled into a club, we made a serious impact. We all had good-looking bodies, wore our clothes tight. We'd wear that double-knit shit. Clinging. No underwear. Muscles bulging. Attitude. But in any club, Freddy and Timmy always owned the first five minutes. They were the First Line Lovers, got the 10s, everyone else fell in behind them. I was a 10-man, too, but I'd wait for Timmy and Freddy, only then would I take my shot. Jim Brown, Team Player.

It was cool with me. I knew in the end I'd have the girl I wanted anyway. I never deluded myself, knew as an athlete, a celebrity, I had a tremendous advantage over the average guy. If I didn't run over people for a living, didn't make love to Raquel Welch on a film screen, my love life would have been a hell of a lot different. Women revere celebrities just as much as men do. I've often said, as a black man, I get two strikes in life to a white guy's three. Well, athletes dealing with chicks get five strikes.

I can't speak for track men or golfers, but women love those football players. Guys who play football have that manly, physical image—the glad-iator—and women go crazy for it. Talk all you want about brain power, but the intellectual gets the secondary women. It's the physical giant who gets the premium women. You see a guy in the NFL, even a big ugly-ass lineman, with his woman at a party, it doesn't fit. The dude is 300 pounds, 45-inch neck, he's with the head majorette from USC. But he bumps into people for a living, so she's fascinated. He leaves the NFL, her ass is gone. I've seen it a hundred times, and it goes for all sports. Mike Tyson can get a beautiful chick and a beauti-ful chick can get Mike Tyson. It's a good exchange. It works. As long as Big Mike can knock a man out in two minutes. If Big Mike couldn't knock anyone out, he'd be up here on the hill with me, struggling.

I've got a unique perspective on women and celebrities: I've been a pro athlete, an actor, and I've spent a lot of time with musicians. Athletes definitely have it over actors. A lot of actors, with-out their makeup, aren't much to look at. And women know what an athlete does is real, he doesn't have any retakes to get what he does right. He has to deliver, now. To women, that translates to sexual prowess. It isn't necessarily true, but women seem to believe it.

So the Hollywood star is third. Athletes are second. It's musicians who get the finest women. I've been on the road with bands, and I know. For a woman to see a musician perform, especially if that musician appears to be virile, then be with him that night, is like BOOM. Night after night, Melvin Franklin of the Temptations had some of the sexiest women I've ever witnessed. And Melvin only sang bass.

A lot of times I don't tell women what I've done, just my name, what I'm doing now. Those are some of the best nights I've ever had. When women do know who I am, that's precisely why they're coming on to me, I don't mind. Pretty girl can show up for any reason she wants, I'm just glad she's showing up, and looking tight. I don't want her showing up 300 pounds and a great personality. Now, if my fame and my money is *all* she wants, I can detect that in no time, and we can just be physical. If she's going to stay with me, she has to like me.

I've been with famous guys at bars, they meet a woman, they start whining, "Man, I wonder if she likes me for my money." Save it. What difference does it make? You're looking for something superficial—why shouldn't they? I'm not saying you can't find real love in a bar, but not in one goddamn night. These guys just want you to tell them, "No, man, she digs you for you." I'll go the other way, tell them "Yeah, she probably does want you for your money. So what?"

A lot of famous guys think there's no middle ground: women are either out for money and glamour, or a real relationship. Nah. Back when I was doing a lot of clubbing, I never believed in one-night stands. Made it a policy, if I liked the woman, to let her know she was always welcome back. But I *wound up* in a lot of one-night stands. It was the nature of the women. A lot of them were just like guys, all they were after was some fun.

If a girl initially likes me for my fame, I like her for the way she looks in high heels, it's all the same game. And that's what it is, The Game, and both sexes play it. On Monday nights, we go down to a place on Sunset called Carlos' And Charlie's. Monday is Star Night. The club cages off a separate section for celebrities. Prince might be there, Eddie Murphy, Mike Tyson—the big boys. We're all back in this celebrity section—boxers, comedians, rock men, football players—and the chicks are damn near panting to get in there. And they run right to Eddie first. He's the biggest right now, making so many millions per film. After Eddie comes Prince. Musical genius. Me? I'm old. I get the women who are looking for something different.

I also attract a lot of curiosity sex. I've got this public image, which I'll talk about. People think I'm the guy who roughs up women, threw one girl off a balcony. I'll meet a guy and his chick, later she'll ask him what I'm like, that cat will run my ass into the ground, tell her every negative thing he's heard, though he's got no idea if they're true. And it's a mistake. Women hear one guy dog another, they're fascinated. "If my man says don't go out with Jim Brown, Jim Brown must have something different. I'm gonna find out what that is." I know for a fact that's true. I get a lot of girls, and they come to me, just that way.

My reputation has also driven away many women. By now the pattern is familiar: if the woman likes me, doesn't know who I am, we usually have a great night. I call her the following day, I hear this new tone in her voice. She's uptight. Distant. Or confused: she wants to trust her own instincts, but she's afraid to, afraid of me. She's gotten the word on me from someone. And she'll tell me she can't see me. When that happens with a girl I have high hopes for, it hurts. I try and remind myself: if a woman is not going to see me because someone tells her not to, chances are good we'd never have lasted anyway. My main women have always been independent thinkers.

If I'm feeling wistful, or playful, at times I can't help musing what might have been. *What if my reputation had been good?*

Million chicks a day. Minimum.

12
MISADVENTURES IN HOLLYWOOD

I BROKE INTO HOLLYWOOD the old-fashioned way: I knew somebody.

I was in Los Angeles for the 1964 Pro Bowl when a guy from 20th Century Fox asked me if I cared to try out for a movie. I told him I'd never acted, he said don't worry, they would give me a screen test. I went to Fox, read for the part, they gave me the part. The film was *Rio Conchos*, with Tony Franciosa, Stuart Whitman and Richard Boone. It was a post civil war western, I played an officer turned cowboy. Gordon Douglas, the director, relaxed me on the set, taught me tricks about the camera. I was very lucky when I got into movies. I met all the good people like Douglas, did not meet any of the trash.

After the film, Gordon told me I had some talent, should probably get an agent. He introduced me to Phil Gersh, who helped me land my second role in *The Dirty Dozen*. It was directed by Bob Aldrich, adapted from a huge bestselling book. And I loved my part. I was one of the Dozen, a quiet leader and my own man, at a time when Hollywood wasn't giving those roles to blacks. *The Dirty Dozen* was an American classic, the most popular film I've ever done, and I've never had more fun making a movie. The male cast was incredible. I worked with some of the strongest, craziest guys in the business.

And London was popping, every day, all night. London, before New York or California, dove into the Revolution. The Beatles and Rolling Stones were running all over the city, and Muhammad Ali was coming up, working out in the park, chasing girls by night. Everywhere you looked you saw miniskirts. English girls—in London they called girls "birds"—started wearing very short skirts, all the way up to their butts.

The film set was a blast. It was only my second movie, I had a major role in what we all knew would be a hit, I was acting with Hollywood heavyweights, yet I didn't feel a shred of resentment. Those guys were so sure of who *they* were, I think they got off on that fact that I had paid no dues. Those guys were hellraisers. After we'd shoot they'd be out on the streets of London, alone, looking for action.

I flew over to London with Charles Bronson. He was the strangest mofo I had ever met. I sat right next to him, man did not say one word to me. He stared straight ahead, appeared to be brooding. I spoke to him once, but I knew not to say too much. After that, I was surprised at how much help he gave me on the set. I like men I can't intimidate, and I liked Bronson. He was tough and forward, if you were weak you'd be scared of him. He used to be a coal miner, never pretended he hadn't. Bronson was in tremendous physical condition. He would walk to a car, stop, jump right over it. The London women were after his ass. He wasn't a face man, but they liked his body and they liked his walk —Bronson had a great walk, tight and contained. Watching Bronson, you could tell he thought he could fight. I don't know if Bronson could fight or not, but you didn't want to fuck with him. The mental thing he carried around was no joke.

I've never seen a more straight-talking guy. I took a girl to a party one night, Bronson and I were on one side of the room, she was sitting in a chair about ten feet away. She didn't know it, but her legs were open, and she was in a dress. Bronson walked over to her.

He said, "Look, close up your crotch. There's a guy over there who's staring up your crotch."

That was Bronson.

Lee Marvin was brilliant and witty and cerebral. He would speak in riddles, crack up the crew. Lee was a nice man, powerful actor, but he was hitting the bottle pretty hard that summer. He'd show up on the set, some days, still high, be weaving and slurring, saying, "All right, you Dirty Dozen, line up." An understanding man, Aldrich would tell Lee's friend, Robert Phillips, or Lee's woman, Michelle, to take Lee home. Michelle sued him for palimony years later, and I think she was

213

totally correct. Michelle had to drag Lee home every night, out of the pubs, care for him like a baby.

One day Lee asked me if I ever took acting lessons. I said, "No, but I've got the best acting teachers in the world. I've got you guys." And I did. Marvin helped me, Ernest Borgnine helped me, Bronson helped me, George Kennedy helped me. It doesn't get much better than that. And I had John Cassavetes. In his heart, John *was* a teacher. When John died last summer I was heartsick. What a bold little man. Each day on the set, it was Cassavetes who set the emotional tone. He was a Method actor; whatever mood his scenes called for, he would remain in that mood all day. If it was John's day to be a lunatic, he'd show up crazy, make the rest of us crazy. If he was withdrawn, we'd pull inside with him. John was our spiritual leader. I guess he was for a lot of people who knew him.

Telly Savalas was a gambler, he'd bet a pair of shoes on when a light might change. Suave and well-read, not handsome, Telly talked that good shit, loved the girls and they loved him. Telly felt he was the star of the movie. When his character Maggot got killed, Telly told me, "Well, Maggot got killed. This movie is over. No one's gonna want to see the rest of it." And Telly did nail that psychopathic part.

Donald Sutherland was just getting started. Aldrich was such a skilled director, he recognized Donald's acting ability, his quick wit, encouraged him to improvise. Donald's improvs added so much humor to the film, Aldrich repeatedly increased his part. I always considered Donald one of the finest actors I knew, but he was a distant man, difficult to know, and I don't think he's ever been truly happy. I always figured Donald was susceptible to strong women. One of his wives was a revolutionary, I think she was involved in gunrunning. Later on Donald hooked up with Jane Fonda when Fonda was at the peak of her activism. Donald was a pawn in Fonda's hands.

Sutherland was the hottest rookie on the *Dirty Dozen* set. The Flavor of the Month was Trini Lopez. Trini had just released the giant hit "Lemon Tree." After we would film, Trini would be surrounded by teenage English girls. In the movie, Trini played the part of Jiminez, the little Mexican guy whose comrades berated him at the start, but was later to emerge as a hero, diving on a grenade, saving the lives of his fellow Dozen.

Trini's success was making his head fat—he wanted a larger part. One song about a tree, Trini thought he was bigger than Ernest Borgnine, Lee Marvin, people like that. Trini called his friend, Frank Sinatra, for instruction. Sinatra told Trini to *demand* a larger part. If he didn't get it, Sinatra advised, just leave. Trini went back to Aldrich, threatened to walk out if his part wasn't pumped up. He said Sinatra was right behind him; Sinatra, in fact, said Trini *deserved* a bigger part. What Trini didn't comprehend was the nature of Bob Aldrich. Bob was one of the few directors in Hollywood with the mind and the balls to handle a gang like ours.

The next day we showed up for work, we were handed some new pages of dialogue. We had just parachuted into enemy woods, now we were huddling up.

Lee Marvin said, "Where's Jiminez?"

Charlie Bronson said, "His chute didn't open. He fell in a tree."

I said, "He broke his neck."

That was the end of Trini. No big heroic scene, no nothing. Aldrich wrote his ass out of the script.

Two years after *The Dirty Dozen* I moved to Hollywood, bought my home up in the hills. And the party continued. The Candy Store, on Rodeo Drive, was THE Hollywood club. It was a small club, private, run by a man named Gene Shakov, and some other investors. Gene Shakov was THE Hollywood hairdresser. In the film *Shampoo*, a lot of people thought Warren Beatty was playing a less intelligent version of himself. Nope. Warren was playing Gene Shakov.

When you're making movies, starring, Hollywood opens wide for you. I became a certified regular at The Candy Store. I'd head over with Freddy Williamson and Timmy Brown; Sinatra, Dean Martin, Clint Eastwood, Tony Curtis would all have their parts of the club staked out. Sinatra would always take a table in the back with his man Jilly. I would hang by the steps. Each group had its territory, everyone else respected that. We mingled, but mostly we'd be dealing with the high octane ladies. Aptly named, The Candy Store was quite a hunting ground.

By starring in *The Split*, I had graduated to leading man status. Hollywood had me pegged as some new sex symbol. In many of my films I started doing love scenes. If I found my leading lady unattractive, physically or spiritually, love scenes for me were uncomfortable. If she was pretty, had some heart, I welcomed love scenes. Actors talk about being professional. They say you can kiss a person, hold a person, not feel a thing. Man, if that person you're kissing and holding is fine, love scenes are dangerous. God did not make the human body so you could talk to it, tell it exactly how to act. It will do some shit on its own.

I've been asked how far love scenes go. Some go nearly all the way. But some love scenes are overly orchestrated, they look it, watching ESPN is more exotic. Sometimes in a love scene, you're on your own. The director throws a man and a woman together, tells them to deal. That's what they said to me and Stella Stevens in the movie *Slaughter*.

Stella was blonde and buxom, with full, pouty lips. For our love scene they cleared the room, except for the essential individuals: director, script guy, camera operator, a few necessary crew members. The camera started rolling around the bed, director said, "I'll leave it up to you two." It was the sexiest, hottest, most realistic love scene I've ever done. Stella Stevens was unbelievable. Had they not said Cut, we might have done it.

I later did a movie called *Black Gun*. I knew they were casting for an actress to play my lover. I persuaded them to hire Brenda Sykes. Brenda had dark skin, a small waist, luminous big brown eyes. She was gentle, spoke almost in a whisper, never moved quickly. For five years I tried to make her mine, for five years Brenda ignored my advances.

At my urging they hired Brenda. When it was time to film our love scene, it called for us both to be naked. I was protective of her, tried to calm her nerves, and Brenda began to see that I cared about her. We removed our clothes, slid into bed, did our scene. By the time we got out of the bed Brenda was my woman. Though we didn't make love, all the fires were burning. But I didn't kid myself for a second: I *used* the movie industry to catch Brenda. Otherwise she never would have been with me.

Normally, I don't care to have an actress for a girlfriend. Either I'm too insecure and too stupid, or I'm too intelligent, I'll let you decide. The fact is, people who make films together wind up having sexual flings. Sidney Poitier once did a movie with an actress named Joanna Shimkus, who was engaged to the film's cinematographer. When the movie wrapped Joanna was still engaged—to Sidney Poitier. Before that, I had done a film with Diahann Carroll. Though I didn't learn it until later, Diahann was still in love with . . . Sidney Poitier. They had been intense lovers, could not make it work, and Diahann was still scarred by that relationship when she did her film with me. But Diahann became romantic with me, because that's what happens on film sets.

Sometimes an actress isn't left with many options. If she's beautiful, and often she is, the arrival of a leading lady on a film set is a major event. There's a goddamn line waiting for her to see who can go to bed with her first, and in that line is the producer or producers, the director, cinematographer, male star or stars, all the way down to the gaffers and publicists. She may not want to fuck anyone, but she does have to work with these people, so it makes no sense to be *too* anti-social. So she compromises, decides she'll be cordial but not sexual. She agrees to have dinner with someone, the cat wants to go to bed with her, she finds a diplomatic way to get rid of him. Now she has to fend off the next guy. And the next and the next. For eight weeks, she's rebuffing guys, and trying to do her job. And a woman can only be so strong. And that's why I don't want my girlfriends to be in the movies.

I used to get a huge kick out of the women who had been around, knew how to work the industry ropes. Before Stella Stevens arrived on our set, guys were ringing their hands. It was, "Stella's coming. Oh boy!" Stella breezed in, said hello to everyone, was perfectly congenial—Boom—went right to her apartment. No one saw her once off the set. She'd do a scene, deal with whom she had to, be nice, and be gone. Stella was too savvy for them.

I once did a film called *Dark of the Sun*. It was shot in Jamaica, Yvette Mimieux was cast as the female lead. Yvette was lovely, not to mention French, and Jamaica was Jamaica: guys were getting carried away with their fantasies. Yvette arrived. She was as gorgeous as she appeared on the screen, she was wonderful to everyone, and she got the hell out of there. After our first day of shooting, Yvette went off on a yacht, alone. She did that for several days, then announced that her boyfriend was coming to the set. Everyone started grumbling. I heard one guy say, "Shit, how much you wanna bet he's some old man, some sugar daddy. Or a fat fucking producer." I was laughing. In the short time I saw her, Yvette and I became decent friends.

That weekend Yvette's boyfriend arrived. He was roughly 6'6", solidly built, with dark hair and blue eyes. The guy was a lion tamer. Yvette Mimieux is bad.

I also performed a love scene with Raquel Welch. Everybody wanted me to say I slept with Raquel. When I wouldn't, they said it themselves.

The film was *One Hundred Rifles*. Later Raquel would have some trouble on another film set, Hollywood would basically blackball her. She didn't receive any film work for many years. At the time we did *One Hundred Rifles,* Raquel had some power. She was sexy, exotic, her husband Patrick was a canny promoter, and her face adorned the cover of numerous magazines. But the film was made because of me. There was no financing until I agreed to do it. I was the lead star, Raquel was second, Burt Reynolds was third.

Today people don't know that I was the top star in films with some famous people. Though Gene Hackman and Donald Sutherland and Ernie Borgnine and Jack Klugman were all in *The Split,* I played their boss, in an attempt to rob the Coliseum. I recruited my men, I strategized—I was the leader. And although my role had nothing to do with being black—although most of my roles were not defined by race—today people think I made black exploitation films. Not only did I not make black exploitation films, I was playing roles that normally went only to white guys. But that's how people are. They talk but they don't do their homework.

Anyway, some producers had an idea. They would match Raquel Welch and Jim Brown as lovers. It would be the first time in history that a black man would make love to a white woman on an American film screen. We took a publicity shot of me, with no shirt on, and Raquel, behind me, her arms seductively across my chest. For American film it was revolutionary stuff.

And I knew it. I was paired with Raquel Welch, one of the top few sex symbols in the world, the movie industry was stepping out, breaking ground, and America was watching. I thought, *Brother, you better be careful. You are the first big black shiny sucker kissing this pretty white angel. The one thing you will not do is make a pass at this woman.*

Raquel's husband Patrick was a good guy, but even if Raquel was single I would not have made a pass. Politically it would have been suicide. I knew the film was big news, and the one thing I didn't want America to say was that I was the black guy who got with this beautiful white girl, made a movie with her, and hit on her. I wanted to break down stereotypes, not give white folks fuel to foment them. I wanted to make the film, make it right, let it be history.

That was my posture when we arrived in Spain. Raquel brought her little daughter, Tahnee, her son, and Patrick was in and out. Raquel was nice, I liked her, everything was cool. I was not particularly attracted to her. I liked my woman slim, with small breasts. Raquel was a small woman, yet she *looked* big. She had ample hips, large breasts, those big teeth. She was not my physical type. At night, she and I would dance a few dances, and that was that. Then trouble arrived. Patrick had been promoting Raquel's career, had arranged for a celebrated English photographer to take all of Raquel's photographs, including those for the promotion of the film. When the studio sent another photographer to our location, Raquel was adamant: she did not want this man allowed on the set. She tried to enlist my support.

"I don't want him, Jim," Raquel said. "You and I won't let him on the set."

I said, "Raquel, you know this guy has come all these miles, and the company wants him. I don't see any harm in him being on the set."

"No," she said. "He's not coming on the set."

I said, "Well I'm not going to stop him."

"Well, I'll stop him."

"I don't think you can."

And she couldn't. I refused to back her up, the guy came on the set, Raquel and I stopped speaking. That was our big feud. Everyone thought it was over romance, that I had hit on Raquel, she had refused, and stories started filtering off the set. And it was all over one photographer.

A few weeks later we were returning from the desert set in a land rover. Raquel and I hadn't spoken in days, it was getting kind of dull. I decided to mess with her. I turned toward Raquel, stared at her.

She said, "What are you looking at?"

"Looking at you."

"*What* are you looking at?"

"Looking at you."

"Shit! Stop this land rover!"

Raquel jumped out, stormed all over the desert. We were just playing star games, acting like fools, but no one knew *why* Raquel had jumped out, so now *everyone* thought I had made a pass at her. The rumor mill started cranking overtime.

It gets better. There was a Spanish guy, with a bit part, who began hitting on Raquel. I'm watching all this, amazed. I'm supposed to be hitting on Raquel, here's this Spanish guy, who doesn't give a damn about politics, or Patrick, or anything else, he wants what he wants, what a lot of men wanted, and that was Raquel Welch. Then Patrick came back in town. He heard about the Spanish guy, purchased a bottle of booze, went to the Spanish guy's room, tried to whack him over the head with it. The Spanish police took in Patrick and Raquel and the guy . . . and they hushed it up! Here is legitimate, sexy, perfect fodder for the press, and it never even gets out. And back in America, they have all these stories about me.

When it was finally time for our sex scene, the director told me to act as if I was sex-starved. He wanted me to snap mid-scene, rip off Raquel's shirt. In Hollywood they babble a lot about Motivation, I figured this director had one of two: he wanted some bosom on the screen, particularly as it was Raquel's bosom, or he just wanted to piss off some white folks.

We began the scene and I started slowly, with sensitivity, suddenly started pawing at Raquel's clothes. Her bosoms were exposed, I was kissing her and holding her and . . . she became incredibly sexy to me. She wasn't lying on the bed, being submissive. She was wild, defiant, she kissed me with her lips, her teeth, it became a sexual contest of who would conquer who in that bed.

Cut.

During that first take I had noticed that Raquel preferred to have her face to the camera, as most stars do. I didn't care, knew her face was prettier than mine. So when we returned from the break, resumed filming, I put my face on the side of Raquel's, gave her access to the camera. While I was over on the side I kissed Raquel's ear, and her body jumped. Hmmmmm. I stuck my tongue in softly. Raquel started heating up, so did the scene. She was sensitive in the ear.

We took another break, Raquel strode over to me.

She said, "Jim, if you don't mind, please don't stick your tongue in my ear."

"Why?"

"It'll mess up my makeup."

I burst out laughing. It was bullshit, both of us knew it. But I did stay away from Raquel's ear, even when we dated, though that's another story.

I also had the pleasure of working with Jackie Bisset, a lovely human being, in the film *The Grasshopper*. The script called for Jackie and me to make love, and on the set there was a definite and mutual attraction. Jackie nipped it short.

Jackie said, "Jim, you know I could be attracted to you, you know that. But I have a man that I love. So please don't put any pressure on me."

I didn't. And my appreciation grew for her, though I'd liked her the moment I'd met her. I'm not a one-woman man, but that's my way. Jackie had a code of her own, I admired her for sticking to it. Years after we completed the film, Jackie would do interviews and they'd ask her from time to time about her leading men. By then she'd worked with

Sinatra, other major stars, and she would mention me, respectfully, along with those guys. Her questioners would be astonished: "What do you mean Jim Brown? You just said *Sinatra*."

Certain guys in this town are so into being Macho, they've become cartoon characters.

Robert Conrad, battery shoulder dude. Tom Jones, bulging crotch. Sylvester Stallone, king of the flex. I look at guys like that, their affectations, what I see is weakness. I see self-doubting. A guy who is tough, for real, doesn't need to wear a neon sign.

Frankly, I find a lot of male stars to be confused human beings. Some guys start to believe they're actually the roles they portray. Stallone is a prime example. Stallone kills three hundred guys in ninety minutes, he thinks he's Rambo, Rocky—multiplied by five for each sequel—rolled into one. He doesn't know who he is. I'd be willing to bet he's the most insecure guy in the world.

Stallone is not the first movie star to be blinded by his image. When Nixon was President, occasionally I'd go see him when he was in San Clemente. Nixon loved football, liked me, I tried to utilize our friendship to push through a program that would benefit black folks. While I was down on the beach with Nixon and his boys, I'd often see John Wayne. Man, John Wayne came off like he could whip anybody's ass. He did it on the screen, pretended he could do it in real life. There were 2 million guys who could kick John Wayne's ass every day of the week. Deep inside, John probably knew it, too. So he played to the image.

I can understand, though, how some actors get confused when they hit it big. Star actors aren't like star athletes, who are pampered from high school on. Actors are humiliated at the beginning of their careers. Stallone once did a pornographic movie. How could he not be strange? Guy goes from porno to international stardom, people who were kicking his butt now can't kiss it hard enough, it has to spin his head.

I guess it all depends on the individual. One guy I liked a lot was Arnold Schwarzenegger, who I worked with on *The Running Man*. Arnold is smart, much more so than people may realize, takes his work seriously but not himself. Arnold didn't play any macho BS, didn't seem hung up about his muscles. Good guy to spend time with.

I can't say the same for Tom Jones. People said Tom used to stuff his pants. I don't know, don't want to know, do know he's a ridiculous person. One night as I was walking into The Candy Store, Tom was walking out with Marjorie Wallace. Marjorie was once Miss Universe, I knew her when she was merely Miss Indiana. I met Marjorie in Chicago at the Playboy Club, we hit it off, she came west to spend a few days at my home. When we stopped being lovers we continued being friends. By the time I saw her and Tom our affair was long over. Marjorie said hello, we embraced, that was it.

A few nights later at a party I saw Tom Jones. He walked up, did not say hello, began to ask me about Marjorie. Tom said, How do you know Marjorie, blah, blah, blah.

"She's a nice girl," I said. "I used to take her out once in a while, that's about all."

That wasn't good enough for Tom. Tom wanted to know, Did I fuck her?

I said, "Man, what kinda guy are you? I'm not going to tell you about my sexual relationship with Marjorie. I don't go with her now, she's with you, go have a wonderful time. Whatever we had, whatever that was, it's over."

That wasn't enough for him. Tom Jones spent half the evening following me around, asking me in slightly different forms, if I slept with the woman he was seeing. I wasn't even angry. I just thought, Man, this guy must be WEAK.

Enough about Tom. What I find more interesting is the mutual fascination between entertainers and athletes. I've known a lot of actors, lot of athletes, and I think many would've traded professions in a minute if they thought they could've pulled it off.

Movies are pure illusion. The actual making of movies, because you're filming a series of contrivances, and contrivances take a long time to set up, can be painfully dull. Acting entails a lot of standing around, or sitting in trailers, punctuated by brief fits of work. It's mostly a passive process.

Sports are fast and real, no retakes, no special effects, no editors to disguise a careless performance. An 180-pound cornerback taking on Herschel Walker has to be a bad motherfucker. He can't fake anything. So an athlete knows he has the manhood. Now he wants the Fantasy Thing. He wants to shoot one bullet, kill eleven hoods. Fall off the Sears Tower, bruise a kneecap. Make *my* day.

The actor has done that, but unlike the tiny cornerback who has the courage to tackle Herschel, an actor can't do a scene, get up woofing. He can't say, "Well, Ray, I really kicked your ass in that scene." Ray, stunt man, might say, "Yeah, but that was celluloid. Kick my ass *now,* pal." So an actor wants to do the Real Thing, the Physical Thing, and it isn't only actors. Nat King Cole wanted to play baseball. Marvin Gaye wanted a tryout with the Detroit Lions. I know why. The athlete, in the minds of American males, is the epitome of manhood. And bottom line, man is a physical being.

That's why we have wars. We *could* talk things out. But the underlying philosophy of man is not Help Thy Neighbor. It's I Will Kick Your Ass. And that's why we've got all these world leaders—usually they're little guys—who can't kick anyone's ass with their fists, so they kick ass with their henchmen and their weapons. Jimmy Carter wouldn't kick any ass, so people screamed for Ronald Reagan. Man used to *be* an actor, thought he *was* John Wayne. Ronald Reagan started kicking ass around the world, bombing people. Went to little Grenada, kicked its ass, said, "Hey, we are *America.* We won't take it anymore."

Take what? And that's what happens when you put an actor in the White House. Guy kicked a little ass on the screen, figured he'd do it in real life.

Sampling both worlds, I have not found entertainers to be half as secure as athletes. And I think I understand it, at least regarding guys who played football. A man who has experienced fear and physical hardship and overcome it, doesn't have to lie. He doesn't have to advertise his toughness.

He's just tough, you know? Men like Bubba Smith and Ray Nitschke now live gentle lives. Give them sufficient reason they could still whip ten men. That kind of man doesn't have to stuff his pants.

There's a Hollywood proverb about seven years lucky and seven years unlucky. It's only a proverb: in Hollywood actors and actresses and directors flash brilliantly across the horizon, only to disappear, seemingly overnight. Others float in and out of the industry, in a series of crests and low tides. Hollywood is a fleeting, peculiar universe, even tougher to predict than real life. You have to enjoy your run while the run is good.

Though I never pursued my film career with excessive vigor, at first I was doing nicely. My first three or four years in the business, I made eight films. A handful even made some money. You're not supposed to talk about things you almost got in Hollywood, but I'm talking about a lot of things I'm not supposed to, so the hell with it: I was one of the finalists for a Best Supporting Actor nomination for my work in *The Dirty Dozen*. I acted with some of the cream of Hollywood and I like to think I didn't embarrass anybody. When I starred in *Tick, Tick, Tick*, a racially conscious film years ahead of its time, it opened at Radio City Music Hall to an excellent review in *The New York Times*. My movies always did well internationally. In the Philippines, though I don't know why, I was their second most popular actor.

Though they didn't stay broken, I also broke some taboos. I played the big-time gangster, the boss, the cowboy, the lover—all traditional "white" roles. It was the end of the 1960s, the market was ripe for a black leading man. Hollywood already had the perfect candidate in Sidney Poitier. Sidney was the real pioneer. He won an Academy Award for Best Actor. He acted powerfully, beautifully, and that attracted audiences. And he wasn't light-skinned and curly-haired. Sidney was black. Sidney did a tremendous job for himself, for black people, for Hollywood. Yet Hollywood never saw him as a romantic lead. Even in *Guess Who's Coming to Dinner?*, in which Sidney's fiancée was white, their one kiss was shown in the reflection of a mirror on their car.

Then I came along, rough and tumble football player. A black John Wayne type. Hollywood wanted to capitalize on that image, which was fine with me, because those were the roles I basically wanted to play. And Hollywood gave me roles that weren't specifically written for blacks. I didn't plan my career that way, but I understood the significance, albeit temporary, and I enjoyed breaking down some barriers.

In the 1970s, those barriers went right back up. America regressed, Hollywood did the same. Hollywood opened its doors to blacks in the 1960s, pulled in the money, slammed them back shut. If you wanted to see a black woman in a major role, it was Cicely Tyson or nothing. Cicely is a fine artist, but I got Cicely Tysoned out. The industry is replete with talented, attractive black actresses. To represent an entire race with one woman is ludicrous.

As for the men, Hollywood moved away from

black heroes. It started looking for comedians and clowns. Comic relief. In serious films, the black presence was virtually nil. I had a conversation once about a comedy with a white film distributor. We were discussing a black comedy.

He said, "This will go good anywhere."

I said, "This will go good in Mississippi?"

He said, "Yeah."

I said, "They like all black movies in Mississippi?"

He said, "No, they like comedies."

"Why?"

"They like to see a bunch of niggers making fools out of themselves. Then they can laugh at them."

A lot of people don't feel that way, but there's no denying that all you ever see is black comedies. Even Richard Pryor and Eddie Murphy, two of the past decade's biggest stars, don't get dramatic roles. You can take any white man's story, make the drama as heavy as you want. Hollywood does not make black dramas. If one does get made, Hollywood serves it with a twist: they make it into the story of a white guy, who's *involved* in a black drama, and the black people are merely background. They take a rich, heartfelt black story, pervert it so it can play in Peoria.

In the case of *The Great White Hope*, the story of the boxer Jack Johnson, they softened the edges, put in some comedy, transformed it into fiction. They didn't want to deal with the real Jack Johnson. Jack Johnson was so bad he took a long white car, a white woman, and a white poodle, drove through the state of Alabama. And that was sixty years ago. Hollywood didn't want that on the screen. It knew white America would not respond in a positive manner. Even though it's one whopper of a story.

In the 1970s, if a black actor was fortunate, he went back to playing second honcho to the white hero. More frequently, blacks played killers and halfwits and butlers and slaves and guys in purple hats, who seemed addicted to giving high fives. Blacks went back to being degraded and humiliated. I guess that's no scoop. Historically, the manner that blacks have been portrayed on film has been atrocious. Walt Disney, with his jive-talking black crows, was famous for making fun of blacks. The man created some blatantly racist images, yet even in death, he's as American as apple pie. Apparently blacks and apple pie don't equate in this country. Mickey Mouse has a star on the Hollywood Walk of Fame. Paul Robeson, the enormously talented actor and civil-rights activist, does not. And black women still play maids so loyal they would kill for their white boss. Black men are still portrayed as stupid, shiftless, lazy, and untrustworthy, incapable of leading other men. In jail movies they have lots of parts for blacks. Black guys can always get that part.

It should be noted that these negative images are not only created by white folks. Alice Walker, a black woman, wrote *The Color Purple*, which created some of the most blatantly racist images in recent fiction. In the subsequent film, which Alice did not write, there was not a single redeeming quality attributed to black men.

In film, there's often controversy over black

actors who take those bad parts. I think you have to be careful before indiscriminately attacking actors. No man or woman is pure, and the dilemma is hardly a simple one. I was once offered a role in the sequel to *Mandingo*. Ken Norton played the original; in the end they stuck him in a huge pot, then the master pitched him down into the boiling water with a pitchfork. (Nice.) In the sequel they wanted me to play Mandingo's father.

I said, "Give me a billion dollars. I'll do it."

Obviously I didn't want the role. For the sake of argument, if they had met my unmeetable price? I would have taken the part. Would have taken it, played the hell out of Mr. Mandingo, come back, made *twenty-five* films, all with black people. My point is, Hollywood isn't football: you can't fight every battle frontally. In Hollywood, sometimes you have to stay alive to fight another day. As long as you know why you're taking a bad part, as long as your heart is in the struggle, I don't think you need to be ashamed. Provided you don't make it a habit.

As for myself, the 1970s marked the virtual end of my film career. People stopped calling me, I could not get work, producers who said they wanted to work with me came back with their minds changed. In essence, I was blackballed from the industry.

Today I'm still on the outer limits. The only time I work is with some maverick producer, who does what he wants, which is what happened with *The Running Man*. The film that was released last winter—*I'm Gonna Git You Sucka*—was a spoof of the old black action movies. It was co-produced, directed, and written by Keenan Ivory Wynans, who also co-wrote *Hollywood Shuffle* with Robert Townsend. For *I'm Gonna Get You Sucka*, Keenan raised the $3 million himself, so he could hire the cast he wanted. One of the guys Keenan wanted was me. The film did well, I made relative peanuts, and I didn't mind. I believed in the project.

I also receive an occasional call from a television producer. It's usually a show that is sinking, needs a pop in the ratings, or an attempt at a pop. But what I get most of all are calls like this: "Jim, we have a role for you. It's small but I think you're going to like it. You get murdered with a hatchet."

I'm not alone. Blackballing is a Hollywood tradition. In the days of the Communist witch hunt, people lost their jobs forever, or were forced to write under pseudonyms. Raquel Welch had a blow-up on a set, was fired, wasn't seen on the film screen for many years. There are many reasons why people get blacked, or semi-blacked: too politically active in what Hollywood perceives as not the Right Causes; too difficult, when you're not a big enough star to get away with it; too wild in your private life, although in Hollywood you have to be seriously wild for anyone to flinch; or by filing a lawsuit against a studio or prominent producer. It happens to blacks and whites. Do whites receive more leeway to rock the industry boat? Of course, there's more leeway for whites in this world. The case of Jane Fonda was absolutely extraordinary. Jane went to Hanoi, posed with the Viet Cong, said and did things I've never seen done by an American actress. And she actually returned to Hollywood's graces, had a long, superb career. Had Jane been black, no matter how much talent she had, no way she pulls that off.

Since I was on the outside peering in, I can only speculate on why my career ground to a halt, and I think there were multiple factors.

In 1969 I received national headlines for supposedly throwing a woman off a balcony. It didn't happen, I was never even charged, but trial by headline is a powerful force. I want to be fair about this, and if I was a producer, and an actor got the same headline, I might have been reluctant to hire him myself.

I was also a casualty of timing, just as timing had been my ally when I broke in. In the 1960s Hollywood reacted to the liberal mood of the country, some of its own liberal leanings, the pressures exerted on it by the civil-rights movement, and gave blacks some decent roles. I played in scenes that were unprecedented: I made love to white women on the American screen. In America, in Hollywood, that is not small potatoes. When Hollywood returned to business as usual in the 1970s, it made sense that I would be the first guy they'd prefer to forget. I symbolized a screen image they wanted nothing but distance from, and have been avoided to this day: it's been twenty years since a major Hollywood studio has filmed an interracial love story.

And it wasn't only white folks who were upset about my love scenes with Jackie Bisset and Stella Stevens and Raquel Welch. A lot of blacks didn't care for it either. They felt by having white girlfriends on the screen, I was putting down black women. I didn't quite follow that logic, and I didn't hear too much about it—black folks know my social track record—but I did get some criticism. When you're a black in Hollywood, it's simply hard to win. Some folks say you should stick to acting, others say you're not doing enough for other blacks. I recall when a black writer in *The New York Times* tore into Sidney Poitier, said Sidney was not taking the right roles, was not doing for blacks what he should be. I thought the guy missed by a mile. I thought Sidney was the best thing we had going, and should be roundly congratulated. Then, maybe it was one of those karma deals, I saw Sidney. We were both returning to Los Angeles on the same airplane. Sidney was alone, I went and sat down in the adjoining seat, we exchanged greetings, some small talk.

Then I said, "Look, Sidney, I don't think you should care about what these people say or write because what you're doing is fantastic for black people. You can't do it all, and what you've done so far has pioneered some things for us."

I had no idea if Sidney took that to heart, until I read his book. He mentioned my words, said I gave him some comfort at a time when he was depressed from being criticized. I felt good because I said it from my heart, had no idea it would ever see public light. It was just a quiet thing between the two of us.

Returning to why I was blackballed, deep in my gut I think the primary factor was my activism. I was increasingly perceived as a militant. I had spent time with Malcolm X, made no attempt to hide that fact, and Malcolm made many people nervous. Even after Malcolm was killed, many people believed I was a Muslim, despite the fact that I was never a Muslim, though I had Muslim friends, and despite the fact that Malcolm himself had broken from the Muslims before his death. Regardless, when people want to bring things out of your past, pit them against you, they do, and my personal relationships did not endear me to Hollywood. Nor, later on, did my friendship with Louis Farrakhan. I also used my celebrity status as a platform to make statements about the oppression of blacks. Historically, Hollywood has felt more comfortable when one of its white liberals says, Yes, let's free the blacks. When a black man stands up there is an entirely different reaction.

Is there racism in Hollywood? Absolutely. Just look at the images. There is also nepotism, cronyism, chauvinism, and economics. Once again, in America the discussion of race is tricky. If you want to be sensational, you just say everyone in Hollywood is racist. No, it doesn't work that way. There are some wonderful color-blind people in Hollywood and Hollywood is a place that makes business decisions. When Hollywood makes a film with its own money, it can make the film it wants. In search of profit, Hollywood tries to determine what the market wants, then gives it to them. Unfortunately, Hollywood seems to think America wants to see blacks degraded. And while you can try and be balanced and fair, you don't want to ignore the fact: Hollywood may only be a microcosm of American consciousness, but it has awesome power to shape that consciousness. If it wanted to, Hollywood could be a major force in the liberation of black people.

The hope is in the young guys. Spike Lee. Robert Townsend. Keenan Ivory Wynans. These guys have the winning formula. Make a small film. Make it black. Don't hide from your blackness, celebrate it. Make your points about life in America, be balanced in your presentation, and laugh at yourself while you're at it, because black folks are fucked up, too. Do what Richard Pryor did in his early comedy: say it from the heart, let it be what is. Get your core audience, black folks, then white folks will see the fun, want to join in.

I'm optimistic about the 1990s, but it's tinged with caution. Black folks are partially responsible for the current state of Hollywood. As an industry Hollywood is almost unique: if you can get the Cash, you can be a Player. Even if they have the money, blacks are exempt from buying a Mercedes franchise. In Hollywood, if a black can get financing he can produce a film. If he can raise enough money, combine it with a good script, he can hire almost anyone. If I had $20 million and a dynamite script, I might attract Steven Spielberg.

Where blacks have been remiss is in developing a financial base. The audience is out there waiting for black films, but they're not getting any. And again, if blacks are going to scream at everyone else, I say first you should look at your own. Eddie Murphy is the top box office draw in the world. Michael Jackson has so much money he doesn't know what to do with it. If Eddie and Michael would stop making symbolic gestures, took some of their money and clout to support the young black talented filmmakers, we could be in strong shape. We could keep making comedies, also do dramas and historical films and not distort the spirit of the stories. If guys like Eddie and Michael stepped up, *impacted* the industry, we could break through. Until then, why should a white producer, working with his son and his brother-in-law and his cousin, taking care of them, step out and help blacks? When Eddie and Michael don't?

The world doesn't turn that way, neither does Hollywood. We have to reach out to our own.

13

SUBSTANCES

WHEN I PLAYED PRO football very few sportsmen used drugs. The NFL was Square City. The only drugs I saw were Bennies and other pep pills, and judging from the looks on their faces, the only guys using those were defensive backs. The first time I saw an athlete smoke a marijuana cigarette was after I retired, when Leroy Kelly came by my home, lit one up while sitting on my couch. I was astonished. I had never seen an athlete smoke pot.

There were Cleveland Browns who smoked cigarettes, but never around the team. Had he caught them Paul would have died, killed them first. When I played football, I never even smoked a cigarette, because I thought it was silly. Didn't want to fill my lungs with that garbage, thought it might inhibit my performance. Smoking cigarettes simply did not make sense to me.

I did not refrain from smoking because I considered myself a Role Model. No one convinced me, "Hey, you're Jim Brown, you can't smoke. The kids will hear about it." Kids? I didn't smoke because I didn't want to smoke. The guys that wanted to smoke, smoked. Athletes aren't characters in a storybook. Athletes are living their *lives*. They will be weak and carnal and greedy and confused. They will also be loyal and brave and sweet and compassionate. Human beings can be all of that in one week.

To say that Mickey Mantle smokes and drinks, how dare he, what about the children, sounds to me like a bunch of adults fooling themselves, and copping out. If a kid doesn't receive a life foundation at home, at church, at school, he isn't going to get one. He certainly will not receive wisdom from a guy who's twenty-five years old, never had a dollar as a youth, now has a million in his lap. That guy figures to have a bumpy ride. I don't think kids are dumb, I think they can come to understand that. They only have to be told.

I used to study master athletes. I eyed Arnold Palmer, Joe Louis, Muhammad Ali, Bobby Mitchell, Bill Russell, many others. What I was seeking was a lesson in style. Athletic style. Once they left the arena, I knew they were no more heroic or evil than the man who delivers garbage, nor was I better or worse. Being a celebrity doesn't make a man great. Greatness is inward.

I still hear people say that athletes should stop using drugs. Because it can kill them? No. Because they're role models. A guy strung out on cocaine cares about kids? About setting an example? He cares about filling his lungs with freebase, stuffing his nose with cocaine. Period. And if he hates himself, he doesn't give a fuck about others. A person controlled by cocaine has no dignity, no loyalty, no judgment. He will lie, steal, cheat, betray his woman, his closest friend, to feed his addiction. You *cannot* overestimate the power of addiction. Tell a cat on cocaine to Just Say No, he will laugh in your face, or he'll nod his head, say what you want to hear, go back to the pipe. I see famous athletes on TV, know for a fact they're still using drugs. And so does the guy on the street. To get a person off drugs, you can't sell them sobriety the way you peddle cereal. You can't stick a guy in a clinic for thirty days, watch the symptoms subside, say the problem is over. Drugs is a people problem. You have to deal with the individual. You have to change the way he *thinks*. For that you need programs run by people who know the terrain, are not afraid to soil their hands. You have to burrow deeper than Just Say No.

In sports, until people who say they're trying to wipe out drugs become educated to the real issues, they will look terribly naive to drug users. Cocaine is the No. 1 dilemma in modern sports. Guys that get addicted are in much deeper trouble than people realize. And while everyone on the inside knows cocaine is there, no one knows how to deal with it. The owners continue to fool the public, say the problem is "under control." I think the owners do this for two reasons. They do not understand the power of drugs, have no idea despite their rhetoric, that people's lives are in danger. The second factor is commerce. If the owners wanted to crack down, they could. They could admit they have a major problem, take the time to treat the guys correctly, acknowledge that thirty days is a trifle. But an owner faces an extremely difficult choice: does he tear apart his team, lose some of his top ballplayers, diminish his product? Or does he take small, symbolic steps, hope a miracle happens?

The double standard is remarkable. A normal guy gets caught by the police for using cocaine, he's convicted, and usually goes to jail. An athlete gets caught, they discuss it as if it's baseball: You get three strikes, then you're out. I'm not saying I want to see any athlete go to jail. As an intelligent person, I am saying that drug use is a criminal offense, and if they truly wanted to clean up sports, they would treat it as such.

As long as owners remain naive about the severity of drugs, sophisticated about protecting their business, public confusion will continue to reign. So-called experts such as Joe Theismann will still get paid $100,000 to go on the air, analyze and criticize the cases of a Lawrence Taylor and a Dexter Manley, who should have been suspended thirty days, sixty days, during exhibition or the regular season, blah, blah, blah. Even while Theismann is criticizing the NFL for its double standards, he is making his living off them. If the NFL cracked down, treated athletes on drugs as they do the man on the street, the industry would shut down, the Theismanns of the world would be out of a job. They know that, so they'll continue to tell half the truth: a little scandal is good—it sells—but too much can jeopardize profits.

Some fans ask, Why would a man making millions, a man who's playing a game for a living, risk it all on drugs? People who understand drugs never ask that—it's a question that presumes an existence of logic. A guy using cocaine doesn't have any logic. Cocaine becomes his God and his mistress, and those who freebase cocaine typically lose it all—job, friends and family. They're headed for one of three destinations—insanity, death, or rehabilitation. Smoked or snorted, cocaine is rougher than any man. Cocaine is the heavyweight champion of the world, the baddest motherfucker on earth.

I had a friend named Buzzy Willis, who used to manage Kool and the Gang. Before that he was the vice president of RCA records, and one of the first black VPs in the music industry. Buzzy came to me when he was managing Kool, said he and the group had been doing drugs. To try and get clean, he felt he needed to put some distance between himself and the boys. He didn't have any money, said he wanted a real place to stay. Together we could sign some groups, like the old days. Would I help him out?

I said, "Yes, I'll help you out."

Buzzy came to the house, we worked on some potential projects. Every time Buzzy was supposed to do something meaningful toward closing a deal, it wouldn't happen. Then Buzzy left for two weeks. I didn't hear from him, he reappeared with some excuse. He left again, I *never* heard from him, and that was three years ago. After it was clear that Buzzy wasn't coming back, Big George went back into Buzzy's room, looked in the drawer, found the equipment used to freebase. The cat had been freebasing while he was staying here. He played a total game on me. Lying, wasting my time, embarrassing me by attaching my name to projects, then pulling out. That's what cocaine does.

A few months before he died, Marvin Gaye did Motown's 25th Anniversary show. I was one of the consultants, spent a lot of time with Marvin. At one rehearsal we spoke for two hours, Marvin told me all about his life, including the drugs. Marvin was freebasing heavily. I knew right then if I could somehow travel with Marvin for the next year or so, if Marvin could travel with someone who he could talk to the way he could to me, who loved him, and who he trusted, he might have a chance. And if he didn't find that person, I knew right then he'd probably end up dead. You can't force yourself on the guy who does cocaine. He has to want you, and he has to have an intense desire to get straight. I felt as if maybe Marvin wanted someone with him, but I don't think he was ready to make that fight. And I do think Marvin killed himself, though his father held the gun.

I know what happened the day that Marvin died, the day he was shot to death by his father. Big George was very close to the Gaye family. After Marvin's death, it was Big George who took that family over. He kept the scandal, as much as humanly possible, out of the newspapers. He took care of Mama Gaye, Father Gaye, worked with the lawyers in a way so that justice would be served, but that would spare the family additional grief. When Mama Gaye became ill, Big George would go to the hospital, sit with her, even after she had fallen asleep.

After Father Gaye shot Marvin, Mama Gaye picked up the phone, called Big George. Big George arrived at the Gaye home first. Mama Gaye told him herself what happened. Marvin had been hitting the pipe, when he and his father had an argument. Marvin threatened to strike him. Mr. Gaye said, "Son, if you ever hit me I'm gonna kill you." Marvin knew his father had a gun. He struck his father anyway, more than once. Father Gaye walked downstairs, got the gun, came up, shot Marvin twice. When people get gripped by the pipe, they will literally play Russian Roulette. I think Marvin was doing much the same thing. I don't think Marvin felt loved, felt trapped, in fact, by his misery, knew his father would give him a way to escape. Though he didn't pull the trigger, I believe Marvin committed suicide.

I think Rick James tried to do the same thing. Rick is a wonderful, bright man with one dangerous problem—cocaine. He admits it. Rick came by my home once at four in the morning.

He said, "You know something, Jim? I almost OD'd twice. The second time I said to the doctors, 'Why the fuck'd you bring me back?' I got twenty-some people on my payroll. And nobody loves me.'"

That's not true. I love Rick. I'm sure others do, too, but the cocaine won't let him see that. Other than that, I didn't know what to say to Rick that night. Now I'm praying Rick can hold himself together.

When we played pro football we were fortunate. I doubt if many guys knew what cocaine even looked like. Today in pro sports it takes a strong-willed individual to not try drugs. Guys who set their own agenda get ostracized. To ensure that they're perceived as one of the boys, I've seen athletes do cocaine with a knowing grin, even as their eyes were saying, What the fuck am I doing?

A lot of athletes find cocaine with their dicks. Athletes want sex, cocaine lures the women. Athlete has a tight body, fame, *and* good cocaine, he can hook the finest chick in L.A. Even an ugly athlete with a belly, guy used to getting 6s, if he can score cocaine, he can now get 10s. I've seen guys at parties with a pocketful of money, no cocaine, chicks want nothing to do with him. Anyone can have money. The cat with the coke is the cat who runs the show. He's the ultimate Star. Women will offer their bodies to him in ways he's never seen. Athletes learn that lesson quickly. It's how a lot of them discover cocaine, how a lot of them get hooked.

In Hollywood, after the clubs close at two, everyone goes back to a private home, continues the party. I've seen hundreds of episodes of cocaine and sex. To me it's all intertwined—athletics, money, cocaine and sex. With the addictive power of coke, with men enjoying pretty women and sex, you're not just fighting drug dealers. You're fighting an entire culture entrenched within the sports world.

In the 1960s drug-taking was standard. In the music industry, drugs were given a high degree of respectability. Cocaine was utilized in business deals. If a businessman could supply good drugs to a musician, it would go a long way to cementing their relationship. A major recording contract was signed with a friend of mine when the other side broke the stalemate by delivering him some high-grade cocaine.

I'll talk about drugs, my opinions, my experiences, but I never preach about them. Obviously I've seen my share of cocaine. I've helped many individuals try and get off it, and some have stayed off. I'll help anyone who wants to get clean. I don't advocate the use of cocaine. It has destroyed people I've loved, and damaged relationships. But I don't go around condemning. Unless it's someone who has asked me for their help, I don't criticize or tell them to stop. I'm here for them, they know it, but I'm not a preacher. It isn't my style.

I also know a man who isn't pure shouldn't preach to others. And I have definitely not been pure. For one thing, I drink. I think drinking is a miserable practice. And yet sometimes, on a weekend, I feel like jumping around, talking a lot of shit, want to *think* I'm having a great time, I will drink. I don't enjoy beer, wine makes me sleepy. I can't stand scotch, can't stand gin, have no taste at all for Courvoisier. I used to drink Southern Comfort. Now if I have a drink, it's usually involving vodka. In my entire life I've never thrown up from booze, and that underscores why I have to monitor my drinking very carefully: I can consume a lot of alcohol. When you have a high tolerance for anything, it can become addictive.

Truth is, I shouldn't drink at all. I'm strong enough to admit what it does to me and what it does to me does not make me strong. Drinking alters my personality. I speak more freely, and sometimes my words aren't worth much. Alcohol makes me less tolerant, more impatient. When people do things, say words I don't care for, I take a more aggressive stance. Sometimes I'll stop drinking for months and when I look back, envision myself drinking, I'll think, Why did you *ever* do that? I should stop drinking on any level, and I'm critical of myself because I haven't. For me, alcohol is the one substance that could be dangerous.

I've never smoked a cigarette. Sometimes I'll see people smoking, think they're the biggest fool of all. It sure doesn't improve your sex. You don't get high, don't even have the illusion of feeling good. You have to force yourself to like it, then you tell yourself you honestly do. And it gives you cancer. The way I see it, cigarettes are the one thing you can't even explain away with a good rationalization.

I've never touched heroin, LSD, peyote, none of those drugs. I never had any curiosity for them. Even in the 1960s, when everyone was talking up LSD, I didn't buy it. I have smoked marijuana. I only use marijuana in a particular way. I would never smoke a marijuana cigarette and drive down the street. I think that's asinine. If I smoke marijuana, it's usually in my bedroom, with a girl, and sex is involved. I've found that marijuana makes the sex good. It also sensitizes my taste buds. But I would rather have a drink than smoke a marijuana cigarette. I have no fascination for it, there is no chance for addiction. Within the course of a year, I might smoke five marijuana cigarettes.

I have never taken cocaine in my life, I will not

take it. No one in the world is even going to talk to me about taking it. People know I don't touch it, so they keep it out of my face. But even with cocaine I have not been pure. I've enjoyed the sexual atmosphere it can create at parties. I've been at parties with pretty girls, they've wanted wine or marijuana or cocaine, someone has given it to them, or they had their own, and I've had sex with those girls. In that respect, I've been guilty of being like all the other guys.

Perhaps five times in my life, I have bought cocaine. I bought it for certain girls, who I knew were coming over, who I knew liked to use it. Those girls would lie on my veranda, naked. They were beautiful. And it was almost as if I had a cowbell. And I could ring that cowbell, and they would do anything to get their little portion of cocaine. They'd make love to me, to each other, they would say right out, "Give me some cocaine. I'll put it on her pussy, and lick it off." The cocaine made them into slaves.

I used to run with a cat named Darrell. He was an intelligent kid, and friendly, yet he never attracted many women. Darrell started dealing with cocaine. He got meaner, and he started showing up with fine women. Darrell came by one night with a sexy young girl. I liked her, and I wanted to be with her.

Darrell said, "Look, man. Take this little package. I'm going away. But this will get you anything you want."

I was naive at the time, I just gave her the package. She did the cocaine and left. She didn't want the sex, she wanted the powder. We were both using each other.

One summer night I was sitting with a famous athlete in my living room, heard a car pull up in my driveway. Looked out, saw two girls dressed in long, formal gowns. They were on their way to meet their dates, then to their college prom. They were snorting cocaine, of course wanted more, knew my buddy had some. He turned them on, they gave him sex. Then they went to their prom.

I'm not proud of the times I've utilized cocaine in a sexual manner. What transpired with those few girls on my veranda, because it involved cocaine, was dehumanizing. But I won't deny those experiences. I'm not writing this book to make people like me. I've lived in worlds where cocaine is ingrained. I've seen it everywhere, being done by men and women. The only fact I hold sacred, to be very honest, is that I don't take it, that I never have.

I learned a lot of what I know about drugs through my relationship with Richard Pryor. I've known Richard for fifteen years. Though Richard was radically funny, he was never simply a comic. Even while he had you laughing, his perceptions cut to the bone.

Richard is also the most skillful actor on earth. Not on the screen, in real life. He can cry tears, cut them off, be warm, serious, mean, wonderful, at his instant command. Richard fooled me about something emotional. That doesn't often happen to me.

Even before we met I identified with Richard. He was always getting in scrapes, so was I. One of the first times I saw him, Richard was sitting behind bars. I went to the jail to visit, didn't say much. Told him I liked him, appreciated his comedy. Next time I saw Richard he was in a hospital, for drug abuse. I stuck around. We had a bond.

Richard won the part in *Silver Streak*, did that classic comedy scene with Gene Wilder—"We bad, we bad"—graduated from cult status to national star. Several months later I was in Manila, co-producing a film. The crew was there, the locals had built several sets. The Filipino government was putting me up at the Manila Hotel, in the presidential suite, I was having meetings with Ferdinand and Imelda Marcos. Financing fell apart. The bank accounts had been opened, but the money had never been deposited. The island was under martial law, there was a general curfew, a specific tenseness. Now, after their hospitality and work, our hosts discovered we were broke. I started getting these looks: "You don't hold up your end of this affair, get used to Manila. You won't be leaving."

I dashed for my credit cards, wired home for my savings, came up well short. In two weeks we were supposed to fly to the island of Corregidor, begin shooting. We started calling America, looking for backers. We called Carroll Rosenbloom, Carroll came through. Called Dr. Woods, a black psychiatrist in Beverly Hills, wonderful man, Doc put up some money. We flew to Corregidor, began shooting, still needed about $20,000. I told my partners we had one other chance—Richard Pryor. I called Richard, told him we were ten to twenty thousand short.

He said, "Shit, I can give you twenty thousand. Just have your guys come over, I'll give them the money."

I said, "Whew! That's fantastic."

Richard saved my ass, came through like a champion. We made the film, returned to the United States. Short time later, I heard Richard was messing with the pipe.

The reason I heard that, didn't see it, is that Richard and I had never been party buddies. Most guys severely into cocaine normally don't indulge around non-users. They're not proud of using cocaine, they're not standing up on Wall Street, hollering, "I'm a fucking drug user, and I'm great!" They're essentially hiding out, from life, will stay in their bedroom for several days at a time. I've seen exceptions, guys who act bold, their expressions saying, "Yeah, that's right, motherfucker, I'm doing drugs. Got a pound of cocaine in front of me. Now what?" It's false bravado. Drugs turn men into cowards.

When Richard was hitting the pipe, he never came by, rarely called. Then one day he did call. He had just returned to his lady, Jennifer, after shooting a film. He had poison in his mind. He said Jennifer had been cheating, that people were out to kill him. He said crimes had been committed on his property, spoke of bodies buried in his backyard. I had never heard more intense paranoia, knew it was the freebase. I couldn't disregard it, he was talking to me. He needed someone. My purpose was to get Richard into a hospital.

I'd drive to Richard's house in the Valley, we'd talk for hours. We met almost every day. I would gently try and convince him to enter a hospital, knew he was not a man to push, that would only fuel his defiance. Later, in a concert film, Richard would perform a routine about this time in our lives. The pipe would tell him that I was coming over. It would whisper to him, "Fuck Jim Brown. You don't need him. All you need is me, Richard. It's just you and me, Richard."

In the film it was frightening and hysterical. You could hear the nervousness in the laughter of the audience. In real life it was painful. Richard would progress, then he'd step backwards, to the pipe. One fantastic day, I thought I had kicked the pipe's ass: Richard agreed to seek help. Next morning, we would meet at a designated spot, drive to the hospital together.

Richard never showed up. My heart sank.

I called his house, received no answer. I went roller skating that evening in Reseda, at my usual place. They paged me. It was Jennifer.

"Richard burned himself," she said. "And I wanted to let you know."

I figured Richard had burned his arm, something minor, was dealing with it, and I continued skating. Next morning I received a phone call from the Sherman Oaks Community Hospital Burn Center.

A man said, "Richard needs you. He's calling for you. Please get over here as soon as possible."

I said, "Oh God." I still didn't know what had happened. Richard was in the record industry where you often have to deal with the Mob. He was into drugs, dealers, large sums of cash. My imagination ran all over the place. I called Big George.

He's a policeman, always packing, strong as a gorilla, and a level-headed sort.

I said, "Big George. Something has happened to Richard. He's out in the Burn Center, I don't know what the hell is going on. It's an emergency, they called me, I need *you* to go with me."

We arrived at the Center, the nurse rushed up, told me to get right in. I told Big George to hang back, for the moment. I walked into Richard's room, could barely tell it was him. Richard's head was swollen, looked twice its normal size. His lips, nose, and hands were scorched, there was a burn the size of a football on his chest. This poor motherfucker, somehow, comprehended it was me the instant I entered.

He whispered. "Jim. Jim. Oh man, Jim."

I cut him off. I said, "Look. You wanna live?"

"Yeah, yeah."

"All right. Let's get it on."

That's all I said. I didn't get into a bunch of bullshit about where and why and how could you. What I was saying to Richard, by not saying those things, was "Let's deal with this problem, this thing of your life. Because you're in fucking danger."

I understood what Richard needed from me. He had always appreciated my attitude of strength, my history of playing football, running over people. So we went to work. I gave Richard my undivided devotion, I received his unconditional trust. Richard said, "Jim, do anything you have to." In effect, I took over Richard's life. The two burn specialists—the Goldman brothers—worked with me in every possible way, and I've never seen two men work as hard to save another man's life. Richard's nurses and his psychiatrist were also fantastic.

And so I had power of attorney. I dealt with the press, police, family, friends, and adoring fans. I helped Richard with his bodily functions. Sometimes I surprised myself, because I always thought I was a Nice-Nasty person: a Nice-Nasty person is a guy who will kiss a girl, but then won't drink out of the same cup. With Richard I felt so close, I figured I'd do whatever it took. We shared a lot in that hospital. I don't know if I'll ever share that much again with another person unless it's my woman or my child.

Richard's recovery was agonizing, excruciating work. Not only was he burned to an inch of his life, Richard was withdrawing from cocaine and booze. While Richard was fighting to live, the whole world wanted to see him. They didn't understand what he needed most was rest, that a card or message was best for *Richard*. They didn't understand that a serious burn is about as bad as it gets, and the doctors must treat it almost twenty-four hours a day. So I had to turn people away, take the heat from all these folks who loved Richard. I'd ask Richard who he wanted to see, he would tell me who to let in. The energy and will and preparation it required of Richard to see a person for *two minutes* was un-fucking-believable. Richard didn't want to look weak, burned up. He would say, "My God, look at my face." By the time a guest had arrived, Richard would be upbeat, almost vital. I said, Damn! This brother is strong!

There was also turmoil outside the hospital walls. There was still the matter of what had transpired the night that Richard had been burned. Now it's public record, about as public as it can get: Richard later went on Barbara Walters, admitted there had been no "accident." Richard had tried to end his life. He had poured a flammable fluid over his head, then put a lighter to himself.

The first few days in the hospital, I didn't know that. I suspected foul play, had poor Big George investigating everyone. Then Richard told me he had tried to kill himself. He didn't say why, didn't have to. Trapped by the pipe, Richard saw one way out. I spoke to Richard's Aunt Dee, who had been there. When Richard had lit himself up, his uncle had panicked, bolted from the room. Aunt Dee ran for a blanket, wrapped up Richard, saved his life. Richard jumped up, began running down his street, where he was spotted by the police, who called an ambulance.

After Richard told me his secret, it would remain a secret. What went out to the press was a brief statement, that Richard had an "accident." While Richard had been tearing down his street, he had reportedly said to one policeman something about "smoking that shit." Taking that to mean Richard had been smoking cocaine at the time of the explosion, the LAPD announced that Richard had blown himself up while freebasing. That became the public perception. The police even came to the burn center to confiscate Richard's clothes, try and prove he'd been using cocaine. I had become close with the nurses, and they loved Richard. The nurses slipped me Richard's clothes. I snuck them out of the hospital, into the trunk of my car, stashed them in my home.

The last thing Richard needed was additional trauma—the doctors thought he might die. As I walked into the hospital one morning, I was waved over by one of the Goldmans.

He said, "Jim, if Richard dies in a couple of days, I want you to be the spokesman. I want you to tell the public."

I said, *"What? If he dies?* What the hell are you talking about?"

Dr. Goldman said there were complications with disease, that Richard's condition was grave.

I said, "Doc, it's not that way, he's *not* dying. You understand what I'm saying?"

Dr. Goldman said they were doing everything. I had watched them, knew how relentlessly they'd been working. I told Dr. Goldman to keep on humping, went into the men's bathroom and cried.

The following afternoon I left Richard's room to take a break. Two minutes later the nurse rushed out, insisted I come back. I walked in.

Richard said, "Come on, come on. Take me back in the back room."

We went into his little back room. Richard stared at my eyes. He said, "Man, I saw on television I was gonna die. Is that true?"

I looked Richard in the eye. I said, "That ain't true, man. The shit is not true. Don't you worry about *any* shit like that."

Richard went limp with relief. He knew I was telling him the truth: I never once believed that Richard would die. It was one of the contradictions of Richard. He had let the pipe control his mind, yet his will was now uncommonly fierce. The little sucker was fighting burns and drugs and booze and the fact that he and Jennifer weren't quite right. I'd watch him in the hospital, wonder if I could be that strong. I didn't think I could be.

Richard's relationship with his family was unclear. Richard was always a suspicious man. He also couldn't understand how anyone could love him. He would say to me, "How could a motherfucker like me get these fine bitches? They don't really love me. They want my money." Richard was equally paranoid toward his family, was certain they were after his wealth. As an observer, I wasn't sure he didn't have ample reason. Aunt Dee was always in his corner. With the rest of his family you couldn't tell. Their deepest interest did not seem to be Richard's life, but his worth, and what they would get if he died. One day I received a phone call from the company that had installed the safe in Richard's home. One of Richard's relatives had called, asking for the combination to his safe.

The safe guy said, "Mr. Brown, we thought we should call you. What should we do?"

I said, "Don't do anything! Don't give that combination to *anyone.*"

At that point Richard was so weak he could barely write. His family called me, said they needed $25,000 to pay bills. I told Rich what the deal was, he was sure his family was fooling him. I convinced him to scribble out a check, gave the check to his family.

Gradually, Richard began to regain his life. He had never lost his boldness. The nurses had been trained to "rap" to burn patients. Richard was so intelligent, that amateur psychology they'd lay on him was absurd. He'd analyze *them*, or be crude, they would laugh so hard I thought they might pee.

As Richard grew stronger, he would try and defy me. He wanted to show me he was just as strong as me, or stronger. I would arrive in the morning, we would say hello, Richard would show me his latest advancement. Now he could pull his ass out of bed, now he could make it to the bathroom by himself. He was asserting that he was a powerful SOB. I knew that was purely healthy.

It was during Richard's defiant phase that Marlon Brando came to the room. There was a big closed-circuit fight, Richard wanted to see it, felt up to doing it. Marlon persuaded the hospital to let him bring in a special cable. The three of us watched the fight. Marlon was beautiful to both of us, Richard was happier than I had seen him. It was one of those nights that you think about forever.

Then it came apart. Richard's family had come to resent me. I had been the one who refused to give out the combination to Richard's safe, I had been the one who his family had to go through for money. While Richard slept, he gave me the right to make crucial decisions. In his time of crisis, Richard had turned to me, not his family. For all of that, the resentment was wired into his relatives' faces, and I didn't really mind. Richard and I had kicked some ass. Everyone knew it.

One day Richard told his family I had become like a father to him. Wrong words at a wrong time. His family got angry and emotional. A few mornings later I arrived at the hospital and Richard's family was rushing out. Apparently they had hurried in early that morning, which was not characteristic. Now, leaving, they hardly looked at me. When I got to Richard's room he was upset, it seemed that he perhaps had been crying. I asked him what was up.

He said, "Well . . . look . . . I don't think I really need you anymore. I think my family can take care of everything."

I think my mouth fell slightly open. I said, "Well, damn, okay."

Richard said, "You know, my family didn't like something you said . . ."

I said, "Yeah, I see. What do you want?"

Richard said, "Man, it would probably be best."

I said, "Okay. What I'll do, I'll just let them handle it."

Then I left. But I knew Richard's ordeal was not close to being over. He would be working through so much pain it would be horrific. To leave it alone after coming so far seemed madness. I felt my job was half-done, and I think Richard knew it. That scared me.

It was also hurtful. In my life, very few people have known anything about who I am. Known me. Sometimes I thought Richard didn't care about anyone *but* me. At the start, when Richard's life was most fragile, he entrusted me to help save it. The one time in my life I have seen Richard Pryor terrorized, when he heard that he might die, feared that he could, he called for me to give him the truth. That drew me to Richard in a way I can't really explain.

What Richard did was not out of loyalty to his family, that I know. I'm not heavy enough or bright enough to dissect the complexities of Richard's mind, but I have an idea why he has ripped off so many people. It's not that he wants to be cruel. I think it's that Richard can't love anyone. Richard was *idolized*, and he knew that shit was false, that they were in love with an image, not the man. Richard the man did not feel worthy of love: the drugs, perhaps other things, had filled him with deep self-hatred. If you can't receive love, how you gonna give it?

I knew a lot of Richard's tricks when I was dealing with him. I knew what the drugs and the idolatry were doing to him, I saw how he treated people. And yet he fooled me. He's the only person who has ever fooled me about emotions. I can feel. I felt Richard. And I said, "This motherfucker here, he's tough on people. He's a game player. But he cares about me!"

The cat was brilliant enough to make me think so.

14

FLESH AND BLOOD

I'M NO TECHNOCRAT. I'VE always felt that people make this world turn. I've always marveled at the flow of human nature, tried to sample it in all its puzzling forms. I've known mobsters, policemen, politicos, gang members, visionaries, movie stars, down and outers, black folks, white folks, and other folks. Of the people I've known, I have never felt bored or cheated. I've mentioned many people you've never heard of. For now, I'll discuss a few whose names you'll recognize.

One man that has always intrigued me is Howard Cosell. Howard pretended to know more about certain sports than he did. At the end of his career he started overreaching, began to parody himself. Not significant. Howard had passion and insight and courage. Bullies take on unworthy opponents

—Howard's enemies were powerful. He confronted the Establishment, saved his loyalty for justice. Howard was shrewd, knew meaty issues would entice people into the tent. Once inside, Howard had a way of finding new angles, making people think in a way they might not have tried yet. I used to love listening to Howard. Loved the nasal tone, even the shameless vocabulary. To a lot of athletes, particularly black athletes, Howard *was* sports broadcasting.

When I had trouble, Howard was the one guy who was not afraid to invite me on the air, allow me my side of the story. He never lobbed me hanging curveballs. His questions were hard but fair. Dealing with the press, I'll take that every time. Howard was always giving black athletes quality air time, and for that he was respected. When Muhammad Ali went to jail rather than war, Howard was the one TV guy who didn't run away from him, who stood up publicly for Ali's right to practice his religion. Religion and war are minefields, and here was a much disliked white man defending the rights of Muslims. Had events unwound in a slightly different way, Cosell's career could have been destroyed. Howard had the grit to take that gamble.

Howard had scores of detractors, many of them his journalistic peers. Howard wasn't an apologist for the sports he covered. I think the guys who were, knew they were, looked at Howard, saw what they might like to be. Howard was egotistical. Good thing. It allowed him to stand alone, on principle, against weighty institutions. Howard Cosell was a warrior. I consider him one of the most significant figures in the history of sports. In the broadcasting end, no one comes close.

Speaking of electronic stars, I also did "The Tonight Show" several times. Johnny Carson was always too nice to me. When a guy is totally on your side it's hard to light a fire, and I always felt I was boring when I was with Johnny. The one memorable incident was the time I took The Friends of Distinction on the show. I had put the group together with a good friend named Paul Bloch, a major PR guy here in Los Angeles, and a lawyer named Richard Covey. The group was ascending quickly, we booked them a spot on Carson. The producers were giving us *three* short songs, we knew the exposure would be fabulous. Unfortunately, the band was not only tight, it was young and foolhardy. Throughout the rehearsal, they complained about the mikes, the lighting, the sound, as if they were major stars. I was standing on the side, giving them small, violent head shakes, they just kept on harping.

"The Tonight Show" cut us down to one song. I said, "Man, you guys are *dumb*."

Another time I went on, Johnny and I started discussing younger women, the dating of them, a subject we both knew a little about. A few weeks later I was at The Candy Store, everyone said, Jim, Johnny Carson was looking for you. I received a few more messages saying Johnny needed to speak with me. I figured it must be important, finally got through to him. He was calling me about a girl. A freak. Johnny wanted to turn me on to her. I met her, she was wonderful, a wonderful freak. That was my gift from Johnny.

I guess we all meet women in unusual ways. When Bill Cosby was first getting big, with "I Spy," he developed a part for me as a guest star, and the role was excellent. Bill Cosby is always trying to be a father to people, even then he was paternal to me. I thought, Bill Cosby. Very straight, but a hell of a guy.

About a year later Bill phoned me.

He said, "Jim, come on out to the studio to see me."

I said okay, drove to the studio, found Bill's dressing room. Bill was there with a beauty, said he wanted to introduce me. Bill left, the girl and I started talking. She asked me out. She told me her hotel, asked me to come by, go out for dinner. I said that would be nice. Later, when I went by her hotel, dinner was not what she had in mind. She wanted sex. She also wanted one hundred dollars.

The girl was a hooker.

My first thought: *What?* Cosby thinks I'm so denied I gotta buy a damn hooker?

I told the girl I wasn't in that market, there must have been a misunderstanding. She was friendly about it, I left. To this day I don't know why Bill Cosby would fix me up with a hooker. Maybe Cosby didn't know.

Prostitutes are people, I don't condemn them, but I also don't buy them. And hookers don't normally approach me. I guess there's something in my manner that says I'm not a likely customer.

Frank Sinatra has his own theory. Frank and I were at a club, it was late, we'd both had more than a couple cocktails. We started talking about chasing women. Frank said it's better to get yourself a couple of prostitutes, pay them a few hundred dollars, get exactly what you want, get rid of them, rather than using valuable time chasing chicks all night long until five in the morning, and *still* not know if you're gonna get anything.

To me that made good sense. I've seen guys who've spent ten hours and $300 buying drinks, hitting every bar, trotting out every line they've used since high school, still finding themselves alone at five A.M., broke, bummed, already hungover. Though I never followed Frank's advice, coming from him it was fun to hear, and I couldn't deny the logic.

Lester Maddox was another guy who never lacked for a point of view. When he was Governor of Georgia, Lester and I did one of the all-time classic Dick Cavett shows, so vintage they always replay it when they do a Best of Cavett. While I was waiting in the Green Room, Lester was already on. Lester is a country boy, and a wildman. To block integration, he had stood in the doorway of his own store, with what was reportedly an axe handle, to stop black folks from entering.

I was watching them on the Green Room TV; Cavett got right to it. He said, "Mr. Maddox, you've blocked integration on national TV. You had an axe handle—"

Maddox interrupted. "See that? That's what I've been telling you. The press distorts everything. I didn't have an axe handle. I had a pick handle."

I thought, Well, well, look what we have here. A crazy Southerner.

Preparing to go on, I knew Lester had a quick

mind, quicker mouth. He also had a state trooper, standing in the wings, watching. They announced me, I walked on, did the hi-how-are-you thing, sat down, asked if I could ask Mr. Maddox a question. Cavett said of course. I turned to Lester.

"Mr. Maddox," I said, "could you tell us something? Is there any discernible difference between an axe handle and a pick handle?"

Lester was surprised, quickly recovered.

He said, "Hey, you must be the guy James Brown. You're a hell of a singer and dancer!"

I laughed. Old Lester could deal. Right before the break, I thought, I got one. I know I can get him on this one.

I said, "Governor Maddox, I've followed your career, your activities in the state of Georgia. In a quiet way, you've done a lot of things for black people in that state. How does this go over with the people who voted you into office?"

I had stuck him with another sharp jab. Lester's mouth opened, nothing came out. Luckily for Lester, they cut to commercial. During the break I kept a straight face, inside I was grinning. I knew I had him in a no-win deal. He couldn't quite say, "I did *not* help black people!" If he admitted he had, certain white folks were going to cause Lester some problems. I could practically see Lester's brain working, was curious what it would produce.

We came back from commercial—Cavett leaped in with a paraphrase.

Cavett said, "Before we went to commercial, Governor Maddox, Jim Brown asked you how your bigoted friends feel about you helping black people."

Maddox detonated. "Bigoted friends! How dare you?! Apologize! Now! Or I will walk off this show!"

Cavett backpedaled. "Well, it was a quote. I was . . ."

Maddox walked off the set, Cavett started rushing behind him. "Mr. Maddox, Mr. Maddox!"

Suddenly I was alone. I saw the camera was on me. And I burst out laughing! Mr. Supposedly Serious, laughing his ass off on national TV.

The Cavett show was my idea of good TV—unpredictable. I once went on Dick's show during the Vietnam War. Jane Fonda had recently gone to Hanoi, posed with the North Vietnamese. The guests that night were myself, the United States Attorney General, Ramsey Clark, and Charlton Heston. While Heston was in the Green Room, the Attorney General and I were discussing Jane's amazing actions, then we segued to a visit the Attorney General had paid also to Vietnam. George McGovern was running for the presidency, the Attorney General was behind him, and the concession I wanted him to make was that his visit wasn't motivated solely by patriotism, but also to benefit McGovern. I probed gently, was able to get him to admit it. I liked him, he was thoughtful and soft-spoken. I could also tell, underneath, where it counts, he was rough.

Back in the Green Room, Heston was bouncing off the walls. He couldn't wait to leap on Ramsey Clark. How do I know? Heston, being Heston, came snorting onto the set, like Moses crossing the goddamn Red Sea. He ripped into this quiet man, *tore* into him. Clark waited for Heston to finish.

Then he cut out Heston's asshole. Heston didn't have his facts straight, didn't know shit, the Attorney General owned him.

There isn't any theater in my relationship with Bill Russell. I don't trust a lot of people. I trust Russ with my life. Bill has been a brother to me. Whenever I've had a love affair end, if my head was wrong, I needed to cool out, I could fly up to Seattle, stay at Bill's. Bill would leave me alone, unless I asked for help, and if I did, Bill would be soothing, also pull no punches. To me that's a perfect friend, or as close as you can get.

The public has no idea what type of man Bill is. It's hard to know with Bill: he doesn't reveal himself unless he trusts you. On one level, I wasn't sure what to make of Bill at first—I didn't know if his heart was in the struggle. Then he wrote that article about the city of Boston, what its racial malice made him and his family feel like. Boston is a dangerous city for blacks, and I knew then that Russ had a special courage. As I got to know him, I saw that Bill loved being black, and hated discrimination. And he was willing to *work* for the freedom of black folks.

Bill the adult is a strong individual, and funny, and intellectual. As a child, Bill had a bad self-image. He thought he was unattractive, he lacked confidence. Even basketball couldn't bolster his ego—he didn't become a star until he got to the University of San Francisco. After Bill became famous, had been divorced, he began dating a lovely black girl. One day she confessed her surprise at the fact that Bill was attracted to her. Bill asked her how that could possibly be.

She said, "Because I'm so dark. I always thought I could never be beautiful."

Bill was touched, and gratified. As a child, being dark, Bill had felt the same way, but had never said it aloud. He said it was the first time in his life he realized he hadn't been alone.

Russ isn't a politician, if he thinks you're wrong he will say so. A lot of people attribute that to a lack of sensitivity. They've got it backwards. Russ is highly sensitive, that's why he doesn't let your words pass right by him: he's *listening* to you, and that is a rare art. As soon as a guy starts agreeing with everything I say, nodding his head like I'm Plato, I know he doesn't give a damn about me. Russell cares enough to tune in.

If you were a Celtics fan, you got to tune in to a whole lot of winning, and some classic battles between Chamberlain and Russell. Did you know those guys once were buddies? They fell out after they met in a championship series. Bill wrote an article venting his frustration that Wilt had left the game with an injury, denying Russ the chance to win a title with Wilt on the floor. That's all it took. From that day on they were chilly.

I like Wilt, he's a friend, but I'm much tighter with Russ. Wilt lives an independent life, doesn't seem to need strong friends. The buddies he does have all know Wilt parties with young, rich white girls. Wilt once wrote in a book that he didn't deal with black girls because they weren't on his level, and there was a storm of protest. I know Wilt and I think he misspoke, wasn't intending to disparage black womanhood. In the circles in which Wilt runs, there *are* no black girls. So he deals with the goodies around him, and most of them are youthful beach girls. Why not? Wilt is a beach *guy*.

Wilt invites me to some of his parties and believe me, the man knows how to get loose. No matter where I see Wilt, he's always been kind. But if there's ever a black fundraiser, Wilt is one brother I never call. Wilt's idea of a right-on sponsorship is woman's volleyball. He lives a Hawaii, Beverly Hills, top-of-the-shelf life. Without going into my revolutionary spiel, I've always accepted that. Wilt is not a fraud, Wilt is Wilt. The guy is just different.

In the NBA, Wilt is the most dominant individual I've ever seen play. I saw a film of Wilt when he was in high school that made my eyes bug. I saw this giant sprinting down the court, leading the break, wrap a pass *behind his back* to another kid on his team. When he turned pro they eventually widened the lane—because of Wilt. Anytime a guy makes them change the rules you know he's Nasty.

Wilt also used to frustrate me a little. I felt there was something in his heart that was counterproductive. Wilt had rabbit ears. If someone said Wilt couldn't pass, next game all he'd want to do is pass. If his dribbling was criticized, Wilt would make it a point to bounce that ball. Despite his monstrous talent, Wilt was never secure with Wilt. I always wanted Wilt to say, Fuck every one of you. I'm gonna score 50 MILLION points, get every damn rebound. If I don't dribble the ball once, I don't care. I have no time to argue with coaches, spite the peanut gallery. I am here to kick ASS.

If Wilt had that attitude, they would have made the entire court the lane.

Bill Russell, on the other hand, was not an exceptional scorer. He wasn't particularly graceful, or physically powerful. What Russ had was brains up the yingyang. Russ understood the games of every Boston Celtic, what he could do to complement those games. He understood concepts and nuance and psychology. Bill understood Sam Jones's psyche maybe better than Sam. Bill said Sam Jones probably could have done anything he wanted to out there, but Sam didn't want to do too much. That would draw attention to him, and Sam thrived when he felt unburdened by expectation. By holding a little back, Sam found his optimum niche.

His teammate Bill Russell also didn't care about personal fame. Russ used to say to me, "We won the championships. The hell with the rest." Russell was a basketball visionary: he understood team defense, its value, years before his peers or the press. At the very same time, he was the quintessential pragmatist: other guys would swat shots ten rows into the stands, the crowd would Oooh. Russ kept his blocks in bounds, gave the Celtics another possession. That's detail, and it's artistry.

How do you argue with nine championships in ten seasons? You don't. No player in NBA history has made a larger contribution to winning titles than Bill Russell.

And no man has introduced me to more intense women than Hugh Hefner. When Hefner had his mansion in Chicago, Bill Cosby used to tell me all about it, urge me to go. I didn't know Hefner, the thought of calling him embarrassed me. Eventually Hef and I met, briefly, he invited me to his place in Chicago. I remember it had a pool, and you could sit in the lower-level bar, have a drink, look straight into the pool, and the girls would swim by. Those were some good drinks.

When Hefner opened the Playboy Club in Hollywood, that's when I really got to know him. Hef has been good to me over the years, I've spent a lot of time at his place. Usually, wanting to show off, I'll take some girls there with me. I drive up to the gate, announce myself to an electronically rigged rock.

Rock says, "How are you, Mr. Brown, good to see you today."

Gate swings open, I look at my chicks, they're impressed, we roll on in there. Funny thing is, I can bring ten pretty girls to Hef's, and I'm cool.

Rock says, "Jim, who's that in your car?"

"Well, I've got Mary, Willamina, Sue, Henrietta, Rosie, Debra, Barbara, Shelly, Iris, and Betty."

Rock says, "Okay Jim, come on in."

If I show up with one single dude in my car, rock says, "Wait one moment." Three minutes later: "I'm sorry, Mr. Brown. He is not acceptable."

And I have to tell President Bush he can't come in.

Hef's rock taught me something: I wasn't the only guy who liked to have women around and not a whole bunch of dudes.

Once I'm through the gate, I stop, gaze up at the castle-like home, park, go in the front door, sit down, order the finest food, some drinks, unwind, let it hit me: Yes! I am at the *mansion*. The mansion is paradise. Beautiful trees, beautiful animals, beautiful gymnasium, beautiful Jacuzzi (beneath the side of a mountain), beautiful bath house (showers, sauna, giant pillows, classical music), long, deep, beautiful pool, in which you can wear a suit, or not, and beautiful girls, eighteen to twenty-four, tanning around that pool, only in tops, only bottoms, or neither.

Sigh.

Hef used to throw his Midsummer's Night Dream parties. He'd enclose the entire yard with a tent, install two outdoor discos, serve shrimp, lobster, crab. The Manhattan Transfer would sing, Clint Eastwood would be there, Steve McQueen, all the Hollywood power hitters, and there would be one guy to every three girls. Keeping with the evening's theme, the girls would wear negligees, shorty underwear, exotic garters, and even if you were a shy unit, didn't want to see their exquisite gifts, you had no choice. It was all right in front of you.

Beautiful women make many men strange, almost paralyzed, but Hef seemed to have less insecurities with women than just about any guy I know. I've seen famous guys in a room with ten comely women, not want anyone to talk to *any* of them. Messing with Hefner's steady woman was strictly taboo, but otherwise he was never territorial. All these big shots would come into *his* home, chase after *his* female friends, yet I never saw Hef get remotely jealous or competitive. In fact, Hef's is the only home where it sometimes appears the host is a visitor. You see Hef in the garden, say a quick hello, keep moving after some girls. That's how he likes it, the way he sets it up. Unlike many celebs, with Hef you don't have to pay homage every time you see him. As long as you had a good time at no one's expense, Hef seemed content.

Then again, what did the guy have to be bummed over? His playmates were Playmates. I used to wonder, What the hell does Hefner fantasize about? I recall one of Hefner's birthdays. The Bunnies decided the focus that night would only be on Hef. They decided it might be nice to take Hef out to the Jacuzzi, surround him with twenty-five wonderful Bunnies. Good deduction. Meanwhile, Hef is in the Jacuzzi with twenty-five Bunnies, we're stuck inside the damn house. Guys started talking. "Should we go out there? Should we peek? What are they doing out there?" We never did find out.

I've spent many days and nights at Hef's, always felt welcome. Hef and I have an understanding. If someone doesn't care for me, it has nothing to do with Hef, he doesn't care. I appreciate that. The mansion is a white-dominated world, celebrity-dominated world, and when certain people get access to it, they get pompous, even more puffed up than they were to begin with. Sometimes I'll turn, catch a pseudo blue blood looking down his needle nose at me, thinking, Why is this big, black football player *here* with *us?*

They can kiss my populist ass. As long as I'm honest and loyal with Hef, carry myself properly, I know we'll always be OK. And I know there will always be surprises. At the mansion you never know who'll you encounter, or what form of union. One day at the mansion I met a frisky little girl, and

I do mean little. She was about 4'8". She said she wanted to meet Wilt Chamberlain.

I said, "What?"

She said, "I know he's been coming here. I'd love to meet him."

Thing about Wilt is, the man is not only tall, he is big. But she was earnest, so I said, "Well, I think he'll be here later."

Wilt arrived, I introduced him to the girl, she came up to the bottom of his baggy shorts. I left them alone, walked around the grounds, an hour later I was in the vicinity of the Jacuzzi, all I saw was this giant knee, and a big, long thigh. Took about ten steps to the side, new angle, saw that Wilt was lying on his back, one leg cocked up, the girl was on her back right next to him. My odd couple was naked.

One night at Hef's, Jim Aubrey, fully dressed, walked over. Jim had once been president of CBS, and I had befriended his daughter during the filming of *The Dirty Dozen*. Jim's daughter had fallen hard for a man named Victor, one of Hefner's associates. Victor was an unbridled playboy, so I spent a lot of time in London consoling Jim's lovesick kid.

Aubrey said, "Jim, my daughter is very fond of you. Could you do something for me? I'm here with Raquel Welch. She's wondering if you would talk to her."

I said, "Of course I'll talk to her."

I hadn't seen Raquel since we'd filmed *One Hundred Rifles*. In the interim she and Patrick had been divorced. I walked over to Raquel, before either of us spoke we both burst into laughter. I guess we knew we had both acted childishly, also realized beneath the BS, we liked one another. We danced most of the evening, never even mentioned the film.

Raquel and I went on a couple of dates, and they were platonic. Though doing our love scene hadn't faded from my mind, I didn't want to have a sexual relationship with Raquel. I knew that sex could deepen a relationship, or kill it off completely. Raquel and I would go out for dinner, I'd come by her house, we'd simply enjoy the company. Raquel was also dating Henry Kissinger at the time, then she met Warren Beatty. She gave him her number, he would call her at her home, and according to Raquel, all Warren would want to do is talk dirty. And not about things he wanted to do with Raquel. He'd have another girl at his place, tell Raquel what he was doing to *her*. Then he'd say, "So when do you want to go out?"

Raquel was more than a little confused. She said, "Jim, what do you think about this? The guy is good-looking, I would go out with him. But all he wants to do is tell me who he's got on the other end of the phone."

First I laughed. Then I said, "Raquel, I think I'll stay out of this."

Getting back to Hefner, behind the pipe, inside the pajamas, there's actually a real person in there. I've seen Hef debate renowned intellectuals, distinguish himself as a worthy foe. Hef throws charity parties, helps out friends in economic need, including me once, at a time when the IRS was kicking my ass, and does it all without fanfare. Hef is also a gentleman; as a result almost all his old lovers still care for him. If Hef was remotely evil, I guarantee, you'd see fifty books chronicling why.

I've seen Hef go through so many changes. For Hef the gallavanting is over. After his stroke, he scaled down his lifestyle. The legendary Friday nights are over, the mansion has become more private. Hef is *married*. Man, do things change.

Hell, even Berry Gordy sold Motown. Berry built it, made it the top black-owned company in America, symbolic of black achievement. Berry is still one of the few black entrepreneurs in America who can sit across the table from the most powerful men in Hollywood and on Wall Street and call many of his own shots. Berry broke black entertainers into the Vegas-Tahoe-nightclub-hotel axis. He worked the Temptations in there, the Supremes, at a time when that world didn't want to be cracked. As a black man, as a person whose life has been enriched by the music, I have gigantic admiration for Berry's accomplishments.

The last thing in the doggone world that Berry Gordy wanted to do was give up his baby, sell Motown. Berry had nearly sold it one year earlier, but millions of people wrote letters citing Motown's symbolic value. Berry pulled back. He said he would regroup, rebuild the company. One year later Berry sold it. Though the deal was right, that's not why Berry changed his mind. Once you've been young, built a Motown, made fortunes, made history, developed the Supremes and Marvin Gaye and Smokey Robinson and Stevie Wonder, it takes an awful lot of energy to try and top that. I think Berry knew he couldn't. So the great Berry Gordy, who has always been a master at adjusting, turned around, sold Motown for $61 million, proving, again, that he's a man for all seasons.

In my opinion, Berry's deepest sense of loss did not come from losing Motown. It came from losing Diana Ross. For the past twenty years, I've always felt Berry Gordy was in love with Diana Ross, and Diana Ross was in love with Berry Gordy, that they were meant to be together, but events and people in their lives prevented it. When I think of Berry and Diana, I think of this immense but frustrated love.

I've been a friend to both of them. Berry is an extreme competitor, and challenge is one of the glues in our relationship. At backgammon, chess, golf, we try and beat each other's brains in. Once Berry and I and Bill Russell drove to Palm Springs for kind of a sportsman's weekend. Berry was supposed to leave, he had plans to visit Diana, but he wasn't motivated, stayed a few extra days in the desert. Our final day, there was a news flash on TV. Diana Ross had gotten married. To a guy named Silverman. Bill and I were shocked. Berry was punched in the stomach. He didn't know a thing about it. Though he wouldn't reveal it, I knew Berry was devastated. Eventually Berry came to view Diana's marriage as a positive thing, but I've always felt it was a spite marriage, that if Berry had gone to Diana as planned, she'd never have married another man.

Though I was much more intimate with Berry, I was also friendly with Diana. She and Timmy Brown used to date and Timmy brought her by the house once. At the time we were all compulsive for chess and we invited Diana to play. First Timmy beat Diana, then I did. After the second game, Diana told Timmy she was going down the hill to get some cigarettes, would be right back. Diana left and never came back. Guess she didn't dig losing at chess.

Over the years I came to know Diana for real. I had a radio show in Las Vegas and whenever Diana would perform there I would go and see her in her dressing room. Diana always seemed pleased to see me: she knew I was aware of her and Berry, and I was someone whom she could speak openly to. She would ask me how Berry was, if he was happy, and I could see the love and hurt in her eyes. I'll never forget one of her concerts. Diana began singing, "Somedaaaaaay, we'll be togeeeeeether," and she started crying on stage. I knew she was crying for Berry, and after the show I went backstage. Usually I would get right in to see Diana, but this time they kept me waiting for over an hour. I was with a girl and it started to get embarrassing. She was looking at me: Do you really know Diana Ross?

I waited, knew Diana would need to talk. When I was finally let in, Diana immediately began discussing Berry. Then an unusual thing happened. Berry walked in. I didn't even know he was in Vegas, yet here he was. I had seen the two of them together, but only at industry events, when they were surrounded by people. In the quiet of Diana's dressing room I could see the deepness of their thing. So I left.

The next day there was a tennis tournament at Caesar's Palace. When I arrived twenty minutes late Berry and Diana were sitting in Diana's box, saving a spot for me. I sat down, checked out the crowd behind me, and there was Grace. Grace is the lady who had been with Berry for many years, and when she saw me she smiled. Grace looked perfectly serene and I thought that showed unusual strength. She knew that Berry was her man and she was secure enough to let him and Diana work out what they had to work out. Still, I doubted if many people, men or women, would be that gracious.

The next time I went to Berry's home, just after his birthday, he said Grace had given him a wonderful gift. That surprised me: Berry doesn't care about gifts. He's not the kind of man to get all gooey over some fancy shirt.

When I asked Berry what Grace's gift was, he said, "Come on, upstairs." In his bedroom, Berry picked up a videotape, popped it in the VCR. It was Grace. She had taped herself reciting a message to Berry. Rather than an object, she had given Berry something of herself. Grace said, "Hi Berry. I didn't know what to get you, so I thought I would tell you how much I love you, and how much you've taught me about myself. Berry, I love you so much."

It was a bitch, and I nearly started crying. Then I glanced at Berry, always so fierce and powerful, who may let you get close, but never *too* close, never close enough to glimpse his softness, which he prefers to keep wrapped up. That moment, Berry could barely keep it wrapped.

15
ALI

BRAVE. OUTRAGEOUS. INDOMITABLE. IN-CANDESCENT.

To Muhammad Ali, all those adjectives apply. He was also one of the nicest human beings you would ever want to meet. I like to remind people of that. It gets lost in the legend.

Ali always wanted to be a street guy, but he was not a street guy. Look at his early pictures, with that little face. I knew him then, when he was a kid, Cassius Clay. He was innocent, almost square, but he had the gift of gab, could make you believe he was anything. Could make you want to believe he was anything.

Ali claimed he didn't like white folks, but he liked anything walking. If they were decent, Ali loved all people. But he was a champion of black folks. Especially the black man who was poor. In New York and Philadelphia, Ali would meet me, and he would drive us into the black ghettos. Those people were Ali's army, and he was their king. It was Ali's idea for him and I to walk the streets together. We'd go into barber shops, shoe stores, barbeque places, Ali would shadow box and tell jokes, put me in a headlock, brag how he could whip my ass. We'd sit around, just talk to people. They loved that Ali was world champion, they loved that I had been a star football player, but there was something more real going on. They knew we both loved black folks, would never turn our backs on black folks. We were on their streets, on their terms. The energy was incredible. For hours Ali and I would stay on the streets, no agenda, soaking up that feeling.

In early 1964, when Ali was still Clay, he was training in Miami for his fight with Sonny Liston, and the Browns were also in Miami. We had finished second to the Giants in 1963, and were now playing the Green Bay Packers in the now defunct runner-up game. Though he hadn't yet announced it, Ali was already a Muslim in the Nation of Islam, led by a man named Elijah Muhammad (Elijah's son, Herbert, would soon become Ali's manager). Malcolm X was also in Miami. Though he and Elijah had once been allies, the two powerful leaders were estranged. When Malcolm made his break from the Muslims complete, he wanted Ali to come with him.

Malcolm and I spoke a lot that week. I found him brilliant and reasonable and I would leave our talks exhilarated. I'm not a man who believes in heroes, but for me Malcolm came the closest. He was the only black man who was speaking out in a manner I appreciated. He spoke of economics and voting rights and political power, questioned the goals of the integration movement. Did black folks really want to sit down next to white people on the toilet? Malcolm asked. Was that a goal for black people? Malcolm also said, If someone hits you, hit him back twice as hard. If someone comes to your home to fuck with you, protect yourself and your children at all costs. I believed in all of that. Still do.

Of course there was also a fight going on, which meant there were lots of gorgeous girls around the two camps. The week of the fight I saw Ali about every day. I told him we had planned a huge post-fight party at the Fontainebleau Hotel, there would be all these sharp chicks, and that he should come. Ali said he would. After he beat Sonny Liston.

Few believed he could do that. Liston had twice dismantled Floyd Patterson, had the air of an invincible killer, and was reputed to be backed by the Mob—there was not a fighter on earth who seemed qualified to take his title. Only Ali, twenty-two years old, publicly said he would win, and he was wildly arrogant and hysterically funny. He said Liston "was too ugly to be the world champion." He said, "I'll beat him like his daddy." There was speculation that Liston was older than his reported thirty-one, and Ali said to his face, "You big ugly bear, you're forty years old if you're a day." Then came the famous proclamation: "I'm young and I'm pretty. I am the greatest!"

People said the Muhammad Ali act was born in those final weeks before the fight. Muhammad Ali wasn't born, just introduced, and I don't know how much was act—that boy really was crazy. So crazy, he went out and defeated Sonny Liston. Psyched Liston out, withstood his early rage, then hurt him with his fists. The manic kid had whipped the bully.

After the fight I ran to find Ali. I was so happy I couldn't stand still. I said we should get our asses to that party, all those happening little girls.

Ali said, "No, Jim. There's a little black hotel, let's go over there. I want to talk to you."

He had just stunned the world, revolutionized his sport, was the new heavyweight champion. In celebration of him, all hell was now breaking loose at the Fontainebleau. And Ali wanted to chat.

When we arrived at the motel room, Malcolm was there with three or four Muslims. To my surprise, Ali took me directly into a back room, sat me on the bed. For the next two hours, he told me about Elijah Muhammad and the Nation of Islam. He told me about the Mother Ship, how it came out of the sky, gave birth to all the little ships. I'm thinking girls and booze, and girls, and Ali is trying to convert me.

Ali would forever try and sell me on Islam, but this seemed a bit outlandish, considering the timing. Finally, Ali arrived at the real point: he had decided not to go with Malcolm. Ali said Elijah was a little man, but extremely powerful, and had always supported him. Ali said he loved Malcolm, but from that day on, he would never again be his friend. (And that indeed was the end of their relationship, which I thought sad. It was largely Malcolm who had brought Ali into the Nation of Islam.)

When Ali and I emerged, Malcolm still was there. He said, "Brother Brown, now that Ali's won the world title, don't you think he should stop having such a big mouth?"

I said, "Yeah. Now that he's the champ, he shouldn't do all that talking. He doesn't have to."

Well, Malcolm and I were both wrong. If Ali had stopped being brash and verbose, he would not have been Ali. Though I never understood his mouth as well as Ali did, that much I came to realize. Ali *had* to talk. That was the way his motor ran.

Trying to predict Ali, or telling him how to live, was an equal waste of time. When Ali made his first comeback, fought Joe Frazier in the first of their three epic battles, it was perhaps the most anticipated fight in history. Ali was returning from the ring after three years of hotly debated exile. He was a hero to an entire anti-war movement. He was fighting Joe Frazier, and that alone is enough said.

And the night before the fight, Ali did not go to sleep. I was with him most of that night. I kept suggesting he try and rest, kept talking only to myself. Ali was messing around all evening, not fucking, not drinking, but chattering, playing, being Ali. I'm not sure he had a choice: I've never seen him more adrenalized. The following day, Frazier beat him. However, I'm not convinced, had Ali been tucked in bed by nine, that he would have won that fight. Frazier was a savage fighter. No amount of sleep could do much about that.

Years later, before Ali's fight with George Chavalo, I hooked up with Bob Arum. Arum and

Don King now dominate boxing promotion; back then, Arum was still on the come. Arum and I wanted to form a company. Our company would handle all of Ali's fights, including the all-important ancillary rights. At that point in boxing history, fighters didn't understand ancillary rights, how lucrative they could be. Boxers received about ten percent, much, much too low. If Ali's people would work along with us, we could make history— for the first time ever blacks would televise heavyweight title fights, and the champion would receive his rightful cut. And Arum and I would be Major Players: in boxing, the heavyweight champ, the men who run his career, are the most influential forces in the industry.

It was decided that I should approach Ali. I called, Ali was amenable to the idea, told me to contact Herbert, his manager. Herbert was intrigued, set up a meeting. There were five of us: myself, Bob Arum, Michael Mallets, who would be our closed-circuit TV expert, Herbert Muhammad, the son of Elijah, and John Ali, the National Secretary of the Nation of Islam. It was an unlikely consortium.

But we put a company together, called it Main Bout. Then an odd thing happened. Here I was, the guy who put most of this deal together, a black man, and when talk began of percentages, Herb Muhammad wanted to cut me out! It took Arum and Mallets, two white guys, to say, "Herbert, look! This guy has value. He knows all the athletes. He knows the people that can promote these fights, televise them. And he's the guy who put us together in the first place!" Arum and Mallets won out—I was given ten percent of the company. We were ready to take on the industry.

History intervened. Ali announced he would not be inducted into the Army. He said his religious beliefs and his conscience would not allow him to fight in Vietnam. That was the end of Main Bout, my chance for boxing czardom. No Don King do for me.

There wasn't much time for regret. Ali's announcement, in the prime of his career, shocked and angered; quickly there was talk of recriminations. We all started scrambling. I called my teammate, John Wooten, our Executive Director of the Black Economic Union, told him to call a group of black athletes, ask them to come to Cleveland. Rumors were flying about why Ali "really" wouldn't fight in Vietnam. I wanted Ali to sit down with these athletes, explain his declaration. I knew Ali would need support, broader than what he had. By having a community of famous black athletes behind him, it would show the press, the public, Ali was backed by more than just the Muslims.

Before the meeting, I received a call from Herbert. He had been working, too. He said he had reason to believe that the United States government would make a deal with Ali, allow him to enter the Special Services, where he wouldn't have to go to war, could perhaps retain his title, continue boxing. Though Herbert was not a religious man, his father was the leader of the Nation of Islam. Herbert wanted *me* to broach the idea to Ali. But he wanted me to do it without telling Ali who I received my information from, or even that my information was concrete.

I said, "Damn, Herbert, this is a sticky one. But I'll try."

I didn't call off the meeting. Knowing Ali, I doubted strongly he would make a deal. I did call Ali, though, asked him to come to my home the night before the meeting. I raised the possibility of a deal with the government. Ali knocked me down.

Ali said, "Man, you know I believe in my religion. My religion says I'm not supposed to get in any wars and fight. I don't want any deals. I don't plan to fight nobody that hasn't done nothing to me, and I'm not goin' in any damn service."

I already knew that, but I wanted to hear Ali say it. I knew if Ali had a legal leg to stand on, it would be his religious beliefs.

The following morning we convened in my office. Along with several other black athletes, Bill Russell, Kareem Abdul-Jabbar, Willie Davis, and John Wooten had been brave enough to come to Cleveland, attend this controversial meeting. Though I knew Ali was not going into the Army, the other guys did not. They were there to hear him out, determine if he was sincere, whether they would support him. Unaware of Ali's intransigence, they were also there to raise questions and potential alternatives. Ali started preaching! He delivered a sermon on the Mother Ship, Elijah, the Nation of Islam. Despite the tension outside, it was funny as hell. Ali was in there with some of the top black athletes in America, whose intent was moderation and balance. But Ali was such a dazzling speaker, he damn near converted a few into the Nation of Islam. Guys were nodding their heads, going Hmmmm.

So much for the question of Ali's sincerity. Every man in the room was convinced. The reporters were waiting outside my office, so I said to the guys, "Look fellas, obviously the only reason Ali's not going into the service is based upon his religious beliefs. What we're going to tell the press is that there have been many rumors about Ali's reasons for not going into the service. We have just conducted a lengthy meeting with Ali, and what we've found out is that the man is not going into the service because of his religion. That's the only reason."

That was roughly our statement, issued right outside our office. There were photographs of all the famous athletes and it was weird how a portion of the press reported the story. In this unusual turn of events, they wrote, *even* Lew Alcindor is dealing with militants such as Jim Brown and Bill Russell. That was okay. While the story was new and volatile and confusing, we helped to clarify some points, and give Ali a broader coalition.

They stripped his crown anyway.

They stole it. Then they exiled him from the ring. They didn't know that Ali was larger than any ring. Ali is one of the bravest individuals I have ever known. They tested him, threatened him, denied him what he loved, yet he never gave in. Other than Jackie Robinson, has there ever been a sports figure more important than Ali? I believe Ali and Robert Kennedy lit the spark that became the firestorm that finally ended the war in Vietnam. And Ali gave fuel to the civil-rights movement, was a source of black pride, not only here but across the world.

Later, when Ali came back and earned millions, the white press wrote that the Muslims were exploiting Ali. Ali did *not* get exploited. Elijah Muhammad didn't even care about Ali's money. Elijah told Ali, "Look, son. I can get fifty cents from each of my people, and make more money than you'll ever make in the ring. That's not what I'm interested in. I'm interested in the way that you carry yourself, and the way you represent black people."

And that's exactly the way that Elijah felt. It's true that Elijah's son, Herbert, made a lot of money from Ali. But Herbert was one individual—even if someone wanted to, there was no one else who could use Ali. And in fact, Herbert was not exploiting Ali. Herbert earned millions off Ali because that's what fight managers do. Ali's relationship with Herbert was similar to the one Mike Tyson used to have with Bill Clayton and Jim Jacobs. They all received large percentages because they were there at the start, hustling and sweating to start their man's career.

I don't hear anyone saying Eddie Murphy is being exploited. That's because white folks run Eddie's career. Whenever black people are around black people, the white press says there's exploitation. Muhammad Ali was the pawn of no one. He chose two people to help him make certain decisions: Herbert Muhammad, and Angelo Dundee, who is white. And with the Nation of Islam, Ali received as much as he gave. I used to talk to Ali about it. Having the support of black people around the world was fantastic for him. I remember what Ali told Sonny Liston before their first fight.

Ali said, "You have a few fast people pulling for you. I have every Muslim in the world behind me. I have a family of power."

Ali was a man of the people and men of the people don't always look for money. Ali spent a lot of what he earned. He also gave a lot of money away, because he wanted to.

He was also, in one facet of his life, a hypocrite. When it came to sex, Ali was one of the biggest bullshitters on earth.

When Cassius Clay got tossed onto the fast track, he saw only green lights. It happens all the time, it happened with Ali. He had always liked women, but being heavyweight champion of the world allows a man to do certain things. Once Ali became champ, women knew he was champ, Ali went wild. This kid would give a girl who was not a hooker a hundred dollar bill, have some fun, he'd buy real prostitutes, he'd pretty much do anything. And the whole time he was lying to the public and his friends, saying he was pure. Pure? Ali was a superfreak.

Ali's greatest fascination in life was with gangsters and pimps, and other men who could control women. He always wanted to be known as a Mac Man, a bad brother who could rap to any chick.

Ali used to run with a man named Lloyd Wells. Leon Isaac Kennedy explained Lloyd's mystique to me.

Leon said, "Lloyd Wells without a doubt is the greatest finder of women who ever lived."

I thought, *If Leon the Lover is saying that, Lloyd*

must be serious. He was. Lloyd could do magic. Ali knew it, kept Lloyd around. Lloyd would have four rooms in a hotel, in each room would be a couple of chicks. He'd tell me, "Go down and get you some." And I would. And sometimes I'd run into Ali.

Ali was a sexual hypocrite, and a man of immense contradictions. Had another guy done some of the things Ali did, you'd say, "What kinda fuckin' guy is this?" Ali, though, would get that damn twinkle in his eye, and if you wanted to stay mad you couldn't even look at him. With Ali there was always the twinkle, and the whimsy. Above all, Ali was damn fun to be with, and when a man can make you laugh, you allow him to break many rules. It's probably why all of Ali's wives still like him.

Initially, I bought Ali's rap. He blew so much smoke up my ass, I should have climbed on a table, given him a better angle. That time in Miami, Ali was training for the fight with Sonny Liston, he told me he'd been celibate for one year.

I said, "No! You been celibate for a year?"

Ali said, "Yeah. Because of my religion, I've been celibate. Gonna stay that way, too."

I accepted that, even more so when he passed on that party at the Fontainebleau. Being a sexual creature, I was deeply impressed by the depth of his devotion. I ran back to John Wooten and the other brothers on the Browns.

I said, "Fellas, that Ali is incredible. He's a fighter man, got all those pretty girls around, but he's celibate, because he believes in his religion. He hasn't screwed around for one year!"

The guys were shaking their head in admiration. One guy said, "Man, that's fantastic."

Three weeks later, our season over, I went to meet Ali in New York. I went to his hotel room, he had just been with three women.

After that, when Ali talked about sex, I didn't take him real seriously. No matter what he'd say the weeks before a fight, when he was feeling all spartan and mean, after every fight, he'd have four, five, six, seven naked women up in his suite, and he loved it. He might screw five women, move from room to room. Ali started earning a reputation, and not just for being prolific. Ferdi Pacheco, now The Fight Doctor, used to be Ali's personal physician. Ferdi came out one day, said Ali had just done the ugliest girl that ever walked. And it was probably accurate. Ali would screw the finest chicks, and the most ridiculous. We'd laugh at him, he didn't care. He thought *he* was so damn pretty, what the chicks looked like didn't matter.

It got to the point where I didn't want to party with him much. His girls might be beauties, might be beasts. When Ali fought Buster Mathis in Houston, I came in for the fight, as I always did. After Ali beat Mathis, his people started calling me, saying Ali wanted me. Ali always liked to party with me after his fights, but I didn't want to go, and they talked me into it, said Ali had been looking all over for me.

I said, "OK, OK, I'll go."

I got to the suite, opened the door, saw about six bogus-looking chicks, all naked.

"JIM! Come on in!"

It was Ali. He said, "Come on, man. We're gonna party!"

I smiled at the girls. Smiled at Ali. Snapped my fingers. "Damn Ali! This is some *great* shit you got here. But hold the phone a minute—I forgot something. I'll be right back. Don't let nothing go! Be right back!"

The rest of the night they tried, but they couldn't find me.

When Ali was young his mind was quick as silver. People would sit around, listen to him talk—the kid talked *fast*—and be astonished at his inventions. Sometimes he'd disappear for an hour, come back with a whole new rap. One day he started calling Howard Cosell "The Greatest Mouth of All Time." I'm not sure if that was before or after he yanked off Howard's toupee on national TV. The week of a fight in Vegas, Ali decided he would have multiple wives. The Muslim can do that, he explained. Ali was with two of his former wives, and his spouse for the moment. He was calling all of them his wife. He had *three* of them.

In that great voice, Ali said, "Look at me, Jim, look at me. I have three wives. Am I bad, am I bad?"

I said, "Man, leave me out of that, Ali."

Ali actually carried it off for awhile, though not a long while.

When I was in London filming *The Dirty Dozen,* I was sharing a flat with Danni Sheraton, my girlfriend from England. Ali flew out to visit with Herbert Muhammad and John Ali. One night Danni had several fine girlfriends up in our flat, and here come the Muslims, who supposedly don't dance, and, according to them, definitely don't mess with any white girls. Ali took one look at Danni's friends, started partying hard. So did Herbert. And so did John. I laughed until I cried. There was no animosity in that suite. Those brothers got flexible, quickly.

I pulled Ali to the side. I said, "Ali, I thought you didn't fool around with white girls."

Ali said, "Well, Jim, Elijah taught us that it's only the German white people and the American white people who are bad. These English folks are all right!"

It was true that Ali loved it in England. Because they loved him. They simply had no bias toward the man. But even when I returned to the States, Ali was dating an Italian girl.

I said, "Damn Ali! You're always preaching to your brothers, don't mess with any white girls, and here you are messing with this girl."

He said, "Jim, you know Italians aren't white."

He always had a perfect line, and he loved the hell out of people, so Ali got away with murder. Because Ali had another habit: He would mess with everybody's women. A friend of mine would bring around his lady, Ali would joke with her, kid her, pull her in a back room and start feeling on her. It would embarrass the shit out of me. Guys would look at me like, Hey, nice buddy you got there.

When Ali was training for his fight with George Foreman, he set up camp in the hills of Pennsylvania. I was sent there by ABC to interview Ali, Foreman, for a prime time special. There was a girl in Philadelphia who I was crazy for. Her name was Diane and we were actually engaged. I invited

Diane to join me at camp, but before she arrived I decided I'd better talk to Ali.

I said, "Look man, I don't care what you do with everybody else. But my woman's coming up here, so I'm telling you beforehand. Don't fuck with her, or I will kick your natural ass."

Ali said, "No way, Jim, no way."

Then he started joking. But I was being real. If Ali even started with Diane, we would have gone to war. Now the average person would wonder, "How could Jim Brown kick Muhammad Ali's ass?" See, Ali was extremely bright about people. He was a champion, and champions can read people. Ali would look at a fighter, gauge his technique, also his mindset, and he'd sense, no, he would know, how to fight him. In the ring Ali was a master.

Yet on the sidewalk, even Ali was vulnerable. Ali knew me. He knew I was stronger than him—he was always wrestling with me, testing his strength, seeing if it had increased since the last time we'd been together—and he knew I had no fear of him. Ali also knew I loved him, and when you betray someone who loves you, *you* become weak. That's a mighty combination and Ali knew he'd better not mess with Diane, and he didn't.

Ali was always trying to get me to put on the gloves with him. One day he came by my house with Angelo Dundee, who I love very much. In fact, if there was a pair of guys I could hang out with Monday through Saturday, still want to see them Sunday, it was Angelo and Ali. This time Ali brought me a gift—two pairs of Muhammad Ali boxing gloves. Three of my kids were there, Kim and Kevin and little Jimmy. I knew why Ali brought the gloves, saw his eyes sparkle, figured okay. I'm not really a boxer, but I always felt Ali's style was reasonably conducive to my personal safety. Ali would play with you, taunt you, so I figured I wouldn't get tagged too often, or too hard. On the other hand, I wouldn't get near a pair of gloves around Joe Frazier or George Foreman. They would crowd me and maul me, be hunting for my head.

I looked at Ali holding the gloves. I looked at my kids. I said to Ali, "Hell, since my kids are here, I'll put the gloves on now, kick your ass right here on my balcony."

Ali smiled and laughed, he was happy as a dog. Angelo and my kids started grinning, too. We all walked outside to the balcony, over on the concrete next to the pool, me and Ali put on the gloves. He started dancing, teasing me. He'd cuff me a little bit, I'd swing and miss, he'd wink. After a while I got tired, slowed down.

Ali said, "Come on, come on, don't stop, don't stop."

Flick, he'd jab me, I'd swing and he'd duck. Ali didn't want to hurt me, just show me how tired I would get, and then, after I was tired, how he would move in and whip me to death.

When we were done, Ali said, "See, Jim, this is what I do to my opponents. I play with them, frustrate them, they get tired, then I wipe them out."

It was a good experience and he definitely proved a point. In the ring Ali would have diced me up.

Bob Arum wanted me to fight Ali anyway. Before Main Bout fell apart, Arum was searching for gimmicks, thought Ali and Jim Brown fit that bill. That went nowhere, but then we got the idea for Ali to fight Wilt Chamberlain. We even had a contract. Cus D'Amato was going to train Wilt, I was going to leave Main Bout and be Wilt's manager. We put the deal together in a motel across the street from the old Madison Square Garden. Then Herbert, Ali's manager, met Wilt in person. Wilt is seven-something, weighed about 290 at the time. Herbert gazed up at Wilt.

He said, "Wait a minute. Ali'd have to be jumping up to hit this sucker in the jaw. No way."

Herbert called off the fight. Didn't want his man Ali in the ring with big Wilt.

I felt the same way when Ali announced he was fighting George Foreman. As an athlete and a boxer, Ali was extraordinary. In the ring, I saw something in Ali that was almost inhuman. I have seen Ali with terrible fear, and within ten seconds, something inside him would trigger, he'd be as brave as a goddamn warrior. I also felt Ali had a covenant with God. Ali would be in a fight, no hope of winning, he'd sneak in a blow, *something* sudden would happen, Ali would triumph. It seemed he was protected.

Against Foreman, none of that mattered to me. I thought Ali had NO chance. Joe Frazier was a bitch, and Foreman made him look like a pigeon. When George knocked Frazier sideways, that famous killer punch, Joe did a dance that defied the force of gravity.

Originally, for that ABC special I was supposed to get in the ring with both fighters, do some sparring. I went to Foreman's camp first, did his part of my segment. I walked into George's camp the first day, saw him hit the big bag. And BOOM! I was watching and he almost broke my rib. I told the ABC guys *they* should spar with Foreman.

The week of the fight I flew to Zaire. David Frost and I were doing one of the broadcasts. Foreman came walking in one day. With him was a huge entourage, including Archie Moore, his trainer, and Daggo, his enormous police dog. George was wearing jeans and coveralls, looking all business. Though we were friends, he would barely speak to me. He was too intense on Ali, how he would kill him.

Ali was everywhere, talking, trying to do a Sonny Liston on Foreman. George knew what Ali was doing, and it appeared to have no effect. One morning, Ali asked me who I thought was going to win. He was with Angelo.

I said, "Man, I'm sorry, you know I love you. But no one can whip that big sucker. You can't beat him."

Ali said, "Don't worry. I'm gonna show you."

Angelo said, "Jim, Ali will knock Foreman out."

Angelo is one of my favorite people. I gave Angelo a lot of credit for Ali's success, but not for the same reason most people did. Everyone talked about his ring tactics. I thought Angelo's premier gift to Ali was the nature of his friendship. Angelo knew when to mind his own business, and when to stand up to Ali. He could hang out with Muslims, and be respected. He's the *only* white man who got along with the Muslims. Angelo liked everyone, everyone liked him. And I'll never forget the fight against Liston, Angelo exhorting Ali back into the ring, cajoling, refusing to let him quit, until the young man had overcome.

Again, it didn't matter. When Angelo said Ali would knock out Foreman, I thought it was the most absurd shit I'd ever heard in my life.

I told Ali, "Take care of yourself!"

Ali thought that was funny.

The fight began. I was right there, ringside with David Frost. Ali started dancing, Foreman was launching missiles, Ali began the rope a dope. Later, everyone said Angelo loosened the ropes before the fight. He didn't, the ropes were just loose. Angelo did not want Ali on the ropes. That was all Ali.

After the second round, Ali came over to me and Frost.

He said, "See Jim? I'm gonna get this mother-fucker."

Frost was aghast, also in heaven.

I said, "My God, this man is bold."

Also incredibly shrewd. While Ali played on the ropes, Foreman kept firing blows. Guess what happened next? Precisely. George started getting tired. He had stamina, but all those big punches stole it. Ali would duck and move, just enough to keep his block on, George would keep unloading. Even when Foreman got leg weary, he kept chasing Ali like he was still the big bad gorilla. Only now George was throwing harmless roundhouse punches, and he wasn't even thinking about his defense. I said to myself, *Son of a bitch. Ali's gonna do it.* And he did. Ali caught George leaning, knocked that hulk out. It was, however, a pretty quick count.

After the fight, I headed toward Ali's dressing room. I wanted to congratulate Ali, tell him I'd been dead wrong. When I arrived at Ali's dressing room, every square foot was occupied, and not only with Muslims and celebrities and women: *George's* entourage was in there. I knifed through the zoo, finally discovered Ali.

I said, "Ali, you were right. You did it."

Ali smiled. "Told you, Jim. You see now?"

I laughed.

Ali said, "Hey, man, it's cool."

That's how Ali was. He never took that kind of thing badly. If he knew you were being honest, he would just laugh at you.

I gave Ali a hug, went to find George. There were three living beings in that dressing room: George, Archie Moore and Daggo the dog. Everyone else had deserted him. Foreman was staring into the mirror. He was looking at his face, fingering the bumps and contusions, as if it wasn't his face at all. He was in shock. He didn't understand what had just happened. I knew Ali was cool, figured I would stick by George, see if I could give him some kind of comfort. We went up to George's suite. Before that, you couldn't *get* in that suite. Now the thing was empty. Archie Moore had to go somewhere, leaving me, George and Daggo. George had "What's Going On," the classic album by Marvin Gaye, and I put it on. We were silent, listening to Marvin, when the phone rang. It was long distance from Jim Marshall. Jim Marshall, who played for the Minnesota Vikings. Jim is a sweet human being, and having played in all those Super Bowls and lost, he understood how low George would be. Jim told George he had been there himself, and that George was a great, great fighter. One loss could not erase that.

Jim must have said it as well as it could be said; when George hung up his spirit was returning. I hung with George for another hour, then I thought that he might want to be alone.

I said, "George, I know you're gonna be going through a lot of things. If you ever need any help, give me a call."

George said he would call, and a few months later he did. And with a guy named Jerry Parruchio, we helped George work his mind and his body back into boxing. I also helped him out of a scrape with his woman. Her name was Erma Compton, a fireball of a lady. She and George had had a few fights, Erma was about to put him in jail. George asked me to call her. I called Erma, said I was Jim Brown, and would like to talk to her about George.

Erma said, "Who the fuck is Jim Brown?"

Duly impressed, she hung up on me. Erma called me back later, and she and George got their thing straightened out.

But this isn't George's story. It's Ali's. After I said good-bye, left George and Daggo with their thoughts, I decided not to join Ali. His suite would be jammed, I wasn't in that mood. I would catch Ali the next afternoon before he left Zaire. I walked into the African night, alone, grinning, thinking about my friend Muhammad Ali.

16

FAME, IN CONTEXT

BACK WHEN I WAS a Glamorous Film Star, I went down to Acapulco to shoot a movie. The producers put me up in a private home over the bay, and the estate had ten servants. For about an hour I was bored out of my mind. I was looking at the servants, the servants were looking at me. I called the producers.

I said, "This house is very nice, but where I'd really like to be is where the party is. Over on the beach."

It was spring break and the strip of hotels along the beach was teeming with stress-avoiding college coeds. The producers complied, booked me a suite in the Holiday Inn, right above the sand.

Walked down the first day, met a gorgeous girl. She went to school at Texas, had just been crowned Miss something or other. She and I became lovers. One afternoon I was lying on the beach with her, surrounded by several of her college girlfriends, thinking, *I'm with all these pretty girls, making a movie, got my own suite, got lots of money—Brother, I am swinging.* If I wasn't the baddest cat in Acapulco, I knew I was close.

I got Montezuma's Revenge.

I'm about to throw up, have a bowel movement, it's hot outside and I'm shivering. Now I have to try and escape without losing my composure, blowing it in front of all these girls. I excuse myself, walk quickly but not too quickly back to my hotel. I'm in the elevator, doubled over, sweat on my face, hands on my knees, praying, Please, just let me hold it all in.

A tourist behind me says, "Hey, isn't that Jim Brown? Look, he's practicing his football stance."

I said, "GODDAMN!"

Elevator opened, I hit the door of my room, my insides exploded. It was the sickest I've ever been. I felt that I might die.

That story illustrates one of my beliefs: life is not spelled out in capital letters. You have to check the fine print. Have to be careful not to get too cocky, think you have it All Figured Out.

The time I went to Zaire to see Foreman fight Ali, I was extremely excited. Gonna spend some time with my black brothers. Gonna relate. When I arrived in Zaire everyone spoke French. Black brothers? I was with dudes who'd been colonized by the French, whose culture was practically

French. Had I gone to Zaire with Mike Ditka, we'd have had much more in common than I did with the people of Zaire.

If I ever met Bobby Knight, my friend Bill Russell told me, I would like him. Though it's uncanny how often Russ and I agree on people, I thought this time we might have to agree to disagree. I thought Knight would be arrogant and intolerant. Eventually I met Bobby at a function. He was gentle and thoughtful and considerate, I liked him very much. I realized I'd sold the man short, from items I'd read, from watching him a couple hours on the Saturday tube. Reminded myself that that isn't fair, or intelligent. Sometimes imagery hides what's inside.

I'm famous, or infamous, about nineteen different ways. My close friends read stories about me, can't believe it's the same person. Same thing happens to me. I'll read a story, the writer is positive he's got me down cold, and I can barely recognize the man he's discussing. It's an odd feeling that you really have to experience to fully appreciate.

A fact of life, when dealing with the press, is that it will tell people what it wants to, when it has time to, and leave the rest out. As a result, often the reporting is vastly oversimplified: you're either Jack Armstrong or Jack the Ripper. I don't think it's a good practice, but I accept it, because there's not a damn thing I can do about it. And I laugh when I hear people say they're declaring war on the press. They may as well declare war on the IRS, or the phone company. In America, the media is God. The press brought down Richard Nixon, one of the strongest presidents we've ever had, insulated by one of the toughest groups of SOBs. It doesn't matter who you are. The media will KICK YOUR ASS.

You can't wage war on the media, and you shouldn't. The media is the safeguard of America. Lot of them are bastards, but I'd rather have those bastards than no media. Without the press, the bureaucracy would run wild and unchecked, even more, much more, than the way it does now. I'm not all for the press, but I'm certainly not all against it.

If you're famous, the media is there to exploit you. If you're smart, you can use *it*. You have to know the rules, play by them. You don't call a press conference when you have nothing to say, or when you're echoing what everyone else is saying. Writers hate that, will think you're crying wolf the next time. You don't call press conferences about rehabilitation of prisoners; the press isn't interested, neither are the readers. You call a conference when you have something new, or newsworthy, to contribute.

The power of the media in the shaping of public perception is awesome. The public can't do the research, takes the quick fix. It can get confusing: whether it's sports or a presidential election, the Conventional Wisdom can't make up its mind. Sam Huff went from demon linebacker to average to press-elected Hall of Famer. Bill Walsh began as Genius, evolved to Playoff Choke Artist, went back to Genius. Does a man really change that much over that length of time?

I have excellent interviews, and moronic ones.

There are brilliant writers and doorknobs. With the dumb writers I don't even have to be in the room—they're not listening anyway. They come in the door, start telling me all about me, though they've never been around me, didn't call anyone who knows me. But they have perused the clips, many of which were written by other guys who scanned the clips. Now, if I say anything that doesn't jibe with their preconceived notions, the head flips on to automatic nod, the eyes go vacant. They don't want me to be a three-dimensional person. It messes up their two-dimensional angle, and then they have to do more work.

I love good conversation, never shied from debate, and I enjoy sitting down with an intelligent writer. I've had many friends who were writers, I respect the power of the written word. Smart writers don't walk in the door, ask me if I'm greater than Walter Payton. They know if they don't try and force me into corners, I'll respond to *them*, and they'll get much richer stuff, might even get something controversial. Even if they don't, they're equipped to write about human beings, not just caricatures, and they don't need ten pounds of dirt to write a compelling story. They might not come down on my side, but they'll allow me to have one. They won't ignore facts to support their own bias.

I think image is a fascinating topic, especially in America, where image is supreme. You know, by not pretending to be a goody-goody, it's actually been easier on me, because people don't like to think they've been played for the fool. And in a sense, I've beaten the game. For all my notoriety, without kissing much ass, I'm still accepted in respectable circles. I still speak to religious groups, and to children. Generally, in the ghetto, people like me a lot. The ghetto doesn't buy into much it can't learn for itself. People in the ghetto know how the police are, how the press is, because they *always* get the shit.

Now take a guy like Lionel Ritchie. I don't even see how he has the nerve to walk down a street. He painted this beautiful facade—white bread, button-down family man. Then his wife came to the home of Lionel's girlfriend, beat up the girl, and Lionel ran away. He was caught living a lie. To me, a guy like that now looks absurd, would probably want to hide his head.

You can believe this or not, makes no difference to me: there are many, many famous guys, with images one hundred times cleaner than mine, who do not live up to their public face. Guys like Dr. J, the Juice, up until recently Steve Garvey, have all been perceived as Goody-Goody, but behind the image is simply another guy who isn't straight. I don't know *one* cat who is straight, and I know a lot of guys. Behind closed doors, *everyone* is human.

Complicating matters of image is the nature of our society. In America, the issue of race always lurks, even when it is not apparent. Blatant racial prejudice usually surfaces behind closed doors; for public consumption, prejudice is often discreet and inbred. The American press is essentially white, and it largely determines which black athletes are Nice Guys. The criteria aren't too heavy. Though there are exceptions, this is the general rule: If a black guy doesn't say anything negative about white folks, he's a Nice Guy. If he's congenial or happy-go-lucky he's a Nice Guy. If he has a serious manner, does not court popularity, or is politically outspoken, he's sullen or cocky or a militant. The first black guy does not have an image problem, the second one does.

Isiah Thomas caused a stir when he suggested that Larry Bird was overrated, had become a superstar not so much for his game, but because he was white, and the media magnified his value. I think Isiah used poor judgment, discussing a subject so volatile at a moment when he was still emotional and frustrated, having made a huge error on the court a few days before, contributing to his team blowing a chance at the NBA title. A passionate heart is fine, but race is best discussed with a cool head.

Even though Isiah's thoughts were not all well-stated, there was truth to some of his remarks, particularly when he spoke about racial stereotypes. Many commentators *do* depict white athletes as intelligent and dedicated—hard workers—while black guys are natural phenoms, who, to paraphrase Isiah, only run and jump, never practice or give a thought to the way they play, as if they came dribbling out of their mother's wombs. Sometimes that sentiment is subtle, but you still hear the echoes.

As for Larry Bird, I think he's a superb ballplayer. I'm a sportsman, and Larry's style suits me. I knew Larry would be an NBA star when I saw him at Indiana State in a tournament game against Arkansas, and Larry was doing it to Sidney Moncrief and Marvin Delph and Ron Brewer. Even though

Sidney held him down at the end, I could see Larry was special. I love the NBA, and I was delighted when Larry came in. Before that the league was reeling. Ratings were done, there were hardly any games on TV. When Larry and Magic came in, I thought Larry was much more crucial to the NBA's revival. The league was so dominated by blacks athletes, had Larry not arrived when he did, I'm not sure white folks would have stuck with the NBA. Larry came in white, and playing his ass off. He had the right talent, had the right color. Larry Bird gave white folks someone to cheer for, and hope that there would be more white stars to follow.

So it isn't that Larry doesn't do it on the court. He does. If Larry was black, Hispanic, or Apache, he would not be "just another ballplayer." But he will get better press, more credit, than if he were in a minority. Not because Larry wants it. Because white America wants it.

I've done some commentating myself. I enjoy it, but I don't get a lot of work. They'll call me when they want something different, which means they don't call me much. I'm direct and outspoken, on TV that is frowned upon. Sometimes I have to smile when I'm in the booth: these announcers make football sound as if it's so goddamn deep. TV pays a lot of money, these guys feel they have to say *something*. What's scientific about Ronnie Lott knocking the shit out of you? Hell, a lot of what you see on Sundays is dumb luck, guys blowing assignments, those mistakes leading to TDs. There's nothing "mastermind" about it.

They bring me in as an expert, so I'll contradict another announcer if I think he's being silly or overly general. I study body language, I can tell when a cat is all-out, or when he's distracted, and how it translates to his performance. TV doesn't prefer that brand of reality. If a guy is over the hill, they want you to say he had a Wonderful Career. Well, sure, but now he's over the hill.

Do the networks censure you? Yeah. They don't hire you. One time I was fired by CBS. Bob Stenner, wonderful producer, lovely man, had finally talked CBS into hiring me despite its protests that I was too controversial. Stenner teamed me with George Allen and Vin Scully. George and I were honest and uninhibited, Vin was simply superb. In no time at all we were No. 2 at CBS, behind Pat Summerall and Tom Brookshier. We were sailing.

One Sunday, Brent Musburger and Jimmy the Greek were doing their thing in the studio. Greek was talking about Earl Campbell, who was having a superlative year.

The Greek said, "You know, Earl Campbell is the best of all time."

Earl had played maybe three years.

Musburger seized the opportunity. He said, "Greek, do you really think Earl's the best ever? Even better than Jim Brown?"

Greek said, "No doubt about it. He's better than Jim Brown. The best of all time."

That was fair enough. The Greek is entitled to his premature opinion. Then Musburger got this smart idea: next week, I'd open the show, right at the top, and Brent would ask me what I thought about Greek's statement. Stenner told me Brent's plan, asked me what I was going to say. I told Bob I'd think of something.

I started thinking: *It's okay for the Greek and Brent to say that stuff. But why bring it to me? So I can say something that will piss everybody off? Make Earl Campbell feel bad, when Earl and I are perfectly cool? They bring that junk to me, they're gonna have to deal with my answer. And I will PUT something on their butts.*

Lights. Camera. Brent.

He said, "Well Jim, you heard Jimmy the Greek say Earl Campbell's the best runner in the history of the NFL. What do you have to say about that?"

Give or take a few words, I said, "Mus, America's a great country. I should be up here talking about Earl Campbell, but now I have to talk about Jimmy the Greek. Okay. Earl Campbell is a graduate of the University of Texas. Known for greatness on the field, and goodness off it. Might have had the most productive rookie season in history. Whether or not he'll become the No. 2 rusher in NFL history, only O.J. Simpson will say. Now you want me to talk about Jimmy the Greek. Graduate from the University of Caesar's Palace. Known for gossip and gambling. Whether or not he'll go down in history, only Mr. Rozelle and the networks can say. Because it's interesting, Brent. Mr. Rozelle and the networks have told all of us who work in the NFL, that at no time should we ever associate with known gamblers. Evidently, Mr. Rozelle and the the people at the networks are not men of their word. Back to you, Brent."

Boy! Those mothers didn't know *what* to say to that. Brent, I know it's astounding, went totally silent. The studio was quieter than that. How was that for live TV?

My ass was finished. CBS called Ed Hookstratten, then my agent, chewed his proverbial ears off. Asked Ed WHAT the hell I thought I was doing. But CBS didn't know how to fire me, so they waited until the end of the season, never said a word about the incident, then let me go. I was sorry I lost the job, happy I said what I did. I thought it was a hell of a way to open the show. I knew I confused some people, they had no idea what I meant, but I knew there was also an audience that knew exactly what I was saying, and that what I was saying held a lot of truth.

Jimmy's the biggest gambler in the world, talking spreads on national TV! Besides gambling, Jimmy has nothing to do with football. I didn't see why I should let him, and Brent, bait me into messing up a good relationship with Earl Campbell. Which is why, at times, the press and athletes are almost enemies. When I was playing football I never gathered my teammates, said, "Fellas, I got to know. Am I better than Jimmy Taylor?" What we talked about was busting the Packers. Athletes don't sit around and talk about Who's the Best. That's that way that laymen think. Laymen ask me, Is the caliber of play higher now or in the old days? I don't know. A million circumstances have changed. The rules have changed. The hashmarks have changed. I might say the NFL today is not as violent, much more commercialized, the In the Grasp Rule should be taken behind the barn and shot. I might say the guys today run faster 40s, can lift more weights, better understand business. But

I can't conclude which is superior. Walter Payton, with all that heart, would have been a monster in 1958. The old Green Bay Packers would still dominate today. And so would I.

I'll tell you how most "feuds" between athletes get started. Guys get sucked into them by the media, as Brent and the Greek attempted with me. The media will set up a challenge, ask each guy to respond. They know how proud athletes are, know if they load their questions properly, most guys will respond. If you do reply, you have one of two choices: either defend yourself, or put yourself down. If you defend yourself, you're bound to say something negative about the other guy. That's what goes in the paper. The other guy reads it, takes a poke at you, or else he says it off the record, and the *writer* says it. The result? Now Walter doesn't feel good, I don't feel good, Earl doesn't feel good. Why should we all feel bad about discussing our careers? We kicked ass. We should feel great.

That time with the Greek I was able to turn the tables. Why comment at all? Non-participation is no good either. Without the press, no one would ever hear of athletes. The press isn't perfect, but it's part of our lives, part of my life. Sometimes you want to talk about things, but you want your words to appear in context. I might talk to a guy for forty minutes, two sentences, uttered fifteen minutes apart, are printed in the paper. Or the words that leave my mouth are not the words that are printed, but my words rewritten in the writer's words. Good writers are meticulous, bad ones don't give a dash. Sometimes it isn't the writer's fault at all. I've seen athletes scream at reporters for asinine headlines, and reporters have nothing to do with writing headlines. Even on the quotes, maybe the first guy got it right, but by the time it goes through the editors it's diluted or cut—it's changed. If the publication has a gossip mentality anything can happen. "Jim Brown said Walter Payton can't run." I might have said Walter can't run with a broken leg.

When I was still playing, we once had a road game against the Dallas Cowboys. Texas Stadium, Texas sun—I had a football headache, and I was irritable and tired. Late in the game I took the ball and broke into the secondary. Runners like myself, the Juice, Gale Sayers, when we'd hit the secondary our computers would turn on. "If I accelerate, *he* can't get me; *that* guy, racing at me, too zealous, I'll slow, cut under; my blocker will shield that final safety."

Flash, we'd know our route to the goal line.

On this run there was one Cowboy left. Don Bishop. I saw his position relative to me and the goal line. I knew he couldn't stop me, and I was weak. So I actually slowed down, stuck out my straight arm, just held it there, toyed with him on into the end zone. I relaxed, Bishop didn't. He was so pissed that I took him lightly, he grabbed my arm, slung me right up against the wall. Whew! I was startled, sitting against this wall like a little kid. John Wooten and a couple of my linemen rushed up. They were all excited.

"Hey man! You tied your own record! Let's break it!"

It seemed I had a couple hundred yards, some

319

change, had a chance to break the NFL single-game record, which I still owned.

I said, "Man, I don't want no damn record. I'm tired! We got the game. Let's get outta this hot-ass place!"

In a nutshell, that was my attitude toward records my entire career. First, there were no records to break except my own. Either way I didn't care. What mattered to me was my performance, and the Cleveland Browns winning. If I wanted numbers, I'd not have quit when I did.

When I retired, people asked me about my rushing record, how I felt about Walter breaking it, I said a lot of nice things about Walter. I meant them. I like Walter. I also said Walter's record will not be the same one I had. Any ballplayer knows that when you go from twelve games to fourteen games to sixteen, the equation is thrown entirely off. It's like giving one guy three strikes in baseball, and another guy four. Give me those extra strikes, I can do anything.

When people would ask me about thousand-yard seasons, or I would volunteer the information, I said thousand-yard seasons stopped having meaning back when I played, when they switched in 1961 to fourteen-game seasons. For a quality back, gaining a thousand yards in fourteen games is like walking backwards, too simple to be relevant. Gaining a thousand yards in a sixteen-game season isn't even worth discussing.

My critics threw a goddamn party. They said, Look now he's *embracing* statistics.

Hold it. I never had a blanket dislike of the numerical system. I felt statistics neglected the human spirit, and that people used statistics to reinforce hoary old cliches, which offended my individuality. And if you are insisting on emphasizing stats over performance, you should temper them with some common sense.

When people said Are you the Greatest, Is he the Greatest? if I pointed to my performance, people said I was jealous. Obviously those people who said I was jealous never saw me play football. For the record, I have never been jealous of another runner. I respect ability, and I've never had an argument with another runner over his ability. The only argument I've ever had is with the media's interpretation of that ability. And this debate is not new. People have challenged my standard since day one. Jimmy Taylor, The Juice, Earl Campbell were all "better" than me at one time. Then the media forgets them. They don't talk about Earl much anymore, don't talk a lot about Jimmy. They talk a little bit about O.J. What happened to these guys in the minds of reporters? I talk about these guys more than the press does.

I used to care about my NFL legacy. Now, they've tried so hard to take something away, they've kind of messed it up for me. Those who cared about my performance, understood it, fantastic. The opinions I care most about are those of my opponents. If those guys want to say nice things about me I will listen, and I will be appreciative. Those who don't understand what I did, that's okay. I'm talking about certain things now because I can put them in context. But this will probably be the last time I participate, the last time I wear my career as a badge. It isn't fair for me to keep reminding the guys today of what I did.

I don't know who the Greatest Runner was, but I know this: when Walter came along, some said he was, the press came to me, asked if I agreed.

Seems to me when the king is dethroned, there is no question. It's absolute. You have a new king, you don't go back to the old one, get a quote.

Spending nine years in the NFL spotlight, I was sometimes noted for my blocking. People noted that I wasn't very good at it.

Truth is, I didn't like to block, and I was not a consistent blocker. To excel, I didn't concentrate hard enough on blocking. That was the result of a judgment I made. I could run the ball with anyone, catch the ball with anyone. To maintain that level of performance, the ferocious concentration it demanded, I decided I had better set some priorities. I knew an athlete could be pretty good at everything, but not excellent at everything. I chose to lock in on running the football, and catching the football. Maybe my blocking suffered in the process.

The professional athlete who masters every aspect of his craft is a sports myth, one of many. One of the shrewdest, funniest most honest sports articles I've ever read was by Jim Murray, the exemplary columnist for the *Los Angeles Times*. Mr. Murray was exploring and exposing cliches. He wrote about the so-called Team Player, who goes 0 for 4 in baseball, pretends to be thrilled because his team won, goes home and kicks the shit out of his cat. It's truthful in any sport. Every athlete wants his team to win, but he also wants to feel good about his own contribution. If he stunk the place up, or didn't get to fully participate, he can't be *that* happy. When the Chicago Bears killed New England in the Super Bowl, afterwards Walter Payton was visibly upset. In the only Super Bowl of his career, Walter felt he should have played a larger role. I saw it as a positive. That level of pride made Walter a champion, and it lifted the Bears. As Mr. Murray put it, "Team play doesn't win pennants. Three-run homers do."

As for football, it's the age of the specialist, including many runners. But no running back, now or ever, has carried the ball twenty-five to thirty times a game and also done a lot of blocking. Not even Walter. I used to see the same clip of Walter over and over, the one where he picks up the blitz, saves the sack, and people would say Walter was a "great blocker." Walter was a strong blocker, but not very often. Usually Walter had the ball.

So did I. Moreover, my priorities were not set in a vacuum. My coaches had more to do with my priorities than they ever admitted to. I played pro football when the running game was dominant. My coaches wanted me to dominate our offense. They never said it, didn't have to—they gave me the football. For nine years they kept giving me the football. Had they given me a lot of blocking assignments, I would have shifted my emphasis. They didn't. When we ran, I was the one who usually took the ball. When we passed, and we didn't pass much until Blanton Collier, I was mostly assigned to drift to the flat. When I did that against the Giants, Sam Huff said they changed their entire philosophy. They would concede the wide receiver on my side the little turn-in, concentrate on me in the flat. My only point is, even if I didn't get the ball, I'd take at least one, often a few of their guys out of the play.

Sometimes I did throw effective blocks. At times I didn't concentrate and my blocking was poor. Sometimes I wish that I could go back, improve that aspect of my game, but I'll have to live with what I do, and if people want to point to my blocking as a weak point they certainly have that right.

They also have the right to ask me for my autograph. One favor: don't ask me when I'm with Bill Russell. Russ doesn't sign autographs. He doesn't like the process or the premise, finds it highly impersonal. He'll shake your hand, look you in the eye, and say, "Pleased to meet you." But he doesn't sign. I do sign, and that's where the problem comes in. If people ask me first, I say yes and I sign. They ask Bill, he says, "No, but I'll shake your hand." The people get uneasy. Then I feel uneasy. Maybe, I think, I should not have signed either, because now I'm being a traitor to Bill, making Bill look bad, when in fact I agree with his basic philosophy. And *that* makes me feel that maybe I'm a phony. While I'm experiencing all these odd feelings, sometimes a person will ask me to try and get Bill's autograph for him. I always say, "Well, I think you should probably ask him." I don't want to say, "No, he doesn't sign. Russ is more pure than I am." Then they'll really get screwed up.

I'm not sure why I sign autographs. It's definitely not to satisfy my ego. Often signing makes me feel low. People sometimes are so insensitive, they don't even look at me, not really, don't say hello the nice way. They throw the paper *at* me. Everyone's crowding: "Get mine! Get mine!"

I'll tell people, "Okay, stand back. Don't put the papers in my face. I'll sign all of them."

That will normally control them, but there will always be one guy who still insists on getting his first. I sign, the instant the ink is on the paper, he rushes off. He wants to take the paper somewhere else, tell someone he's met me, when he hasn't really met me. We have had no human connection. And at times signing depresses me. I can be surrounded by a crowd of people, feel more alone than if I was miles away sitting by myself.

I like to sign autographs when it's for a kid, his little face is so shy and sincere, and I feel that. Sometimes a little boy will come up with my football card, that his dad held on to. That's very nice. I also like it when I'm signing for a group, everyone leaves, and one person, who has waited, gets the nerve to walk up to me, then says, "I don't want an autograph. I just wanted you to know I really enjoyed watching you play. I appreciate what you did."

I literally get chills. Now I want to follow this person, sit down with him. I'll say, "Hey, you really saw that game? You enjoyed it?" We'll talk about a couple games, I'll tell him about a Nitschke or a Unitas, and it's a sweet moment. We say good-bye and we both feel good.

Elvis Presley was a wonderful fan. Elvis knew football and he loved football. I met Elvis, then he invited me to Graceland. Not surprisingly, I wanted to talk about music, he wanted to talk about football. Elvis said he didn't just read the papers, he'd watch football games on TV, go in person, and pay strict attention. He was a fan of mine, and he started telling me about certain games, plays I had made, plays I did not make. Everything he said was perceptive, and true. I thought, *Yeah, this cat knows. He understands.*

If it's not a signing situation, ninety-five percent of the time the public is cool with me. I'm not famous enough for them to want to tear off my clothes. That's reserved more for film stars, people still look at me as a football player. For the football fan, especially as he gets older, it's as if I'm a part of him. He grew up with me, ran the ball with me, felt the disappointments. When we meet he's talking to me, but he's really talking to a part of himself, to his history and his youth. I can relate to that, and to him.

It's the drunk in a bar who can be difficult. Not because he's a bad guy, but when he's drunk, he repeats himself a hundred thousand times. Wants to buy you forty drinks, tell you ninety variations of the same story, when you say you have to move on, he gets offended. Normally I'll send out a vibe, that I want to be left alone, people will respect that. But there isn't a vibe in the world that can penetrate the booze. Man's drunk, vibes just ignite him. So I'll usually call the manager, get some help.

I have a good time with New York taxi drivers. I guess they like me because I'm about as subtle as they are. But my best barometer, to measure how I'm doing at any given time in my life, is walking through an airport, interacting with the porters. The guy who takes bags at the airport is a unique individual. Most of them are black, most of them are highly intelligent, and most of them are wise about human nature. When I walk through an airport after I've said something for black people on TV, or I've announced a game honestly, they'll say, "Hey Big Jim, how you doin', brother? I heard what you said. Right on." They never fawn, "You're Jim Brown! You were a great football player!" It's just one man talking to another, and when those guys show their appreciation, I know I've been doing pretty good.

My relationship with the police is a good deal more volatile. Fame has its perks and its prices, and the one price I've paid is my dealings with the police. There are cops in Los Angeles who would love to be the guy who sent me to San Quentin for 49,000 years. If they can't accomplish that, they'll settle for taking me in, leaking it to the press, getting a headline, their name in print, for the type of incident they would not even respond to if my name was John Doe. With the police and celebrities, it's never about the case. It's about the newspapers. The police are masters at manipulating the press.

My situation is far more complex, because I'm more than just famous. In the eyes of the police, I'm big, black, and arrogant. My Hollywood lifestyle has often been flashy, I had huge parties with white girls and black girls. I've had famous militant friends, who were not well-liked, to put it mildly, by the police. I also speak out against inequities in this country, in the city I live in, and I am a black man. I have touched nerves in segments of the Los Angeles police department. I've said publicly, when young and old black people were getting killed by the hundreds in South Central L.A., that the LAPD didn't appear to get overly upset, or extend a lot of manpower. But when one white woman was killed on a corner in Westwood, the police were up in arms. They ran massive sweeps, arrested hundreds of blacks, went on TV to announce those sweeps, assure the viewers that the police were on this very important case.

As I'll get to, I've also brought on some of my own problems, though nowhere near the extent that people think. I'm not saying the only reasons I've gotten in trouble with the police is because I'm black and outspoken, though if you study American history, those are two damn good reasons. I am saying you can't separate those facts from the equation.

There are cops I care for. I have friends on the force, some of whom were told they would hate me, and we play some great racquetball. I know it's hard on those guys being my friend, and I appreciate their friendship. My closest friend in this world, Big George, is a policeman, and a fantastic one. I know cops who aren't quite friends, but they're decent with me. I would never suggest that all cops are bad. The only absolute about cops is that they're very powerful. Some men will utilize power fairly. Others will abuse it.

After all our battles, I've become somewhat of an expert on policemen. There's something I didn't know when I was much younger: most cops don't see themselves as public servants, and they're not public servants. Cops are businessmen. Like any businessmen, they want to move up the ladder, have an impressive career. To accomplish that they have to win. In order to win, certain cops will lie and cheat, put winning in front of justice. Cops aren't alone: that's the way of the business world.

It's not my position that I will sit here, defend everything I've ever done in my life, or things that people think I've done. But since I've talked about a lot of the good times, I'll talk about some of the trouble.

One matter occurred in 1968. It started, indirectly, with Gloria Steinem. Gloria was assigned to write a magazine piece about me. She came out to the Arizona film set where I was making a movie, returned with me to Los Angeles during a break in the filming. One afternoon we were crossing Sunset, it was busy, I offered Gloria my hand, and I noticed that turned her off. She was a feminist, I suppose my offer offended her. As I spent time with Gloria and her tape recorder, I saw she was extremely bright and vocal, and I was sure many guys had not been able to stomach that. It attracted the hell out of me. So did the challenge, I have to admit, of winning the affections of this particular feminist. Gloria and I started dating, and she was wonderful, physically and mentally. She may hate me after this but she was real fond of me then.

Gloria returned to New York to do some work on the piece, I went back to Arizona to finish the film. Before I did I left my car with the woman I was living with. Her name was Eva Bohn-Chin.

Flashback: I had met Eva in London, while

filming *The Dirty Dozen*. I went down one Saturday night to King's Road, and into my favorite little Italian restaurant. There was a girl in there. She was tall, stunning, with sharp bones and caramel skin; her chest was small and her legs were long and thin. And she was talking shit to everyone. She was laughing and smiling, telling people her mother was German, her father was a Jamaican prince. When I was done chatting with the guy who owned the restaurant, I walked into the dining room, looking a little square, sat right down at her table.

She said, "Who are you?"

I said, "I'm from America. My name is Jim. Who are you?"

She gave me her rap, told me about her parents, how she knew everyone who was anyone, and maybe she would show me around. She didn't know shit about me, and she was going to take this square from America, turn him on to the pleasures of London. We walked around King's Road, Eva told me she was a model and an actress, had done just about everything. She was smart and arrogant and dizzy and very, very sensual. Also, down inside, Eva was a very sweet girl. Eva said she wanted to show me Dolly's, and I asked her what that was. She laughed, told me it was *the* London night spot. We walked into Dolly's and of course Eva knew the girl at the door. She gave her a kiss, and when Eva turned to introduce me, the girl walked right past Eva, who was dumbfounded, and came to me.

She said, "Jim! Where you been tonight? Do you want your table?"

I looked straight at Eva, saw the expression on

her face. I thought, Uh oh. We are gonna be battling from now on.

And we were. I told Eva who I was, she realized I'd set her cocky ass up, and she was fuming. *She* was used to playing the head games. And she fell in love with me, and I fell in love with her. We had an erotic, turbulent, unforgettable relationship, and we conducted it all over London. We made love all over, had other girls make love with us. And we argued all over London. One night I threw Eva's wig out of a window. Another night we argued in a London restaurant, right on into the parking lot, where I told Eva she couldn't come back to my apartment until I'd fallen asleep. I went back to the apartment, was woken from my sleep by a phone call from the London police. Eva had lain down in front of the police station. She had told the curious police her boyfriend wouldn't let her back in, and wanted them to make him. The London cops found that quite humorous. They told me I should let her back in, so I did.

I brought Eva with me back to Los Angeles. As soon as we got here I sat down with her in my living room.

I said, "Eva, we did a lot of crazy things in London. We can't do that stuff in America. In America these policemen are after my butt. Don't be lying in front of any station, messing with police. They carry guns over here, not like in England. Over there they have a different attitude about black folks, and they have a different attitude about us. They find humor in things. There won't be any humor in America."

Eva moved into my apartment, later I met Gloria Steinem. I went back to Arizona to finish the film, left Eva my car, and Gloria called from New York, said she wanted to see me. Gloria flew back to the desert, and I stayed with her there, a couple days longer than I was supposed to. Eva didn't know where I was, or why I wasn't home. When Gloria went back to New York I returned to Los Angeles. When I got to my place Eva was gone. And my car was gone. I had to try and find her.

Eva had gone to a singer's house, a lady named Fran Jeffries. A thought occurred to me: what if they had been romantic. Eva, after all, was sexually adventurous. I was a little upset, part of my sexual hypocrisy. It was cool for me to sleep with Gloria, but I didn't want Eva to stray.

I was calm though. I said, "Hey babe, you're mad, come home."

I talked Eva into coming home, that night we went for dinner at the Old World on Sunset. We had both cooled out from the afternoon, had some food, then saw two sexy girls. We thought we'd invite them over, have some fun. So we invited them, and they said they'd go home first, meet us there later. Eva and I went back to my place. She started grinning.

She said, "You want me to call Fran over, too?"

I said, "Yeah, call her up. We'll have a ball."

Truth is, I still had some animosity about Fran maybe being with Eva. Eva called Fran and told her to come on over. Then Eva started sweet-talking Fran and I got jealous. I slapped Eva and she slapped me back. We started screaming and grabbing and tussling, I guess the neighbors heard the shouting and called the police. They arrived quickly, while we were still angry, and when I heard them at the door, I said to Eva, "Hey, you better go back to the bedroom, because this is gonna be trouble."

While Eva went back to the bedroom, I went to the door, opened it a crack. Two policemen. White guy and a Spanish guy.

One said, "This is the police. We heard someone's getting beat up."

I said, "No, no one's getting beat up. Me and my lady are having a fight."

He said, "Well, we're coming in."

I said, "No, you're not."

I slammed the door. I walked back to the bedroom, said to Eva, "Get yourself together. These guys are gonna try and put me in jail."

She was frantic and the cops were pounding on the door. I went back to the door, cracked it again, the Spanish guy decided he was just coming in. I hit him with a forearm, knocked him out of the doorway, slammed the door again. I walked back to my bedroom, saying "Shit." And Eva was gone. I didn't know *where* she was. I found out later, knowing the cops were coming in, Eva kind of freaked, decided to get the hell out of there. She climbed over the top of our balcony, and then fell, and rolled underneath it.

I went back to the door, let the cops in. I knew I was going in, had no choice but to let them do it. The police came in, put me in handcuffs, took me outside . . . here come those two pretty girls we'd invited over. If a black man can turn apple red, I did it.

They took me to the station. Several other squad cars had backed these guys up, and the cops had searched my place, the backyard, and saw Eva under the balcony. And they also brought her in. They said they were going to charge me with assault on Eva. They tried to get Eva to say I had thrown her off the balcony, tried to kill her. She said I hadn't thrown her anywhere. From day one, she said, "No, It was nothing like that."

The next day there were headlines saying I had thrown a woman off a balcony, and the stories said that I would be charged with attempted murder. I never was charged, but they continued to harass Eva. They tried to intimidate her, threatened her, said if she didn't tell them what they thought was the real story, they would bring charges against her. All they wound up charging me with was striking an officer as he tried to enter my residence, but they never stopped trying to get Eva to say I had thrown her off the balcony. The publicity was sweeping and scandalous. And the toughest thing I did to Eva was slap her.

It wasn't the first time I had slapped Eva, it certainly wasn't the first time she'd slapped me. Eva would jump on my butt in a second, that was the nature of her spirit. However, I have also slapped other women. And I never should have, and I never should have slapped Eva, no matter how crazy we were at the time. I don't think any man should slap a woman. In a perfect world, I don't think any man should slap anyone, and I don't consider slapping people a sign of strength. In my case it's related to a weakness. If I'm dealing with someone, they do something I feel is wrong,

I'll tell them that, and that I don't like it. If they continue to provoke me, I will say, "Okay, you leave now, or leave me alone." That means we're at an impasse, and I'm about to lose my temper. At that point, in that situation, I have slapped women, and put my hands on men. I don't start fights, but sometimes I don't walk away from them. It hasn't happened in a long time, but it's happened, and I regret those times. I should have been more in control of myself, stronger, more adult, should have had the restraint to just walk away when events were turning edgy. I've done it before, walked right out of bars or parties when I felt a problem was coming. I have also acted meanly and foolishly, let my emotions overpower my intellect.

At this point I don't even go out when I'm working on something important, don't want the chance of getting in a scrape. I am not among those folks who get in hassles, resolve them privately. I am a person people call the police on. So my problems get resolved by the police. That means press, and that means my reputation is irrevocable. People take all the things I've seemingly been involved in, combine them, say, "Well, where there's smoke there's fire." But smoke is smoke and fire is fire. When you're famous, or infamous, sometimes there's smoke when there isn't even smoke.

Once a girlfriend's mom, when I was playing in Cleveland, talked her daughter, Brenda, into saying I had forced her to drink liquor, and then forced her into intimacies. I know that her mother made her do this, because Brenda called me two years later and apologized and confessed. Said she'd been young and let her mom talk her into something wrong. It went to trial though, and it was a huge story in Cleveland.

What had happened was that Brenda had come to a hotel where I used to party with my partners on the Browns. Brenda and I had agreed to stop seeing each other, she had changed her mind, wanted to try it again. We stayed up all night, mostly talking, and in the morning I went to play golf while Brenda slept. That afternoon I asked one of my teammates, who was returning to the hotel, to call my room, tell Brenda to go on home, that I wasn't going back to the hotel. But Brenda didn't go home. She went to see Paula, one of her girlfriends. Brenda was under twenty, had been out all evening, and her mother was furious. She cooked up a scheme to try and get money out of me, Brenda agreed to it. Brenda and her mom filed a complaint, saying that I had made her drink liquor, badly bruised her, and forced myself on her sexually.

In court it did not fly. Paula and her family testified that when Brenda had arrived at their house, she had no bruises at all. In fact, they said, they knew Brenda's mom had made the whole thing up. Then the taxi driver, who had taken Brenda from our hotel to Paula's house, said, not only did Brenda look fine, she seemed cheerful. Brenda's sisters got on the stand, started laughing, even while "corroborating" Brenda's story. Even Brenda couldn't keep her story half straight. And the doctor's report—Brenda's mom, trying to be clever, had taken Brenda to the hospital—said that Brenda had one bruise on her entire body, on her hip. The jury went out for one hour, found me not guilty. Anytime a jury returns that quickly, the case is a sham, should never have been on the docket.

That didn't stop Brenda and her mother: after that season they filed a paternity suit against me. They never even called me, said Brenda was pregnant, the child was mine, could I help—they just filed a hostile lawsuit. Certain it was one more scam, I fought it in court, while Brenda was still pregnant, and I won that, too.

About a year and a half later, Brenda called me to apologize, for our first go-around. She admitted her mother had talked her into saying I had roughed her up, and she said she was sorry that so many people got dragged in, and it had to end in court. Brenda sounded sincere, but she was also calling for another reason.

Brenda said, "Jim, there is one thing I want you to know. The child is yours."

The court had ordered me to stay away from Brenda. I hadn't seen her or the child. I was stunned.

I said, "Brenda, I never believed that. The first thing I knew about you getting pregnant was when I got sued. I had to fight. I guess, now that you're saying this, you had to fight, too."

I wanted to believe, but I still wasn't convinced that Brenda was telling the truth. We had definitely had sex, but Brenda was hardly chaste, and I was pretty sure she had also been with other men. Above all, her credibility at that point wasn't very high—she was still living with her mom.

I said, "Brenda, I'll tell you what. I'd prefer not to be around you, I don't want any more stuff. But you bring your daughter into my hotel in the morning. If she's mine, I'll be able to tell by look-ing at her."

Brenda brought her little girl in, immediately I knew it was my daughter. Her name was Shelly. I'm not pretty but she was. And her features made it perfectly clear that Shelly was mine. Brenda had brought her up beautifully, and the moment was wonderful for all three of us. I accepted Shelly as my daughter, after we spent some time, she ac-cepted me as her father. Over the years I've had Shelly and Brenda come and be with me, although we've never lived together as a family. We've strug-gled at times with our relationship, there have been bumps, but we're okay. Now Shelly's a grand-mother . . .

In 1985 I had been friends for a couple years with a lady named Margo Tiff. I knew her good family back in Cleveland, had helped Margo at times with her Westwood rent. Margo had played briefly on the pro tennis tour, she was a fine ath-lete, and we were sports buddies, mostly playing tennis, and some basketball. Margo was a tomboy and a self-admitted lesbian. She used to tell me she had not been with a man for eleven years, and that she would like to someday find a woman whose personality was just like mine.

Margo's current lover was an older woman, whom I had met while giving a party for the wom-en's basketball teams at UCLA and USC. This woman didn't like much about me, or much about anyone, it seemed. She was domineering, didn't want Margo spending too much time with me. Her attitude was clear when Margo needed more help with her rent, and this woman came by my home, not Margo, to brusquely collect it.

At this time a young woman was staying at my home—Carol Moses. Carol was small, cute, with an ebullient personality. Everybody liked Carol, including Margo, who came over one night and was quickly and obviously attracted. Margo made a pass at Carol, who was totally straight and rejected it. Margo became characteristically aggressive, she and Carol had words, then a minor altercation which I broke up. I told Margo to leave: Carol was staying at my house at the time, and Margo had started the whole thing anyway. Margo was pissed. We were pretty close friends and she thought I was siding against her.

Fortunately for me, there were three other people at the house who saw Carol and Margo argue, and Margo leave. There were a couple guys over who wanted me to listen to a sample recording of a new group, and there was Leah Wallace. Leah is a former girlfriend, now one of my best friends. I'm tight with her entire family.

That evening, Leah spent the night at my home. Next morning, after Leah had left, I walked up my driveway to grab my morning paper. Waiting for me at the top were several policemen.

I said, "What the hell?"

One of the cops told me to get down on my knees, put my hands behind my head. After I did he put me in handcuffs.

He said, "We have a warrant. We can go search your house. You're going in with us. When we get in, we'll tell you what's happening."

Carol was sleeping, they woke her up, took her to another room. A detective took me into my kitchenette, told me to sit at the table.

He said, "This will be the roughest day of your life. You are being charged with assault and battery and forcible rape."

I said, "Goddamn!"

He said, "I will read your rights, you can choose to say something or not."

I said, "If I say anything to you, am I still going down?"

He said, "Oh yeah, you're going down. It doesn't matter what you say."

He read me my rights, I said nothing, didn't know what the fuck I was supposed to talk *about*. They searched the house, asked me where my towels were, paper towels, everything. Everything they asked for, I directed them to. I cooperated completely.

They took me down. They said Margo Tiff had filed a complaint, alleging that Carol and I had raped her! What I found out later was that Margo, when she had been interviewed by the police, had been accompanied by an older woman.

Though there were headlines instantly, the police never charged me, and Big George bailed me out. Before he did he asked me one question.

He said, "Did you rape her?"

I said, "No man. I did not rape anyone!"

He said, "Okay. Let's get on with it."

I waited to see what the police were going to do, what their approach would be, what the hell this was all about. A detective did a preliminary investigation, spoke to Leah, apparently looked at the medical report, saw that Margo had had no scratches on her, there was *nothing* to indicate she'd been raped. I was scheduled to go to Chicago to film a movie, I figured I better talk to the detective first.

He said, "Go to Chicago. Don't even bother to hire a lawyer. Everything is going to be all right. We don't want to make this girl look bad, make you look bad, or make the police look bad."

Believing I would never even be charged, I left for Chicago. When I returned I still had not been, but I kept receiving calls from the press, wanting my comment. The reporters had obviously talked to the police, and the cops clearly hadn't told them this thing was over. I called the detective, asked him what was going on.

He said, "Look, I know what I told you, but this thing is bigger than me. I don't know what's going on, or what's going to happen. We want to interview your witness again."

I had no choice but to hire an attorney. I hired Johnnie Cochran, one of the city's top black criminal lawyers, and a former Assistant DA. Meanwhile the police began harassing both Carol and Leah. They didn't take anyone else to a Grand Jury, but they took them. Johnnie Cochran knew I was angry, tried to cool me off.

He said, "Look, man. Don't have a press conference. We might be able to work this out."

I said, "What? It's already in the headlines. I'm going out and telling my side. I am *having* a press conference."

Johnnie's request seemed unusual to me. I mentioned it to Big George, and he and I formed

341

an opinion: in handling my case, Johnnie was proceeding with a certain ambivalence. Johnnie was a capable, scrupulous lawyer, but he was also a political creature, in a political profession. It seemed as if he wanted to keep me under wraps because he didn't want to embarrass the prosecution, which consisted of former colleagues. Big George is as smart as Johnnie or smarter, and will fight for what he believes is right, regardless of potential flack. When Big George said he and I would walk through this thing together, every step, I was greatly relieved.

And I called my press conference. Margo's entire complaint was a fabrication, but I did not say that, did not even try and explain the events of the night in question. All I said was, "I did not rape anyone. The medical report will prove that. That's my statement." The medical report was absolute— if the reporters read it there would be no fodder for speculation.

After my press conference we were contacted by the police. They said if I produced my two other witnesses, the men who'd been at my home, they might not press charges. I said no. Once I had gotten the headline, I didn't want them to ease gracefully out of this. They had wronged me, they knew it, now were attempting to save face. I wanted this to go down, all the way down to the truth.

The other side, meanwhile, had started with an inadequate prosecutor, so they switched to a guy named Dino Fulgoni. He was a deputy DA, and I believe he was their best. Finally, after two months, after searching my home from top to bottom, after telling me not to hire a lawyer, the prosecution pressed charges, and set a date for a preliminary hearing.

Johnnie had hired a detective to find out where Margo Tiff's older girlfriend lived. The detective discovered the apartment, learned that Margo had gone there the night she'd said she'd been raped. He gathered this from two elderly women who lived across from the hall from Margo's girlfriend, and knew both women. On the night in question, both said that Margo and her girlfriend had engaged in a loud, violent fight.

I don't know what happened there that night, I wasn't there. But I learned quite a bit at the preliminary hearing. The detective who took Margo's complaint testified that Margo had been accompanied by a woman—her girlfriend—and there had been a disagreement at the station over whether to file a complaint. And that the two women had asked to confer privately, then the older lover had said to the detective, "OK, we've decided we want to go for it. We're going to get him." The two elderly people also came in and testified, and so did the doctor who had examined Margo. And *we* had to get the doctor to court—the prosecution never called for him. They tried a rape case, didn't use the doctor. Anyway, when Margo got up on the stand, she contradicted everybody, everything, made the police witnesses feel nonsensical, made the prosecution feel nonsensical, after four months of making me look like a rapist.

The morning of the hearing's third day, Johnnie Cochran, my attorney, had an idea.

He said, "Jim, why don't you just put your two

witnesses on the stand? We'll knock this thing out today."

I said, "Uh-uh. Leah has to go back to Chicago, she's working. Carol is at home. I don't need to put anyone on the stand. They got Fulgoni, man. He'll ask them a bunch of wild questions, get that into the papers, try and nullify what their crazy plaintiff said. I don't need anybody on the stand."

After the morning of the trial's third day, I had lunch with Big George. He said, "Now watch what happens after lunch." And that afternoon, as Big George had suggested, both sides went back to the judge's chambers. Johnnie Cochran came out smiling.

He said, "Jim, it's over. The prosecution is going to make a motion to drop all charges. It only proves the judicial system works. This is good for everyone."

What I took that to imply was, Don't pop off to the press. Just get your innocent ass out of here. Do not mess with the police.

When court resumed, Fulgoni stood up, said a great deal of evidence had come forward that had contradicted the allegations, and made a motion to drop all charges. The judge granted the motion. I walked out of the court room, turned to the press, took Johnny's advice.

I said, "I'm glad to be an American. The judicial system works. We have a chance, if we're innocent, for the facts to come out. I'm gone."

We climbed into Big George's car and went home. The press continued to call, I said I would stand by my statement.

There was nothing to say. Everything else was

bullshit. With the help of Big George, a fair human being, a dedicated policeman, I had won. And this is the first time in my life I've told the great Margo Tiff story.

It may not be over. A few days after the trial, Margo sued me for $8 million. Four years later, Margo is still after $8 million. Somehow I get the feeling there may be more depositions. Maybe you'll read about it.

17

NFL, PRETTY MUCH TODAY

IN THE EARLY 1980s I thought the NFL had sold its soul to TV, and the omnipresent dollar. Once the name of the game had been Physicality. Now it was Entertainment. Play Hard, But Be Careful, Don't Want to Risk the Big Money. Above All, Mug For That Camera.

If I didn't love the sport, the *sport*, I would have sat on the hill and kept my mouth shut. I did love football, didn't want to see it turn into wrestling.

Today, I feel good about the NFL again. Toughness is coming back, the running game has returned. There are still cosmetics, but the game is more genuine than it was in the first half of the decade. I regained my hope for the NFL in 1985, when something came along to rekindle it.

The Chicago Bears.

The year they won Super Bowl XX, the Bears played football the way it should be played. The Bears were what I call a True Football Team. They lined up, no tricks, *kicked people's ass*. The Packers did it in the 1960s, the Steelers in the 1970s, and the Bears in 1985. When the 1985 Bears are straight up in your face, what kinda trick you gonna pull?

I thought Chicago's offense was adequate. It was their defense that blew me away. I heard people say it was boring watching Chicago's defense— it was so dominant, when the other team was trying to score, there was no sense of wonder. My turn was 180 degrees: when the Bears were on defense, I was more turned on by football than I had been in many years. Then again, when Mike Tyson beat Michael Spinks in ninety-one seconds, I thought it was a classic fight. To me that fight epitomized boxing: if your foe is inferior, don't waste anybody's time. Beat him up.

The Bears beat people up. Most defenses in the NFL have maybe five hitters. I can honestly say the Bears had eleven hitters, and I've never seen a team that had eleven hitters on defense. The pressure they exerted was severe. Forget about quarterbacks having time to pass—runners couldn't even get started. The Bears were shoving their blockers into the backfield.

I attribute a lot of that success to Buddy Ryan. Buddy's no charmer, but the man is a superior football coach. And that was really Buddy's defense, which I thought was abundantly clear after the Super Bowl when the guys on defense lifted Buddy on their shoulders. That only underscored what already was a fact: the Bears had two leaders, and that wasn't going to last. You put Buddy Ryan with Mike Ditka, you have two guys who could tear each other up, and they tore. When Buddy left, went to coach the Eagles, I thought that was too bad. Ditka and Ryan were a terrific combination. Had they remained together, with the manpower on the Bears, Chicago might have been *the* NFL power, instead of a contender.

After Buddy left Chicago, Ditka changed the Bears defense. Three-quarters of the league woke up, started blitzing and pressuring, the team that planted the seed went conservative. And Chicago's defense had been *scoring points*. When Ditka scrapped it, I thought it was strictly a Personality Thing, Ditka wanting to show the world he could win without Buddy's influence. That was childish and counter-productive and a lot of the Chicago Bears knew it, and didn't like it.

I'm one of those people who likes the Bears, doesn't care much for their coach. I always admired the way Ditka played football. He was maniacally determined, and he deserves his niche in the Hall of Fame. As a head coach Ditka has won a Super Bowl. Those are considerable NFL accomplishments.

The man is also no intellect. Ditka reminds me of many of the coaches back in the NFL of the 1950s: fascist, loud, could talk a streak of paramilitary bullshit, but weren't exactly Phi Beta Kappa. According to guys I know on the Bears, Ditka sometimes used to overdrink, get so hammered that his players had to take care of him. Ditka is still abusive and obnoxious to the people he works with, but his job is secure as long as he wins. If the Bears should start to slide, I don't think you'll see much patience from Chicago's front office. Ditka will be fired quickly.

I could not have played for Mike Ditka. I don't want any man two inches from my face, bellowing at me, and I don't like to see it done to other athletes. I'd never have allowed Ditka to do me the way he did Mike Tomczak. Before Ditka made *me* seek therapy, I'd have tried to kick his ass. I pick no bones with a man who knows he is tough, and has respect for the toughness of others. I admire that. Judging from Ditka's manner, he thinks he's the only tough guy on earth—the Rambo of goddamn football. I think Rambo's an illusion, a stupid one at that. I think Ditka's a lunatic who enjoys humiliating people.

One of Ditka's peers who I like is John Robinson. John is a decent, sensitive, intelligent man. His players trust him, and that can be a powerful motivator. Guys on the Rams say John also gives a good speech. Most pros don't need a strong speech—they drive themselves—but it certainly can't hurt, especially the guy who is only average. Fire up a guy with modest skills, he might tear up the field for sixty minutes. Whether a pro can be inspired by a speech depends on the coach, and the speech. A bad speech—a bunch of lies or threats—is better left unsaid. Corny is terrible: guys who should be primed to kill will be giggling. If the coach is honest, forceful, knows precisely what his players need, that particular week . . . guys still might wake up Monday morning, think, Hmmm, he really didn't *say* anything. But at the moment, they might want to break down a wall.

As for John Robinson, he loves the running game, and runners, which means he can have a sandwich at my house any time. I don't think John knows much about passing, and I don't think he's a great NFL coach. Motivationally, he's right at the top; in his NFL knowledge I think John is still limited. In terms of know-how, he seems more suited to college than to the pros.

Regardless, John has been positive for the Rams. Because of his nature, he has been the glue that has held that unusual franchise together. Whatever degree of peace the Rams have recently maintained, I attribute it to John; without him, I think the organization might have self-destructed. I go back a long way with the Rams. I was close friends with Carroll Rosenbloom, used to play a lot of tennis at his home. That's how I came to know Georgia. And I like Georgia. I enjoy her flamboyance, and she's always been a warm person to me. So it isn't easy to say what I'm about to say.

However, I don't think Georgia's reign as owner of the Rams has been good for the franchise. Georgia can be a marvelous ally, she can also be cold-blooded. When it comes to running her business Georgia is harsh, much harsher than her public image suggests. And when Georgia brought in John Shaw, it was a marriage of overkill—the dragon lady and the hatchet man. As a result, a lot of the Rams have been treated shabbily. John Robinson arrived with some sorely lacking humanity, but it's grueling to be a football coach and a humanitarian and the rope in a tug of war between personnel and management, all while dealing with a giant press corps in a city accustomed to world championships. That would wear down anyone, I think it's tiring John. I'd like to see the Rams get in the Super Bowl, for John's sake. Despite his efforts, I think the organization is still highly tenuous: if the Rams don't make it to the Super Bowl in the next two seasons, I predict you'll see a total reorganization.

That's the way the Rams operate. When Chuck Knox was coach of the Rams, I thought he was impressive. He was a winning coach, taking his team to the playoffs every year. And they fired him. They didn't like "how" he was winning, told him he wasn't winning in an "exciting" manner. To me that isn't football. It's bullshit. They fired a craftsman because his style wasn't Hollywood. It was typical of the modern Rams: hard on contracts, soft on football.

I still admire Knox, think he's doing a fine job up in Seattle, without exceptional personnel. No, he has not gone to a Super Bowl. Man, it's hard to get to a Super Bowl. You need talent and coaching and health and luck. You can't say a man is not a good coach just because he doesn't take you to the Super Bowl. A good coach will take you to the playoffs, consistently, give you a chance at the Super Bowl, but it is not the coach's fault if the team falls short. If a coach is capable enough to take his team to the playoffs, the players have to bring it home from there.

After the Bears of 1985, I didn't know if the

NFL would slip back to lightweight football. So I was extremely encouraged when I saw the New York Giants, then the Washington Redskins, win it all. That made three straight Super Bowls, won by three True Football Teams.

When the Giants were champs I especially enjoyed Joe Morris. Joe, who also broke most of my records up at Syracuse, had a near-perfect year. He was small, smart, and the Giants went to him when they needed tough yards. New York had Phil Simms and Lawrence Taylor and that proud, physical defense. But Joe Morris was the soul of that team.

When the Redskins won Super Bowl XXII, beat the Broncos, it illustrated my point about dominance in the NFL. I think Dan Reeves is one of the top three or four coaches in the NFL. His club has ordinary talent, no size, one real star in John Elway, yet Dan has taken them twice to the Super Bowl in the past three years. With due respect for Dan, look what happened in their last Super Bowl. Denver had the gadgets and the finesse, Washington had the muscle and the menace. And the Redskins made the Broncos look like schoolboys.

I watched that whole game, which is rare for me. I still watch football many Sundays, but if it's dull or sloppy I stop. I like to find one guy who is playing out of his head. Jerry Rice did it for an entire year—1987—and it was one of my all-time favorite performances. And it defied belief: the guy was evolving the art of pass receiving, and there were people discussing his "slow" time in the 40. Say *what?* If I see a man running, no one is catching him, to me that means he's Fast As He Wants to Be.

My friend James Harris says that rap on Jerry Rice was pure invention, created by Bill Walsh. Jerry Rice was so prolific in college, no one could explain it. While the cynics searched for chinks, Walsh obliged them with a manufactured beauty: Jerry Rice did not possess great speed. Walsh desperately wanted Rice, was fearful he would lose him. He didn't: after fifteen other teams passed, the 49ers grabbed him.

Knowing the honesty of James Harris, the fertility of rumor, and the mind of Bill Walsh, I believe that story. Long before he won his last Super Bowl, his detractors fell back in love with him, I was a staunch supporter of Bill Walsh. For years I called him the most brilliant coach in the NFL. I loved his offensive scheme, which his players believed in, and understood beautifully. When you see a quarterback dropping to pass, his first guy is covered, now he's lost, his head is swiveling so fast it looks like he's watching ping pong, it means the offensive scheme is not real hip. Walsh's was the hippest in football. If Joe Montana's primary man wasn't open, he knew instantly where to find his second, third and fourth receivers. That is testament to Montana, also to the precision of Walsh's scheme. I have no inside information as to why Bill retired, don't fully understand why he did, but he left on top, and that's the best way to go. If Sugar Ray Leonard fights until he's ninety, he'll never top the night he defeated Marvin Hagler.

I shouldn't be surprised that Bill retired: things in San Francisco have been strange the past few seasons. Even before he won the last Super Bowl, Joe Montana's bandwagon was also replenished, Joe was one of the best quarterbacks ever. He had overcome a severe back injury, rallied his team from fourth-quarter deficits at least fifteen times, was 2-0 in the Super Bowl with no interceptions. So what was that so-called quarterback controversy? I heard it two years in a row, and it made no sense to me. Steve Young has potential, athleticism, but you do not compare him to a Joe Montana simply out of respect for Joe. Maybe there was more to that "controversy" than what was reported. I know there were rumors that Joe was involved in drugs—maybe certain parties believed that, used it without saying so to try and undermine Joe. I don't know, but I know Joe Montana has *always* been the quarterback of the 49ers. You do not challenge the ability of Joe Montana.

Speaking of misguided notions, I was disappointed by Jerry Rice after last year's Super Bowl. Jerry complained that the press did not respect him, and that he deserved more endorsements. Holding up Joe Montana as a comparison, Jerry suggested he had been a victim of racial prejudice. I don't know about any of that. Of course Joe Montana will receive a lot of press. He wins. And the football has to be thrown before a man can catch it. But that doesn't mean the press does not appreciate Jerry. The press wrote a million glowing articles about the guy, it was the press that voted him Super Bowl MVP. The week after the game, Jerry was on the cover of *Sports Illustrated*. Jerry Rice has been wonderful for Joe Montana, Joe Montana has been wonderful for Jerry Rice. The world has acknowledged that.

Endorsements: you have to lay the groundwork. You have to find a sharp commercial agent, play that whole slick game. Just because you're a super athlete does not mean a company will want to hire you, and it isn't obligated to. And just because they don't use you doesn't mean it's racial. The Refrigerator is black, dark black, and he got more commercials than any seven white guys. Jerry's performance in the Super Bowl was dynamic, it spoke better of him than any commercial, his statements took away from that fact. I feel someone talked to Jerry, told him what to say, and I think Jerry was ill-advised.

Living out West, I can remember when the 49ers weren't even the best team in northern California, let alone the NFL. It used to be the Raiders, not the Niners, who made trips to California somehow seem like punishment. While his peers were drumming players out of the league, Al Davis was reeling them back in, maximizing their value. I've always rooted for Al, always considered him a friend. I used to laugh when I'd hear guys from other teams discuss the Raiders. They *hated* playing the Raiders, knew they would get beat up, even if they managed to win. On the road the Raiders would appear from their tunnel, a horde of black, and after a moment the fans would BOO. First, 60,000 people would GULP. Who are these hellhounds, and what lock did they pick to get in here? Then the Raiders would go out, have twice as many penalties as their opponent, still win. And their games were always exciting, because Al understood the psychological value of the quick strike—the long bomb. For many years I considered the Raiders the most watchable team in football.

Those were the old Raiders, the gashouse Raiders, led by Alzado, Matuszak, Stabler, Lester Hayes and Jack Tatum. Marcus Allen and Howie Long represent the new Raiders. Not only are they talented athletes, they are articulate and softspoken. And they're not what the Raiders need. When the old guys left, took their thuggery with them, they also robbed the Raiders of their edge. Even Al has admitted he got rid of Alzado too soon. Sometimes it's not so much what a guy can still do as he what he reminds people of. Alzado reminded the Raiders that they were in a street fight.

Another team competing with its legacy is the Pittsburgh Steelers, coached by my old teammate, Chuck Noll. Chuck has a rich football heritage: He played for Paul Brown, coached under Sid Gillman and Don Shula. Chuck was devoted to learning, so he deserves the ultimate credit. On the Browns Chuck played guard and later linebacker. He was small for both spots, but fanatical in his attention to the fine points; I thought Chuck was a more acute student of the game than even Lombardi. And with that colorful mix of guys he assembled in Pittsburgh, Chuck was canny enough to allow them their individuality, forceful enough to remain the boss. Chuck won four Super Bowls, made it to the top, never surrendered his dignity.

I don't know if Dan Marino is the top quarterback in football, but he may just be the most arrogant. That's good: on the Browns, the guys I never worried about were the guys who thought they were Bad. No question, Marino is Bad, but calling guys the top this, top that, can make you crazy. Because the minute I start talking about Marino, I begin to think of Elway. And Montana. And Randall Cunningham. And Bernie Kosar. Surround any of those guys with the right cast, they can all win the Super Bowl.

I'm a big fan of Bernie's. I recall doing a Browns game for ESPN and one of the announcers said that "Bernie is slow, but overcomes it." Slow for what? To sprint with FloJo? Different offensive schemes demand different skills. By design, Elway runs sideline to sideline, Marino stays cemented in the pocket, Montana mixes it up. The Cleveland Browns don't want Bernie scrambling and sprinting out—it's not their scheme—so his foot speed is immaterial. Bernie releases quickly, thinks quickly, reads defenses like he's Evelyn Wood, does not throw interceptions. He credits his teammates freely, the players know he means it, and they respond to him on the field. And I just happen to really like him.

I also like the Browns . . . again. For a period in the 1970s I put distance between myself and the team. I followed them right after I left, when Leroy Kelly was there, and most of the fellas on the offensive line were still playing. A few years later some of the Browns made negative statements about me, and a few of the guys had never even met me. That's when I got irritated. I said, "What the fuck do these guys know about me, and why are they wasting their energy talking about me? They're not even playing any kind of football." And they weren't, so I stopped checking them out.

About five or six years ago I resumed following them. I liked the Browns again because they started playing my kind of football. They were hitting people and they were exciting and the team was high-spirited. The renewal of my affection began with Minnifield and Dixon. They were small, brash, doing the Dawg thing, and they backed up their mouths with talent and heart. And of course I love Bernie, but the two guys who got me hooked were Earnest Byner and Kevin Mack. I was seeing all these other runners, tipping around, being cute, and it was shutting my eyes. Checked out the Browns, saw these two big bulls rampaging up the middle, sounding that Pop! when they struck people. I looked at Byner and Mack, said, "Aw, man, that's Cleveland Browns running. I like this."

Today I respect the entire organization. So they lost a couple times, didn't make it to the Super Bowl. But you know they're playing real football.

And now Marty Schottenheimer is gone, 800 miles away in Kansas City. Marty did a tremendous job for the Cleveland Browns. Today, again, Cleveland is a big-time football city. I attribute quite a bit of that to Marty Schottenheimer. I thought Marty resurrected that old Cleveland Browns spirit. He brought in the right kind of people, and with just a couple breaks, his team would have been in the Super Bowl. First Elway knocked them out with that famous drive, then Byner dropped the football the next year—Marty had nothing to do with either. Marty is a nice man to boot—I talked to him about his athletes, and he liked them as men, felt they had guts and class. Marty seemed especially fond of his two hard-working runners.

What Marty didn't see, or refused to, is that there is more to football than football. Football is also a business. When Cleveland's offensive coordinator, Lindy Infante, a man noted for his specialized brilliance, left the Browns, Marty put himself on the spot by assuming that role himself. The fans and the press came to dislike that, and that put a lot of pressure on Art Modell. The fans buy Art's tickets, the press promotes his team. When Art told Marty he could satisfy three elements—the fans, press, and Art—by hiring an offensive coordinator, Marty said no. End of story. In the business of the Cleveland Browns, you do not defy the boss. I'm sorry to see Marty go, but he did it to himself.

I still pull harder for the Browns than any other team. But I don't want them to win on a fluke, because a ref blew a critical call, or the other guy's runner fumbled nine times. If they play uninspired football, get lucky and win, I have no interest in that. I won't call them great until they dominate, win like champions. Browns' fans aren't that way, they want a W anyway they can get it. But I'm not a fan, not in the manner of the True Believer. When I turn on a game, I'm on the lookout for something I'll remember the next morning. I like to see Anthony Carter click into Genius, catch twelve passes, like to watch Eric when he's cutting hot. I may start a game behind one team, but if a guy on the other team starts performing, I may start rooting for the artist.

When Elway worked that drive against the Browns, I didn't pull out what remains of my hair. I felt bad about the Browns, but for me, sitting in my living room, I felt fortunate. I got to see Elway terrorize an entire stadium. Saw him perform a ninety-eight-yard magic show. Why should I have felt more than a little sorry for the Browns? They had Elway on the two at their place, they let him escape, win, end their season. I wanted them to do it, but I had to see it. I saw Elway do it.

I have affection for the Browns, but if they get out there and fold, that's their problem. They get out there and win the whole thing, that's their glory.

Go Browns!

18

COMING BACK
AT 47

MY ALLEGED COMEBACK, AND the Franco Harris affair, both sprang from a protest—mine. In the early 1980s I was disgusted with the state of professional football. Television gobbles up everything, spits it out transformed so it can sell more beer, and TV devoured the NFL. TV stuck cameras behind the bench, in the blimp, it wanted to *wire* the coaches. Monday Night Football the circus took precedence over Monday Night the game. For the networks, hard football no longer was sufficient. TV wanted Show Business. It wanted Television Moments.

With the consent of the league, prodded by TV, guys started manufacturing those moments.

They weren't real and they weren't spontaneous. You had the Fun Bunch in Washington. They're down by twenty points, score a TD, they're still losing, they meet in the end zone, do the Funky Chicken. For three minutes. Still down fourteen, are they really that joyous? Hell no. It's all for the damn camera.

I'd turn on the set Sunday morning, it started looking like the Ziegfeld Follies out there. One team scores, ten guys rush into the end zone, choreograph some bullshit. Big 300-pounders, shaking their asses. What the hell does that have to do with football? Maybe I'm a dumb old purist, but when I played football I didn't want TV cameras in my face. I was taking care of business, didn't want to be interrupted. After a TD I never *considered* doing the boogie-woogie in the end zone. I scored a TD, that was the show right there.

So there was that. I also thought many players were getting soft, too obsessed with the money. I didn't object to them earning it, but not at the expense of the game. When you're out of the game, do what you want, and do what you want in your private life. While you're on the field, you're only there once a week, have a little respect for the sport. Guy would get tired, he'd put up his hand, come out for a rest. A rest? Or a modern guy would get injured, not too badly, he'd sit down a few games. Didn't want to jeopardize his Career. Or a guy would get "hurt," know he was on TV, lie on the turf like he'd been cold-cocked. Then he'd bolt up, trot off to the cheers of the crowd. If a guy did that in my day, he would have been wise to *stay* out of the game. If he came back he would have been in danger.

When I'd look at the modern ballplayer, I'd see an awesome physical specimen, who seemed to be holding something back. I'm a sportsman. I disliked that.

The highest high in the world for an athlete is to have a dynamite game, have his team win. I can understand a guy playing poorly, his team wins, he's mad at himself, though he's pleased for his teammates. But if I see a guy who has a big game, his team gets beat, that fact doesn't bother him, to me he's selfish, has no concern for his teammates. He's a mercenary. To me, so is the athlete who doesn't care where he plays, goes wherever the payday is fattest. People say a large contract robs an athlete of his motivation. No, it depends on the athlete. Larry Bird is a patriot: he makes big money but it's not what spurs him. He's motivated by the game of basketball, has been his entire life. That's why Larry Bird is so driven, unlike the guy who skips from city to city. No matter how much you pay a mercenary, he'll never be willing to die like a patriot.

When I played I didn't want to be traded. I didn't want to play out my contract, go to New York, make more money. I had pride in the history of the Cleveland Browns. To be with the Browns my entire career meant something to me. If they had asked me to play one year at tackle, to help the team . . . I would have told them to back off. I'm not capable of *that* kind of teamwork.

But we were sportsmen. A lot of guys made practically *no* money. Yeah, everyone wanted to be paid reasonably, but business, compared to the game, ran a piss poor last. Today many guys are businessmen first, competitors second. There are exceptions, there are exceptions to everything I'm saying. I'd be the biggest liar on earth if I said there were no more sportsmen. The guy who is true will be true in any era.

And I'm not saying the players are devils, the owners are saints. It's the owners who teach the players the money game. Though the scale has changed dramatically, even in my day the game was a business. And the owners got away with a hell of a lot more than they do today—now the agents have entered the landscape, and the owners can't fool them as they once did the unrepresented players. The Browns used the same tactic on me throughout my career: at times they'd say football was sport, at times they'd say football was a business. When I went in for money, football was definitely a business. During negotiations, the Browns would use every negative they had against me. They'd bring up blocks I had missed, they made a very big deal over a lateral I had tried to a guy named Jim Ninowski. They were never angry or fervent—they were collected and cool, suggested I be collected and cool. Football being a business and all.

I guess this stuff is standard today, and it became standard to me as I learned how things worked. But the first few times it happened, I thought, Wait a minute, fellas. Make up your mind about this—sport or business—because I have never been through this, and it's confusing the hell out of me. And it was, because Paul used to say it all the time: at heart he was an amateur coach, and the

Browns would be the most amateurish team in the NFL. And then when it was time for a game, they didn't want us to be cool and collected. They wanted us feverish. Go for Old Glory! Run hard, jump up, get killed, man. Nitschke ripped out your cerebral cortex? Gee, that's terrible. But tape it up, Big Jim! And get back out there! This is sport!

And I did feel that way, almost—I just didn't want them changing the rules on me. On the other hand, when Franco Harris left the Steelers that was purely the result of a business decision, that an agent influenced him on. His agent, doing business, wanted Franco, though his career was nearly over, to drive for that extra money. Right in the middle of Franco's dispute, the Steelers suddenly released him. Now I have my own feelings about Franco's career, but from Franco's standpoint, I think his agent did him all wrong. Franco had a good owner in Art Rooney. If Franco had gone to Mr. Rooney, put himself in his hands, I think Mr. Rooney would have taken care of him. I think he would have given Franco a contract he could live with, and Franco could have had a pleasant ending. It would have been nice for Franco, the Steelers, and the city of Pittsburgh. Instead, Franco left Pittsburgh bitter and shocked. For money?

It goes round and round, the business spoiling the game. The worst thing I can say about football —pro, college, increasingly in high school—is that it is a business pretending to be a sport. In the NFL, I think the trend is swinging back. Fewer guys are mugging for the camera, more guys are hitting. And even that is related to business. The league milked the game for every last drop of entertainment, forgot what football was about, and instead of growing the ratings dropped off. Rozelle had a cow, the owners had twins—the *dollar* was threatened. TV backed off, the NFL outlawed taunting. Guys started playing football again.

And ratings came back. That was not happenstance either. When a fan watches the Olympics, he doesn't want to see Carl Lewis holding back on one event, saving himself for the next one, because he can cash in bigger, buy more mink coats, by winning four medals, not three. That sucks, and it violates the spirit of sport. A fan wants to see Carl Lewis grunting and sweating and bucking, willing himself to his personal threshold, the way the fan dreams he would if he got that incredible chance. Even if he doesn't know it intellectually, when a fan watches an athlete he wants to see honesty.

I think that's even truer of football. The football fan wants honesty, and he wants crisis. If pro football players don't save a drop, the game is furious, it's about as revealing as human drama can get. I've never been to war but I know there is a common element with football: when the enemy is violent, moving in, human facades are peeled away. There isn't time to bullshit.

Money and TV, I believed, removed much of that peril and purity, and that bastardized the game. But it isn't fair to summarily scapegoat Rozelle, or the owners, or the high-priced athletes. Today the NFL is a different animal, and everyone contributes to the money game. You certainly can't overlook the NFLPA. They've called two greedy strikes in the past seven years, which is two too many.

Gene Upshaw led the players out the last time. Gene will hate me the rest of his life for this, but he made a terrible blunder. Gene got wrapped up in himself, lost sight of reality. Personally, I don't believe in any kind of football strike. Working toward free agency is okay; striking for it is dead wrong. I think the union should not have struck, used that fact to curry public favor. If I were the head of the NFLPA I would have said something like this: "Look, we *can* go on strike. We have legitimate grievances. Our guys do get big contracts, but almost none of them are guaranteed. And when a guy's contract is up, he should be able to play where he wants. However . . . because of our love of the game, because it would visit hardship on many people—vendors and parking guys and others who make modest livings off the game —and it would put hardship on *you,* the fans, we're not going to strike. What we'll do is keep advising you of the issues, and we want you, the fans, to support these issues. One of our *main* objectives will be making the NFL's pension plan retroactive for former players who are maimed, who played football when money was scarce, and the first monies we receive will go to those men, not these mighty motherfuckers who are making $10 million!"

If you're not playing on Sunday, people don't want to hear you. When you take the game away from people, there's nothing to discuss. Fans don't make any money off the game, they get high from watching, whether you make 3 dollars or 3 million. The last thing you ever want to do, PR-wise, is not play the game. Now you are the enemy.

The players got out on the picket line, threw eggs at the scabs. They should have been throwing eggs at Gene Upshaw. Or at each other. If the whole thing was about making a living, why couldn't the scabs try and make some money? You walk out, you can't ask others to sacrifice income for you. It's not like you're a teachers' union. Your union is just a little bit different—its members are rich! I had no problem with the scabs. Guys got to live out their dreams, and a few were so good they're still in the NFL. When I saw strikers messing with the scabs, I was disappointed. I thought, *Leave the scabs alone. Examine yourselves.*

First examine your leader, see if you have a chance to win the war. Gene Upshaw was brutally overmatched. If I was playing two years ago, Gene told me and my teammates to strike, I would have said this: "Your background is playing offensive guard, now you're running the union. You envision yourself a capable opponent of men like Art Modell, Al Davis, Hugh Culverhouse, Pete Rozelle? Gene, are you crazy? Do you understand power? These guys are among the most skillful manipulators of the press in the *world.* You know what type of telephone callers they are? They can call the head of anything, get a conference—they can huddle with the President of the United States. You are not on that level. You've never made that type of money, don't have the training, or the contacts. You want to challenge those guys as an individual, fine. How dare you try and fool *me,* my teammates, by telling us you can whip the NFL owners. And how dare the union threaten me if I say no. I'm a veteran, I have one more year, if I walk out I lose half my salary and I can never make it up. I should walk out for free agency? You won't even get it, not by a strike. For the future? Whose future? The guy who wants to make $5 million instead of $3 million after me and my bad back are long gone? No, I won't get used so you can satisfy *some* of your constituents. Sorry Gene, I'm not getting sold down any drain."

Where does Franco Harris come in? He doesn't, not with the strike anyway. I have to backtrack to 1983, when other former players, certain writers, and myself, were growing perturbed with the modern game. One of the flaws we cited was an odd new trend: professional running backs scooting out of bounds. If a guy took a certain angle to get another yard, and it carried him over the sideline, or he ran out of bounds to stop the clock, that makes sense. But to purposely duck out of bounds to avoid a blow, no, I didn't like that. To me it looked like more modern football—guys protecting their paychecks instead of stinging people.

I never ran out of bounds to escape a hit. In fact, when I could see I was sprinting straight for the sidelines, I would stop, cut back against the grain, and those were some of the most vicious hits I ever received. I'd be turning my body back in, losing momentum, the pursuit would arrive at full speed, full force. It felt like getting smashed by a ten-foot wave, but this wave wore helmets and angry shoulders. I'd always try the cut back anyway, thought they were paying me to get every yard I could.

When I watched modern football, Franco Harris was one of those guys running out of bounds.

He was infamous for it. And it teed me off. I don't think anyone should run out of bounds to avoid getting hit, and Franco was a *fullback*. A fullback running out of bounds is like a Hell's Angel driving a Rabbit. Bogie smoking a Swisher Sweet.

It just isn't right.

Franco also was 6'2", about 230. You're blessed with that size and strength, utilize it. At 230, don't give a goddamn inch. Let other guys worry about *you*.

When he was staying in bounds, Franco was also creeping toward my rushing record. The reason I say "creeping" is this: I didn't see much fight in his running. Even before he caught on with Seattle, I felt Franco was well past his prime, hanging on, in an effort to pass my record, and if he was going to hang around to break a record that Walter Payton would just smash anyway, he should not diminish the sport, or the position, by playing half-assed football. If he was going to represent football history, I felt he should not set a BAD standard. And STOP running out of bounds.

I said it because I believed it, and I still believe it. I don't care if people say I'm the meanest man on earth, I don't think a 230-pound man should slip out of bounds. I will never change my mind on that. Same time though, when he was younger, and a much better runner, I do think Franco played a huge role in the success of the Steelers. First he was the No. 1 man in the offense. When he had to carry the load he did. Later, when Bradshaw and Stallworth and Swann stepped forward, and Franco had to play a secondary role, he adjusted perfectly. That took intelligence and versatility and maturity. If Franco wanted the ball more than Noll was willing to give him it, if he resented the growing role of Rocky Blier, if he was jealous because Bradshaw and his receivers, or Mean Joe Greene and the defense, were now dominating local headlines, any one of those things could have bred dissension. Instead, Franco went from star to supporting character, played both parts well, was instrumental in the Steelers winning four Super Bowls. Even I can't argue with that.

I also think Franco is a decent man. I got to know him a little after my Comeback was over, when we competed against each other in "The Shootout" in New Jersey, a TV show I put together with a pair of buddies who are producers. Franco and I both made some money, and his family got to know my friends, and everyone hit it off famously. In basketball and racquetball, running track and playing "football," Franco competed hard, never once backed down. I didn't change my feelings about his style of NFL running, but I did come away with increased respect.

That was in 1985. Back in 1983, as a professional back, I thought Franco was pretty much out of steam. So, I thought, was the NFL. At that time I used to co-host a radio show out of Las Vegas called "The Stardust Line." My partner was a guy named Lee Peete and we had two hours every Saturday and Sunday nights. I loved that show. Everyone in sports would come on, be very loose. And the two-hour format was very important. In two hours, people start understanding your mind. They start to like you a little when they see you have some balance.

We were never bland though. Lee and I were as spirited as our guests. One night a listener called in.

He said, "Franco Harris is soon going to break your rushing record. What are you going to do?"

I said, "Hell, if the man is going to run out of bounds, limp and crawl to a record, I'll come out of retirement, limp and crawl a few feet, and *re*break it."

That's what started the whole odd thing. One statement. Couple of days later, a story appeared in Cleveland: Jim Brown Thinking of Coming Back. It started slowly, then built, and snowballed —next thing I knew, I began getting phone calls from across the nation. It seemed as if every sports writer, and a bevy of entertainment writers, wanted to hear my story, wanted to know if I was really coming back to football, if I was serious.

I was serious. About as serious as my big toe going to the moon.

Before I answered the press, first I measured the situation. Hmmm. These folks want to use me to sell newspapers. They know I'm good copy. But this time, I'm gonna use their asses right back. Use the hell out of 'em. Play them just like they play me. I'm gonna make some money, make some *points*.

I told the reporters, "Yeah, I am serious. I'm coming back. Today you can raise your hand when you're tired, they pull you out of the game. I can play ten plays a game, get thirty, forty yards, wave my hand whenever I need a blow. I can rebreak the record."

I said it with a stone face, and the press ate it like a Dove Bar. Some writers were outraged and hypercritical, took *it* as seriously as they took themselves. "This guy thinks he can come back? Why would this old man want to get out there and make a fool of himself? He's an egomaniac. He's crazy!" Their reaction tickled the hell out of me. I was NEVER coming back to football. There was NEVER one doubt in my mind.

Franco faded into the background, the comeback became the thing. The national debate unleashed, then I *really* started talking. I said, "Yes, I may come back. But the situation must be just right."

They asked what team I wanted to play for.

I said, "I think the Cleveland Browns still have my rights. I'll have to be traded to the Raiders. Al Davis is a kick-ass owner, the Raiders are a kick-ass team. They're the only team I want to play for."

It started getting wild and fun. Some of the writers had a sense of whimsy, said, "Well, he might be able to do it!" Paul Brown said, "If anyone can do it, he could." Al Davis said, "If he comes to me, I'll talk to him. He hasn't talked to me yet." About this time *Sports Illustrated* was running an article, written by Paul Zimmerman, titled, "Pete, The Way They Play Today Stinks." Paul said the current NFL was weak, quoted John Madden, Hacksaw Reynolds, Ray Nitschke, who all supported segments of his premise. I guess it was a slow week, *Sports Illustrated* figured my shit was the best thing they had. I put on a L.A. Raiders uniform, *SI* shot my photograph for Zimmerman's cover piece. Eighteen years after my retirement, I was on the cover of *Sports Illustrated,* next to a headline proclaiming I was "Just What the Boring NFL Needed."

I was like a cat standing on a corner, spouting bullshit. But while I was doing it, I was achieving one of my objectives: I was making good points. "Why would a 230-pound man run out of bounds? Why is everyone dancing, mugging for the camera? Where's the danger in the game? Where are the characters and the warriors? You talk about records. Why even compare me to Franco? He played thirteen years, I played nine. He played something like fifty more games. Man gets four strikes to my three, where's the significance? My performance spoke for itself. I don't want to hear any shit about Franco."

I wasn't lying. Hell, a lot of things I talked about, the NFL wound up changing. I wasn't the only dissenting voice, but I received the massive press because I said I was coming back—crazy notions sell—and simply because I was Jim Brown. Whenever an athlete hasn't been broken, didn't leave the game because they forced him out, set some standards that fans know are strong, people will still want to hear from you.

Franco wasn't sitting back. At first he was, would only say No Comment. Then he blasted back, said I was basically full of shit. When I said a 230-pound man should not run out of bounds, Franco said the wise man lives to fight another day. I said, "No, not in this case. You weigh 230. You come up to a 200-pound man, let *him* live to fight another day. You go for the yards."

Once people started talking more about the comeback, less about Franco, and the publicity swelled beyond the sports page, to TV and national magazines, I knew I could make some cash on this thing, speaking or whatever. At one point I was invited onto "Donahue," with Franco and Walter Payton. We were there to debate my observations about the modern athlete and the state of the NFL. It was lively, each side trying to break the other, when I surprised them.

I said, "Walter, Franco, you guys are great players and you make a lot of money. But aren't you concerned about the fact that there's not a black head football coach in the NFL?"

I caught Walter off guard, I think he knew it. He was shrewd, didn't risk a statement he might later regret.

Franco dove right in. He said, "Jim, you know football is too tough for me to have to think about things like that."

I let that be. It needed no amplification, Franco didn't need any more rope. To me his reply epitomized the mentality of the modern athlete— self-absorbed. I'd planned the question, knew it would score points for my argument. More importantly, I wanted to provoke some thought about the absence of black coaches while I had a national audience, at a time when people *weren't* discussing it. Unfortunately things haven't changed, but at the time I thought I was doing some good, considered the "Donahue" show the most, perhaps the only significant event in my entire Comeback.

The most fun I had was with Al Davis. I was telling people that I would wait until the current season was over, after the Raiders had won the Super Bowl, then call Al about playing for his club.

Al's reply that he would talk to me if I wanted to talk? It was a joke. If there was one guy who got a kick out of my statements it was Al. It seemed like the Raiders were the only team that understood it. They didn't even object when I used their jersey on the cover of *SI*—some teams would have sued me into next week. The Raiders knew I was having some fun, saw no need to ruin it. It wasn't like Al, his teams had never been outrageous.

Part of my prophecy came true: the Raiders made it to the Super Bowl. That's when Al did something I thought was extremely funny, and entirely characteristic. While my critics were feasting —Jim Brown can't let go of the game, he's arrogant, he's deluded, it figures he'd pose as a Raider —Al invited me to the Super Bowl, as a guest of the Raiders. On their chartered plane and everything. You get the idea that maybe Al likes to stir the pot?

And you think I'd blow that opportunity? I took my girlfriend, flew to Tampa early with the Raiders, we partied every night with the Raiderettes. Al gave us complimentary seats, great ones, close enough to see that the Raiders are relaxed, focused, Marcus Allen is burning, Jim Plunkett is cool, Riggins, Thiesmann and the Hogs can do nothing with Alzado, Lester Hayes and the rest of the incorrigibles. I watch the Raiders demolish the Redskins, 38–9, afterwards I'm part of the celebration, up in the dance hall with the joyous Raiders, superfine Raiderettes, my lady, dancing, partying, knowing I'm not really a part of all this, that belongs to the Raiders, but *feeling* like I am. All thanks to my friend, Al Davis.

Later, that summer, Franco Harris was released by the Steelers. He had a brief stint in Seattle, was released before he could pass my record, and Walter Payton cruised by us both, became the all-time leading rusher. That was the unofficial end to my Comeback. If I had tried to come back, stay on top of Walter, I'd have been playing pro football until I was a *hundred* and forty-seven. Besides, if Eric Dickerson stays healthy, he'll shatter every record there is. Eric will have more numbers than the phone book.

Anyway, I don't have time for that stuff anymore. I'm not above pro football, just beyond it. My life right now is full. I'm the President of Ocean Productions, a Hollywood film company. We've gone public, and though we're relatively young, we have several promising deals in the works. Ocean Productions gives me the opportunity to create opportunities for others, namely young, talented minorities. That prospect excites me.

Vital Issues, of which I'm Executive Director, also continues to flourish. Our Advisory Board recently expanded, again, to include Fred Dryer, Kellen Winslow, Duane Thomas, and Reggie Jackson. They're committed, they want to work, we're pleased to have them. Vital Issues is now in five California prisons and the response from the inmates has been extremely gratifying. Men are reclaiming control of their lives, regaining selfworth. I went to a graduation recently for one of the men who'd completed our program and when he stood up, said Vital Issues had changed his life, maybe saved it, I started crying my butt off.

Human development is the greatest development of all, and that's all the reward I'm searching for. Today, that's where I get my stimulation. Let Walter and Eric battle it out now. I've got life to attend to.

Check you later.

POWELL'S ARMY
BY TERENCE DUNCAN

THRILLERS BY WILLIAM W. JOHNSTONE

THE DEVIL'S CAT   **(2091, $3.95)**
The town was alive with all kinds of cats. Black, white, fat, scrawny. They lived in the streets, in backyards, in the swamps of Becancour. Sam, Nydia, and Little Sam had never seen so many cats. The cats' eyes were glowing slits as they watched the newcomers. The town was ripe with evil. It seemed to waft in from the swamps with the hot, fetid breeze and breed in the minds of Becancour's citizens. Soon Sam, Nydia, and Little Sam would battle the forces of darkness. Standing alone against the ultimate predator — The Devil's Cat.

THE DEVIL'S HEART   **(2110, $3.95)**
Now it was summer again in Whitfield. The town was peaceful, quiet, and unprepared for the atrocities to come. Eternal life, everlasting youth, an orgy that would span time — that was what the Lord of Darkness was promising the coven members in return for their pledge of love. The few who had fought against his hideous powers before, believed it could never happen again. Then the hot wind began to blow — as black as evil as The Devil's Heart.

THE DEVIL'S TOUCH   **(2111, $3.95)**
Once the carnage begins, there's no time for anything but terror. Hollow-eyed, hungry corpses rise from unearthly tombs to gorge themselves on living flesh and spawn a new generation of restless Undead. The demons of Hell cavort with Satan's unholy disciples in blood-soaked rituals and fevered orgies. The Balons have faced the red, glowing eyes of the Master before, and they know what must be done. But there can be no salvation for those marked by The Devil's Touch.

Available wherever paperbacks are sold, or order direct from the Publisher. Send cover price plus 50¢ per copy for mailing and handling to Zebra Books, Dept. 3114, 475 Park Avenue South, New York, N.Y. 10016. Residents of New York, New Jersey and Pennsylvania must include sales tax. DO NOT SEND CASH.

THE FINEST IN SUSPENSE!

THE URSA ULTIMATUM (2310, $3.95)
by Terry Baxter
In the dead of night, twelve nuclear warheads are smuggled north
across the Mexican border to be detonated simultaneously in major cities throughout the U.S. And only a small-town desert law-
man stands between a face-less Russian superspy and World War
Three!

THE LAST ASSASSIN (1989, $3.95)
by Daniel Easterman
From New York City to the Middle East, the devastating flames
of revolution and terrorism sweep across a world gone mad . . .
as the most terrifying conspiracy in the history of mankind is
born!

FLOWERS FROM BERLIN (2060, $4.50)
by Noel Hynd
With the Earth on the brink of World War Two, the Third Reich's
deadliest professional killer is dispatched on the most heinous as-
signment of his murderous career: the assassination of Franklin
Delano Roosevelt!

THE BIG NEEDLE (2776, $3.50)
by Ken Follett
All across Europe, innocent people are being terrorized, homes
are destroyed, and dead bodies have become an unnervingly common sight. And the horrors will continue until the most powerful
organization on Earth finds Chadwell Carstairs—and kills him!

*Available wherever paperbacks are sold, or order direct from the
Publisher. Send cover price plus 50¢ per copy for mailing and
handling to Zebra Books, Dept. 3114, 475 Park Avenue South,
New York, N.Y. 10016. Residents of New York, New Jersey and
Pennsylvania must include sales tax. DO NOT SEND CASH.*